Job Descriptions in Banking

Job Descriptions in Banking

The Complete Guide to Planning, Writing, and Using Job Descriptions

Frank Oldham, Jr.

Jeffrey L. Seglin, Consulting Editor

BANKERS PUBLISHING COMPANY, BOSTON

Library of Congress Cataloging in Publication Data

Oldham, Frank, 1945-
  Job descriptions in banking.

  Bibliography: p.
  1. Banks and banking — Job descriptions.   I. Seglin,
Jeffrey L., 1956-   II. Title.
HG1615.7.J6043   1984   332.1'023'73   84-6443
ISBN 0-87267-049-X

Executive Editor:	Robert M. Roen
Managing Editor:	Nancy Long Coleman
Cover Designer:	William Samatis

To my wife Donna, son Chad, and daughter Whitney Oldham.

To Nancy

"You're God's answer to Job. . . . He would've pointed to you and said, you know 'I do a lot of terrible things, but I can also make one of these. . . .'"

— Woody Allen, Manhattan

Other titles by Bankers Publishing Company:

Bank Letter Writing Handbook, Jeffrey L. Seglin
Banker's Guide to Personnel Administration, Eugene J. Looper
The Effective Bank Supervisor, Paul F. Jannott
The Effective Branch Manager, Albert J. Brown, Jr.
The Encyclopedia of Banking and Finance, 8th edition, F. L. Garcia
Teller World, 2nd edition, Paul F. Jannott
Work Measurement in Banking, 2nd edition, Donald L. Caruth

About the Authors

Frank Oldham, Jr. is currently chairman and president of Security Bank of Paragould, Arkansas. He is also president of Profit Consultants, Inc. of Jonesboro, Arkansas, a bank consulting company, and holds the rank of professor at Arkansas State University.

Dr. Oldham has received a Ph.D. in business administration from the University of Arkansas and an M.A. in marketing from Central Missouri. He is a frequent seminar leader speaking on a variety of subjects of interest to the banking industry. He has conducted several American Bankers Association seminars and is on the Stonier Graduate School of Banking faculty. He has published numerous articles and monographs on a variety of banking subjects. He is a member of many professional organizations as well.

Jeffrey L. Seglin is a writing and editing consultant living in Boston, Massachusetts. His consulting projects have included work as a story consultant and editor for WGBH's 13-week personal finance television series and as a developmental editor for Random House's professional books division. His articles have appeared in magazines including *Financial Planning, Inc.*, *Boston*, and *ENTER*. He has edited and collaborated on a variety of book projects and is the author of *Bank Letter Writing Handbook*, published by Bankers Publishing Company.

Mr. Seglin attended the Radcliffe Publishing Procedures Course after graduating with a bachelor's degree in English from Bethany College in West Virginia. He completed a master's degree with an emphasis in literature and theology at Harvard University.

Contents

Preface

A job well done can increase the effectiveness of all organizations, banks notwithstanding. But it is the rare individual who can arrive on the job and proceed to a stellar performance without some type of guidelines from which to work. In any job there are simply some things that need to be accomplished. Granted, there is always room for the creativity different workers bring to their respective jobs, but when push comes to shove, if there are not duties to be performed there is no need for the job.

Job descriptions give an individual coming to or holding a job a set of guidelines from which boundaries and responsibilities can be established. They can supply these guidelines without being so restrictive that jobholders find themselves stymied from performing up to their capabilities.

Job descriptions set a firm foundation on which the well-qualified employee can build. They can go further to aid employers in evaluating and compensating their employees. As a set of guidelines, job descriptions are a flexible tool that can help increase job productivity, satisfaction, and goals and lead to a more effectively operating bank.

It is our intention in *Job Descriptions in Banking* to show you just how useful job descriptions can be. The first part of the book gives you everything you need to know about preparing job descriptions from job analysis to data organization to writing and using the finished job description. Step by step, in easy-to-follow, clearly written language, we lay it all out for you.

Part two of the book supplies you with job descriptions which you can adapt for use in your own bank. We have developed these job descriptions to be effective tools for all managers and supervisors, personnel staff, and employees throughout the banking industry. We've also included several appendixes and a bibliography which have been specially designed to make your job developing and using job descriptions easier.

The completion of *Job Descriptions in Banking* would not have been possible without input from many sources and individuals. The following people have been generous in lending support and information: K. Linford Loesch, Senior Vice President, Central Penn National Bank, Philadelphia; Marlin Jackson, State Bank Commissioner for Arkansas; Bill Fisher, President, First Pyramid Life Insurance Company, Arkansas; Judy Wetchel and Jean Inness of Security Bank, Paragould, Arkansas; George Shirley, President and Chief Executive Officer, Carl Albright, Executive Vice President, and Gerald Busby, Senior Vice President, all of the First National Bank of Tuskaloosa, Alabama; Sue Roen, Andover, Massachusetts; David Lawrence Palay, Grand Forks, North Dakota; and finally, Nancy Coleman and Robert Roen of Bankers Publishing Company in Boston, without whom this book would never have been started nor completed.

Frank Oldham, Jr.

Jeffrey L. Seglin

PART ONE

Developing
Job
Descriptions

1

JOB ANALYSIS

Job descriptions distinguish one job from another by accurately depicting in a terse format the intrinsic makeup of a particular job. They are clearly written statements of the functions, responsibilities, and duties of particular employees. These descriptions also depict the interrelationships employees have with others in a particular organization.

Job descriptions are integral to many aspects of a bank's organizational structure. (See chapter 5.) They can be used as the basis for recruitment, training, management, evaluation, and an understanding of the corporate structure.

A job description is only as good as the information that makes it up. Just as medical research findings are useless if the information used to draw conclusions was inaccurate, so too are job descriptions if they contain inaccurate particulars about the job in question.

With numerous facets involved in every job from clerical to upper management positions, where do you begin to piece together the information necessary to make up an accurate job description? First, do not try to compose a job description off the top of your head, piecing together all of the information you can recall about your job or the jobs of people you supervise. To prepare an accurate, useful job description, the first step is job analysis.

STEP 1: JOB ANALYSIS

The first step in writing or revising a job description is to complete a job analysis. A job analysis is the process of gathering information about the work done by a particular

3

employee. The analysis consists of accumulating the data necessary to accurately describe the functions, responsibilities, accountabilities, and duties of a given employee and to come to an understanding of how he or she relates to all other employees within the same bank.

The first step in conducting such an analysis is to gather the hard facts about the job. Not only should there be an examination of what bank employees "should" be doing, but also what they are "actually" doing on the job.

The most effective means of gathering the data necessary to describe a job can often be an interview with both the employee currently holding the job and that person's supervisor. Since employees may not always be willing to volunteer all of the information needed to complete an accurate job analysis, it is often necessary for the interviewer (whether it is an outside personnel consultant or an inside bank personnel officer) to guide the interview along so it does not get off track. Whenever outsiders (organizational or departmental) come in asking questions, there is bound to be some hesitancy or resentment among some of the employees being interviewed. Skilled interviewers who can keep their task in mind throughout their encounter with the employee can be particularly helpful in completing this process successfully.

Information for the job analysis can also be gathered by using a questionnaire, handed out to individual employees, requesting basic information such as their title, the purpose of their job, the extent to which they supervise others, their duties, their experience, and how they relate to others in the bank.

The questionnaire is a quick way of gathering a great deal of fairly objective information. You do, however, risk losing some of the insight that may have been gained by talking directly with the employees and their supervisors.

Observation of "bank employees in action" is also crucial to the completion of an accurate job analysis. Hearing and reading what people think they do on the job and

---

Figure 1-1   Generic Job Analysis/Job Description Form.

Name of Company:
Date:
Job Title:
Department/Division:
Reports to:
Supervises:
Job Summary: (brief synopsis of job)
Primary Duties:
Secondary Duties:
Organizational Tasks: (performed in and out of department)
Financial Responsibilities:
Relationships: (in and out of department)

seeing what they actually do on the job is an important way to pinpoint some of the discrepancies between what is said is being done and what is actually being done.

An interview with individual bank employees and a questionnaire filled out by them, combined with observation of them on the job is an effective means of gathering the data necessary for a job analysis that is thorough enough to use as the basis for the preparation of a useful job description. After this data is gathered it can be put together in a somewhat rudimentary form of job description.

Sometimes in the process of conducting job analyses, employees are asked to record what they do for a given period of time (at least a week) on the job. The results of such exercises are often not as useful as the interview/questionnaire/observation methods, because the employees' recordings might range from sporadic and incomplete to compulsive recordings of even the most minute, unimportant details.

OBJECTIVITY A KEY

Although *total* objectivity is never possible, it is important throughout the job analysis process to remain as objective as possible. It is for this reason that an impartial person is often called in to conduct interviews, interpret questionnaires, or observe employees. This professional is often the member of an outside consulting firm or a trained member of the bank's personnel department. All of the job descriptions in part II of *Job Descriptions in Banking* were gathered with this objective attitude.

It should be stressed again that all recordings of information, no matter what method is used to gather it, should use action verbs to describe what makes up a given job. (See appendix I for a list of good action verbs.) If good, clear action verbs are used it helps to depict accurately what a person does on the job.

As a result of the job analysis, you'll have gathered the data necessary to put together a good job description. How this data is organized will affect the usefulness of the job description.

2

DATA ORGANIZATION

There is no universal format to follow in putting together a job description. The information, length, and organization can differ from bank to bank. One bank's job descriptions are not necessarily better than the next's as long as both are organized to be useful and to accurately reflect the details of the job being described.

Once a bank has decided upon a format to follow then, with the possible exception of some upper management positions, the same format should be used for all jobs within the organization. As a result, the finished job descriptions can be used effectively as a comparative tool among a diverse group of jobs.

Although formats may differ, all effective job descriptions should contain some common elements. The format should first and foremost be arranged in order to depict a concise synopsis of the identification, purpose, duties, and accountabilities of a particular job. To achieve this, some common structural features should be used in organizing the data drawn from the job analysis to be used in a job description.

Most job descriptions will contain the following sections:

Job identification
Job summary
Job duties
Job accountabilities

All of the job descriptions in part II of *Job Descriptions in Banking* contain these sections, but the categories are broken down further so that they contain the following sections:

Job identification
    Title
    Department/Division
    Reports to
    Supervises

Summary & Purpose

Duties

Accountabilities
    Organization
    Finances
    Relationships

Not only the content but also the order in which job description data appears can differ from bank to bank. A good way to order the data is to make the various categories appear in a logical order. Obviously you'd want the job identification up front. A summary followed by a duties section further clarifies the job in question. And finally, the accountabilities section should give the reader of the job description a good idea of what all of the work a particular jobholder does will lead to.

Before the various sections of a job description are discussed, another item closely related to the job description should be mentioned. These are the job specifications.

Often job specifications are written on a separate sheet attached to the job description. As its name suggests, job specifications include information about the specifics necessary to complete a job. These specifics could include such things as experience, education, working conditions, mental and physical demands, and other items required to perform the job. For the purpose of our discussion here, we will focus on the job description itself.

JOB IDENTIFICATION

The job identification section in the sample job descriptions in part II of *Job Descriptions in Banking* contains the following information:

Job Title:
Department/Division:

Reports to:

Supervises:

Items included in the job identification section should be things that are expected to remain stable. For example, you don't want to include names of specific people because you never know when these names are likely to change and put the job description out of date.

The most important item in the job specification section is the job title. An accurate job title is important to the jobholder because it can briefly identify his or her job; to other members in the bank because it can be used as a basis for comparison; and to personnel specialists who can use it to compare the position to similar jobs in other banks.

A job title should be as brief and specific as possible. It should be written in non-sexist language, so the job description can be applicable to both men and women. The brief one or two word job title should give a brief indication of the following four items:

1. job content and purpose
2. skill level involved
3. extent of responsibility
4. area of bank activity

Obviously these four items will be further elaborated in the rest of the job description, but the brief job title should be able to trigger some details about the job in a reader's mind.

A good resource to use in determining job titles is the *Dictionary of Occupational Titles* published by the U.S. Government Printing Office. Several thousand job titles and job descriptions are included in this work. For ideas about accurate job titles, you should consult this dictionary. It is usually available in the reference room of a public or college library or can be ordered through the U.S. Government Printing Office.

The remaining items in the job identification section of the job description are self-explanatory: Department/Division; Reports to; and Supervises.

It is important to remember to include the supervisor's or subordinate's title and not his or her name. This will guard against making the job description obsolete before it need be.

JOB SUMMARY

The job summary gives a brief overview of a job, giving the job's general characteristics. The summary gives the essence of a person's job in a few clearly written specific descriptive sentences.

The summary will be most effective if the sentences begin with action verbs (see appendix I), the job's purpose and what is done on the job is depicted. For example, in a job description for a file maintenance clerk in the consumer loans operations department of a bank, the job summary might read:

> *Films and files all pertinent documents. Answers phones when necessary. Checks credit and handles inquiries as needed.*

Note that each sentence begins with an action verb. The job's purpose is set out as to "check credit and handle inquiries," and a brief depiction of what's done on the job is given.

Precise language is crucial to make the job summary as effective as possible. Ambiguous and unnecessary technical words should be avoided. You should be consistent in the way you use particular terms in the summary and throughout the job description. For a quick overview of words that are commonly used incorrectly, see "Words to Watch" in appendix II. There are also many grammar hotlines set up at universities throughout the country. For a list of some of these see appendix III in *Job Descriptions in Banking*.

JOB DUTIES

All job descriptions have a section listing job duties. The section lists the major duties and responsibilities required to perform a particular job thoroughly and efficiently. While the contents are more detailed than those in the job summary section, they should not include every minute detail involved in performing a job.

There are various ways to order the material presented in the job duties section of a job description. They can be listed in order of importance, in chronological order, or in any order that best meets the needs of the bank for which the job description is being written.

What constitutes a major duty can be a somewhat subjective determination. In formulating the job duties section, pick out the major everyday duties, the recurring occasional duties, the contact with other people required, and the supervision given or received. If you pinpoint these items, you will be able to form a thorough list of job duties.

The job duties section is usually set up in list form. Often a numbered or lettered list will make the specific duties easy to identify when reading the job description.

Remember to keep the sentences brief, unambiguous, and in the present tense. Each sentence should begin with an action verb.

The job duties section of the file maintenance clerk whose job summary we already examined reads:

1. Alphabetizes and films material relevant to credit information.
2. Files information on individuals' microfiche.
3. Obtains direct credit reports.
4. Checks credit with credit bureau using credit terminal.
5. Reports any potential new business.

When completed, the job duties section can be used to further distinguish one job from the next.

ACCOUNTABILITIES

The accountabilities section of the job description gives a brief description of what should happen when job duties are performed efficiently. This section can be used as a reference for performance appraisals and as a basis for setting job goals. Making accountabilities clear also eases a supervisor's mind that the person to whom he or she delegated responsibility is indeed held accountable for those responsibilities.

In the sample job descriptions in part III, the accountabilities section is broken into three sections—organization, finances, and relationships. In this way, particular accountabilities are made clear. For example, in the example of the file maintenance clerk, the accountabilities section reads:

Organization
Responsible for making recommendations to supervisor about possible methods to improve department.

Finances
Responsible for making recommendations to supervisor about the budgetary needs of the department.

Relationships
1. Responsible to Consumer Credit Operations Supervisor for the fulfillment of functions, responsibilities, and authority, and for their proper interpretation.
2. Has extensive contact with customers and the public. Conducts relationships in a manner that will enhance the overall marketing effort of the bank.
3. Participates from time to time with community organizations and in community projects.

The most important result of organizing the data in a job description is that it becomes an easily used tool. Once a format, such as the one described early in the chapter, is decided upon, the organization of data becomes relatively simple.

3

WRITING THE JOB DESCRIPTION

There are several questions that need to be asked when preparing to write job descriptions. For the purposes of our discussion, we have pinpointed these as the four chief questions:

Who writes the job description?

Who approves the job description?

When should a job description be rewritten?

How does the position description differ from the job description?

By answering these questions, you will be able to gain a clear idea of what goes into writing an effective job description to be used by many different members of your bank's staff.

The finished job description will result from a process that included collecting, analyzing, and organizing information about each job's purpose and duties. No job description will perfectly outline a job. Good job descriptions will, however, identify the chief tasks involved in performing a job efficiently as well as give the jobholder and his or her supervisor an idea of the scope and limitations of the jobholder's responsibilities.

A good job description will give a clear idea of what a particular jobholder does to someone who does not necessarily have any working relationship to the jobholder. It is like a map of the job with major areas highlighted and boundaries clarified.

It will be helpful if you follow the simple "use" and "avoid" list below. Not everything is mentioned here, but there is enough to get you started on the right track.

1. Use simple words and sentence structures.
2. Use a brief, terse style.
3. Use the present tense.
4. Use unambiguous words.
5. Use job or department titles without mentioning specific people.
6. Use a logical progression in outlining the order of duties.
7. Use an impersonal, objective style.

1. Avoid unnecessary technical words.
2. Avoid ambiguous, imprecise language.
3. Avoid listing every minute job duty.
4. Avoid opinions about the job or jobholder.
5. Avoid many words where one will suffice.
6. Avoid temporary duties or duties to be performed in the future.
7. Avoid negative or blanket statements.

The length of the job description does not indicate the importance of the position. Often jobholders will want to pack their job description with much information that is unnecessary in order to prove, by virtue of the length of the job description, that his or her job is more important than the next person's. The length, of course, is no indication of a job's importance. Just as a puppy's paws need be only long enough to reach the ground, the job description need only be long enough to fulfill its purpose.

WHO WRITES THE JOB DESCRIPTION?

Many people should be involved in the writing of job descriptions.

The jobholder and supervisor

The jobholder and his or her supervisor are of course excellent resources from whom to draw information and get help in editing the final job description. Usually, however, both the jobholder and supervisor are not the best people to write the job description for several reasons.

First, both the jobholder and supervisor would find it extremely difficult to remain objective throughout the process of writing the job description. Something a jobholder might want to highlight because of its prestige is not necessarily crucial to the writing of a good job description. In fact, it may hinder the job description by distorting the relative importance of various duties. Similarly, the jobholder's supervisor may have his or her own "hidden agenda" when writing a subordinate's job description.

Second, the jobholder and supervisor may lack the writing skills necessary to produce a well-written thorough document of the job's details. Finally, both the jobholder and supervisor are not necessarily trained in specialized personnel areas such as job analysis and job description preparation. The jobholder and supervisor are crucial to the process, but are probably not the best people to draft the job description.

The expert

A professional from a bank's personnel department or an outside personnel consultant are full-time professionals in personnel matters. They are trained to be able to conduct job analyses and to draw information from these analyses that can be used to write accurate job descriptions.

If a bank has a trained personnel staff it is usually to its advantage to draw upon it when writing job descriptions. One of the drawbacks of trained outside consultants is the cost involved. But if no personnel staff is available, it is best to rely on the outside professional who can provide the bank with well-written, useful job descriptions.

Working together

Before a job description is finished, the jobholder and supervisor should be allowed to thoroughly review the work completed by the personnel expert. As a result, all duties, procedures, and responsibilities listed can be examined to ensure that they accurately reflect the work performed in the job being described.

WHO APPROVES THE JOB DESCRIPTION?

More than one draft of the job description, after feedback from the jobholder and supervisor is received, is often necessary. Throughout the process of revising drafts, the question that should constantly be asked is whether an outsider or new employee would understand the job after reading the job description.

After job descriptions are edited for consistency, they usually will have to go through some sort of approval process. It is best if the approval process involves more than one person. The jobholder's supervisor, an upper level supervisor, and a personnel department officer should each review the job descriptions and come to a consensus about them. Each of these people can review the job description from a unique perspective and add different input to the approval process. Once these three people or equivalent counterparts decide that the job descriptions accurately reflect what is done in each job, the job descriptions can be approved for use within the bank.

WHEN SHOULD A JOB DESCRIPTION BE REWRITTEN?

When a job description no longer accurately reflects the job that a particular jobholder does, it needs to be rewritten. It's as simple as that. The difficulty lies in keeping job descriptions up-to-date.

When a major change is made in a jobholder's job, these changes should be reflected in a revised job description. As duties shift or are added, the writer should try to keep the job title similar to the previous one so there is little confusion about the revised job description being for the same job.

Jobholders and supervisors should learn to keep track of job changes as they occur so they are prepared to update the job description. It is typically the supervisor's responsibility to ensure that his or her subordinates' job descriptions accurately depict the work being done. The supervisor should bring major changes to the attention of the personnel department or the person responsible for the bank's job description program.

It is most efficient to review job descriptions on a regular basis, whether it be yearly, every other year, or every five years. Obviously, the more often job descriptions are reviewed for accuracy, the more likely they are to be kept up-to-date. The same procedure that was used to compile data for the original job description should be used in preparing the revision.

When job descriptions become out-of-date and no longer accurately reflect the job, they not only lose their accuracy and effectiveness, but also can cause frustration among jobholders and mismanagement by supervisors. The tendency of people to let job descriptions go severely out-of-date is what leads to the belief that job descriptions are restrictive tools that don't accurately reflect the work done on the job. This needn't happen if job descriptions are kept alive and up-to-date. They can remain a useful tool and guide if used and updated responsibly.

HOW DOES A POSITION DESCRIPTION DIFFER FROM A
JOB DESCRIPTION?

Some banks and companies will use a position description rather than a job description for upper level management jobs. Position descriptions differ from job descriptions because they more generally depict the end results expected from a person rather than the specific procedures involved in producing these end results.

There are both positive and negative sides to using position descriptions. The positive side is spelled out very well by John K. Hemphill in his 1959 *Harvard Business Review* article titled, "Job Descriptions for Executives Has Important Implications to the Problems of Top Management." Hemphill argues that:

> *A good method of describing executive jobs should help management in a number of ways. It would:*

Be useful in defining the area of an executive's activity and responsibility.

Aid in establishing an objective basis for appraising a manager's performance.

Provide a rational basis for paying different salaries.

Serve as a valuable guide in the development of management ability. (John K. Hemphill, Harvard Business Review, September/October 1959, Vol. 37, No. 51, p. 55).

It is hard to argue with Hemphill that such a tool would be useful, but a separate program for developing position descriptions presents several problems. These include the length of time it takes to prepare a separate set of position descriptions, the cost incurred by hiring a professional to prepare the position descriptions, and the need to change the position description every time a new person takes over because it is assumed that each high level executive will shape his or her own job in his or her own way.

The sample job descriptions in part III of *Job Descriptions in Banking* are all actual job descriptions. Higher level executives' jobs are included in the sample job descriptions provided. If the job description can fulfill a similar function as a position description used by some companies or banks, it is an effective use of money and employees' time to prepare the job description for the high level executive at the same time other jobholders' descriptions are prepared.

Obviously some jobs will not be able to fit the job description format we suggest. Take for example the president of a bank whose main task is to keep the bank running profitably. It would be very difficult to specify exactly what the particular function and duties of the president are.

Common sense should always be used when preparing job descriptions. In many small companies, job descriptions for top level management might be unnecessary because the overall objectives will be clear to the small group of top level managers.

If you decide to use position descriptions, these questions should be asked:

What is the purpose of the job?

What is the complexity of the problems dealt with?

How much independence is allowed?

How does the job affect the rest of the organization?

What is the financial scope of the job?

The information drawn from the answers to these questions can then be formatted in a manner similar to the way typical job descriptions are formatted. A first draft can then be written, reviewed, revised, edited, and finally approved.

4

JOB
DESCRIPTIONS
AND THE LAW

Legislation which has been passed over the last decade or so has greatly affected the entire scope of personnel functions not only for banks, but for all employers and employees. The continual upgrading of laws to ensure equality and fairness for all workers has sometimes placed a tremendous responsibility on employers to keep abreast of current legislative requirements in the workplace. In the midst of trying to make the workplace equitable for all involved, legislation has also placed a burdensome task on employers who must shoulder the cost of keeping detailed compliance reports for various government agencies.

Banks must meet the personnel requirements placed on them by all state and federal legislation. There are qualifications, not exceptions from the laws. If fifteen or less people are employed, the employer is exempted from meeting the requirements of Title VII of the Civil Rights Act of 1964. Once employers have fifty or more people in their employ, however, a formal affirmative action program must be maintained.[1]

---

[1] For a thorough discussion of legislation affecting personnel practices, see C. Eugene Looper's *Banker's Guide to Personnel Administration* (Boston: Bankers Publishing Company, 1983), from which portions of this chapter were adapted with permission from the publisher. Also see Richard I. Henderson's well-done series of articles titled "Job Descriptions—Critical Documents, Versatile Tools," a five-part series which appeared in *Supervisory Management* from November 1975 through March 1976. Both Looper and Henderson do an excellent job of charting the various government regulations which have affected not only the role of job descriptions but also the personnel relations field as a whole.

There is no question that the changes in the legal framework over the last several years have affected the importance of job descriptions in personnel relations. The Fair Labor Standards Act of 1938 (FLSA), the Equal Pay Act of 1964, Title VII of the Civil Rights Act of 1964, and the Occupational Safety and Health Act of 1970 (OSHA) are four of the major acts which have had an affect on the effective use of job descriptions.

FAIR LABOR STANDARDS ACT OF 1938 (FLSA)

The FLSA was passed by Congress in 1938 to set up minimum living standards for workers. FLSA established a minimum wage and overtime payment for more than forty hours worked in a workweek, and also set restrictions on child labor.

It is from the passage of FLSA that the categories of "exempt" and "nonexempt" from overtime were derived. Employees who meet specific criteria set by FLSA are exempt from the FLSA's overtime payment provision. Part of the criteria for being exempt from having to be paid an overtime wage includes having the responsibility of managing a department or division and directing the work of at least two other people. Exempt employees have a say in hiring and firing people. They must also be in a position in which they are free to make decisions using their own judgment and discretion.

In order to ensure that jobs fall clearly into an exempt or nonexempt status, it is crucial that the work actually being performed by a jobholder be detailed in the job description. To determine exemption status, a jobholder's duties and responsibilities listed in the job description must meet the exemption criteria of the FLSA.

EQUAL PAY ACT OF 1964

Sexual discrimination in salary payment to employees is prohibited by the Equal Pay Act of 1964, which was amended by the Equal Pay Amendment of 1974. Skills, duties, and responsibilities performed under similar conditions must be rewarded equally paying no heed to an employee's race or sex. Performance or varying job requirements can, of course, cause people with similar jobs to be rewarded differently, but these rewards must be on the basis of merit and not race or sex.

Job descriptions should specify the skill, effort, and responsibility necessary to perform the job. If a bank is accused of sexual discrimination because of a discrepancy in pay to a man and woman for the same job performed, the job description should serve as an indicator of whether or not the job in question does indeed require the same skills, effort, and responsibility.

The job description can often be an excellent defense for an employer accused of sexual discrimination in salary practices. It is as important to remember, however, that the job description can also be used by the employee as proof of discrimination if it does indeed indicate that similar qualifications and responsibilities are being compensated inequitably.

TITLE VII OF THE CIVIL RIGHTS ACT OF 1964

The primary requirement of Title VII of the Civil Rights Act of 1964 prohibits basing employment decisions including pay, work terms, conditions, privileges, and hiring and firing on race, color, religion, sex, or national origin.

Of course, banks and companies can still hire the best qualified candidate, but they must be able to prove, if called upon to do so, that they did not discriminate in their hiring process. The job description can be incredibly useful in delineating the performance requirements of a job. Job descriptions can also be used by the bank to show that hiring practices are non-discriminatory and fall under the guidelines of Title VII of the Civil Rights Act of 1964.

OCCUPATIONAL SAFETY AND HEALTH ACT OF 1970 (OSHA)

Safe working conditions and procedures were ensured by the passage of the Occupational Safety and Health Act of 1970 (OSHA).

Some job descriptions feature a section detailing job conditions. If working conditions are particularly grueling, these conditions should be elaborated upon in the job description so the prospective employee can know what he or she is going to face. There are limits, however, to how "grueling" working conditions can be, and banks should be reminded that they must comply with all OSHA regulations. Banks typically should concern themselves with potential problems such as possible hazards in the workplace, sufficient lighting in work areas, care to avoid glare and reasonable noise levels in computer areas, adequate lavatory facilities, and elimination of anything that could possibly cause injury.

Banks must concern themselves with fairness in employment practices. A well-written, accurate job description can go a long way to ensure that banks maintain fair, nondiscriminatory, and legal hiring and performance standards.

5

USING JOB DESCRIPTIONS

Now that you've got a clear idea of how to put together a good job description for the employees of your bank, it's time to examine how the job descriptions in part II of *Job Descriptions in Banking* as well as those you develop on your own can be used. We've been stressing the importance of writing effective job descriptions. Now we'll focus on what an effective job description can do.

We've identified five areas in which we believe job descriptions are most helpful. These are:

1. Recruitment
2. Orientation & Training
3. Performance Standards & Evaluations
4. Compensation
5. Understanding Corporate Structure

RECRUITMENT

When you want to get a good idea of the type of person your bank is looking to hire, the job description is the perfect tool to turn to. Looking at the responsibilities and duties required for a particular position can give you a good fix on how much experience and management a prospective employee may need to have.

Recognizing the need

If all of the job descriptions are examined together you can also identify potential staffing problems. You might notice you are overstaffed in certain departments and understaffed in others. Positions which are unnecessary to keep the bank running smoothly might also be identified.

If you identify understaffing in a particular department, job descriptions should be able to help you identify the kind of person needed to complete a good operating staff.

Filling the job

The job description is an ideal tool to use when advertising a job opening. The information in a classified advertisement can be directly adapted from the job description.

In a classified ad, the opportunities for advancement within the bank can be specified. These can quickly be assessed by examining the job descriptions of both the open job and those to which it relates. If there is a genuine chance of advancement to a supervisory position, this can be highlighted in the ad.

The job description can also be used in the bank's job posting program. (See C. Eugene Looper, *Banker's Guide to Personnel Administration*, Chapter 13, "Job Posting: Job Opportunities Program." Boston: Bankers Publishing Company, 1983.) Employees can be kept abreast of current bank openings if job descriptions for the open position are posted. As a result, employee-supervisor communication can be improved, turnover can be reduced, and untapped talents can be identified.

Job descriptions are very useful for the interviewing process. They can be used to give the employee an idea of the room for career advancement in the job. The abilities of applicants can be matched to the abilities described in job descriptions. Paying heed to the details of an accurate job description can also make the screening process for job candidates easier.

ORIENTATION & TRAINING

By examining the duties and accountabilities detailed in the job description, they can be used as a starting point for orientation and training programs to be developed. Obviously, certain functions to be performed might require training the new employee. The job description is an excellent guide to planning a training program. In addition, the new or prospective employee can review the job description in order to get a clear idea of the skills that will have to be learned to perform the job effectively.

The job description is an ideal way to orient the new employee to the parameters of the job. It should not be used as a restrictive guideline but rather as a kickoff point from which an employee can grow on the job. As a result of using the job description for orientation and training, the employee will be able to form a clear picture of his or her job and its relationship to the other jobs in the bank.

PERFORMANCE STANDARDS & VALUATIONS

An accurate, up-to-date job description can be used as the basis for performance evaluations. The job description can give the employee clear expectations of what is expected on the job. If clear expectations are given in the job description, then the performance evaluation need not be a frustrating experience for employee or employer.

Job descriptions can also be used to give the employee a good idea of his or her future with the bank, in terms of career opportunities and wage parameters. They can be used effectively to develop upward mobility programs if employees can see that their current job can lead to promotions and added responsibilities. If the employee sees this development as a possibility, then he or she can use the job description as a touchstone from which strengths and weaknesses can be gauged. When the time comes for a performance evaluation, there should be little confusion over which areas the employee should have been working to improve since the last job description.

Job descriptions can also be used as a comparative tool when reviewing performance among various employees holding similar jobs or jobs within the same division. If the job description is used to set the standards that must be met to perform the job effectively, it will be an excellent tool when discussions about promotions, raises, or movement within the bank must be held.

If grievances do arise over performance evaluations, job descriptions can serve as an excellent defense for the grieving employee or employer. They can serve to quell disputes over duties, responsibilities, and accountabilities on specific jobs.

COMPENSATION

Deciding the worth of a particular job in a bank is a difficult chore. The data in a job description can often serve as a checklist for determining a job's relative worth within the organization.

In determining a job's worth to the bank, it is important to first establish organizational goals. After these goals are established, a measure of a job's worth can be to determine how the overall duties and repsonsibilities fit into the overall corporate gameplan.

Compensations for various jobs in the bank can be determined after the jobs are grouped according to area and responsibilities. These can be established from studying various job descriptions. After categorizing different jobs, they can be compared for relative worth within the bank.

Job descriptions can also be used to compare similar jobs in different banks to determine competitive pay scales. An accurate job description can go a long way in establishing equitable compensation among the employees of a bank.

CORPORATE STRUCTURE

Job descriptions are integral to almost every aspect of the bank's organizational structure. They can be used to establish hiring and interviewing procedures, to meet legal requirements, and to establish compensation programs.

Job descriptions not only serve to let the employees know their own responsibilities and duties, but also how they relate to other employees within their own division or other divisions of the bank. Furthermore, job descriptions can be used to determine not only the relationships among individual employees, but also the relationships of one division or department with another.

Employees are made aware of the duties they must perform to successfully meet departmental objectives. As a result, the job description can be used by the employee as a starting point to get a sense of where he or she fits into the overall organizational structure of the bank.

By identifying common job duties and responsibilities in the job description, jobs can be grouped into families or divisions. The job description here does not only serve to aid in understanding corporate structure but to establish the structure itself as well.

The job description can be used as a measure of how far an employee can go with the bank. If the bank's overall expectations are made clear in the job description, the employee should know that to move up within the bank, certain tasks must be performed and goals met. If clearly written, the job description should also allow the employee to have a good handle on the limits of his or her authority and responsibilities within the bank as a whole.

Because all corporations and banks change, the job description should be kept up-to-date to accurately reflect the job's place in the overall scheme of things. As time goes on and changes occur, it may be necessary to combine jobs and descriptions or to get rid of those which no longer fit into the overall plan.

Bank managers and personnel officers can use job descriptions to study and make changes in the bank's overall structure whenever necessary. If job descriptions are studied as a total body, weaknesses and excesses can be identified within various divisions and departments of the bank. As a result of studying the job descriptions, the overall structure of the bank can be improved and made more efficient.

PART TWO

Sample
Bank
Job
Descriptions

Now that you know how to write an effective, useful job description, you can examine the sample job descriptions in part II and use them as guides for your own bank's job descriptions. The job descriptions included here lend themselves particularly well to easy adaptation for similar positions in your bank.

All of the sample job descriptions follow the format discussed in earlier chapters. They are divided into chapters by various bank departments, with the exceptions of the senior vice president for planning and development and the executive secretary to the president which are included here because they both fall into areas of the bank which are considered to be top management divisions. Often, the president of the bank will not have a job description or, if he or she does, it will differ substantially from bank to bank. Job descriptions for secretarial positions in top management areas can easily be developed, however, as indicated by the job description which immediately follows.

JOB DESCRIPTION: Senior Vice President – Planning and Bank Development
DEPARTMENT/DIVISION: Planning and Bank Development
REPORTS TO: Executive Vice President
SUPERVISES: Secretary

JOB SUMMARY

Member of the top management team with direct responsibility for comprehensive strategic planning, serving the needs of selected major customers, and management of bank's real properties.

DUTIES

1. Serves as a member of the following bankwide committees:
   a. Senior Loan Committee.
   b. Personnel Committee.
   c. Senior Management Committee.
   d. Long-Range Planning Committee (chairman).
2. In cooperation with the President and Executive Vice President, heads the bankwide strategic planning process. Ensures that short-run and long-run plans are written, communicated, reviewed and evaluated on a quarterly basis.
3. From a bankwide perspective, as it relates to financial management, identifies and recommends changes and new procedures to eliminate weaknesses in practices and procedures for the purpose of control and prevention.
4. Keeps abreast of current trends in banking by regularly reading appropriate periodicals, preparing summary memos for the Executive Vice President and President, and by attending selected seminars and conventions.
5. Participates in and maintains the records for the bank's officer call program.
6. Recommends approved modifications in the strategic planning process.
7. Contacts and maintains relationships with likely sources of community development information such as real estate developers, realtors, the Chamber of Commerce, local utilities, building contractors and architects; directly promotes the bank's services where appropriate.
8. Follows up specific leads offering business development opportunities among high income citizens. This involves promoting the bank's services, placing the prospect in contact with the appropriate bank personnel and following through to determine the results of the meeting.

9. Maintains an active role in community affairs to improve the bank's visibility in the area and offer further opportunity to acquire useful information.
10. Serves on various civic committees, as designated by the Executive Vice President, to increase bank community involvement.
11. Responsible for all bank activities relative to real property, including negotiations for lease of bank's mineral rights.
12. Coordinate investment services for up-scale customer with Investment Division.
13. Supervises bank parking lot attendant.
14. Evaluates potential new branch sites.
15. Prepares new branch applications.
16. Responsible for special projects as assigned by the Executive Vice President.

ORGANIZATION

1. Initiate changes in the basic organization structure and complement of the planning function in order to accomplish objectives as developed in concert with the Executive Vice President.
2. Activate new work procedures and systems to accomplish planning and bank development objectives more efficiently.

FINANCES

Prepare the annual budget for Planning and Bank Development, administering allotted funds in accordance with the budget and approved fiscal procedures; and, recommend capital expenditures for planning and bank development.

RELATIONSHIPS

1. Responsible to the Executive Vice President for the fulfillment of his or her functions, responsibilities, and authority and for their proper interpretation.
2. Will advise and assist division heads, department managers, officers, and staff in their respective functions associated with the areas for which he or she has direct responsibility.
3. Will have extensive contact with customers, the public and the community, and is to conduct relationships in a manner that will enhance the overall marketing effort of the bank.
4. Will be called upon from time to time to participate with community organizations and in community projects.

JOB DESCRIPTION: Executive Secretary
DEPARTMENT/DIVISION: Office of President
REPORTS TO: President and CEO
SUPERVISES: Has no supervisory responsibility.

JOB SUMMARY

Primary: secretarial duties; secondary: assist Commercial Loan Department as time permits.

DUTIES

Secretarial Duties for President and CEO:

1. Take dictation.
2. Serve as receptionist for President and CEO (also for Chairman when secretary is out or away from desk).

Executive Secretary (continued)

3. Answer phone and screen calls (also for Chairman when secretary is out or away from desk).
4. Open mail and route mail that needs to go elsewhere.
5. Route mail from out box.
6. Keep diary of appointments up to date.
7. Make appointments.
8. Personal bookkeeping for President and CEO—pay monthly bills, prepare year end financial statements, make deposits.
9. Filing.
10. Keep a record of subscriptions coming to second floor and handle renewals.
11. Call Executive Committee member's secretaries to remind them of meetings which are held twice a month. Also call Personnel Department to tell them when first meeting of month will be held so they can have payment to Executive Committee members ready on that day.
12. Make airline and hotel reservations.
13. Write Christmas thank-you notes and other thank-you notes during the year for President and CEO.
14. Hand address Christmas cards which are sent to all employees by President and CEO.
15. Buy supplies for kitchen and President and CEO's offices.
16. Call Operations secretary each day to find out the interest rate of the federal funds bought or sold the previous date and write it on the daily balance sheet.
17. Supervise housekeeping for President and CEO's offices (have rugs turned periodically, furniture polished, etc.).
18. Represent President and CEO and the bank at all times.
19. Take dictation from Executive Vice President for Executive Committee Minutes.

Commercial Loan Department Duties:
20. Make sure real estate files are complete.
21. Make sure loans secured by real estate are complete.
22. Type letters to customers when a mistake has been made on the note informing the customer of the correction.
23. Help type purchase order assignments.
24. Help type subcontract assignments.
25. Help type insurance assignment letters.
26. Help type envelopes for outgoing mail (renewed loans, paid loans, etc.).
27. Help with the alphabetizing of notes and interest rate change notices.
28. Help with the filing of the notes.
29. Assume duties of Commercial Loan Department's secretary during vacation, when the secretary is out sick, etc.

ORGANIZATION
Has an inherent duty and responsibility to make recommendations to supervisor concerning possible methods to improve department.

FINANCES
Has the responsibility to make recommendations to supervisor concerning the budgetary needs of the department.

RELATIONSHIPS

1. Responsible to the President and CEO for the fulfillment of functions, responsibilities, and authority and for their proper interpretation.
2. Will have extensive contact with customers and the public, and is to conduct relationships in a manner that will enhance the overall marketing effort of the bank.
3. Will be called upon from time to time to participate with community organizations and in community projects.

By referring to specific job descriptions in part II of *Job Descriptions in Banking* you should be able to put together your own job descriptions and your own team of proficient bank employees.

6

INVESTMENT DEPARTMENT JOB DESCRIPTIONS

The investment department of a bank, in a broad sense, is concerned with establishing and maintaining an investment portfolio of securities which maximizes return and minimizes risk. This desire for regular income clearly contrasts to speculation which is typically a desire for capital gains.

The investment department job descriptions which follow detail the basic jobs necessary in such a department. All of these jobs, whether it be a secretary who ensures the day-to-day operations run smoothly or a securities clerk who implements securities transfers, combine to form a team which works together to successfully accomplish the goals of the investment department.

JOB DESCRIPTION: Senior Vice President
DEPARTMENT/DIVISION: Investment
REPORTS TO: Executive Vice President
SUPERVISES: Secretary
Securities Clerk
Investment Officer

JOB SUMMARY
To manage the Investment Portfolio of the bank in a manner which maximizes return while minimizing risk; to provide information to bank personnel as to interest rates and participate in

Senior Vice President (continued)

decisions involving rate sensitivity; to enhance image of bank in community and promote increases in commercial deposits and ancillary business.

DUTIES

1. Supervise investment portfolio activities.
2. Supervise investment portfolio personnel.
3. Initiate changes in asset structure and yield curve inflection.
4. Formulate interest rate models and methods to deal with each scenario.
5. Keep abreast of capital needs of commercial loan and operations divisions and plan portfolio accordingly.
6. Convey economic outlook and interest rate forecasts to other bank personnel.
7. Manage monthly Investmtent Policy Committee meeting which reviews all investment department activity.
8. Complete statistical and comparative analyses on a constant basis.
9. Work with computer programming as a tool.
10. Work with bank's general ledger concerning both income and assets.
11. Work with bank clearing, settlement, proof and operations divisions to maximize float on securities activities.
12. Complete purchase and sale activities with brokers.
13. Arrange settlements.
14. Deal with brokers and salesmen through constant telephone inquiries.
15. Deal with bank and trust customers about financial affairs through telephone and personal contact.
16. Participate in certificate rate determinations as member of Funds Liability Management Committee.
17. Supply material reviewed by #16.
18. Match assets in money market items to reflect specific short-term certificates and repurchase agreements.
19. Read, review, analyze, and synthesize trade periodical material:
    a. research of approximately 40 brokerage houses.
    b. 20 weekly and biweekly financial publications.
    c. 10 commercial bank publications.
    d. 5 legal or law review publications.
20. Administrative duties for 30 trust accounts (down from 200 from two years ago).
21. Complete knowledge of trust systems and operations.
22. Work with and train trust investment personnel, when solicited.
23. Relate knowledge of 800 trust accounts managed by bank to new trust administrators.
24. Participate in decisions to change and review trust operations through the Trust Administration and Review Committee and the Trust Policy Committee.
25. Work with individuals who are potential trust customers and steer them to use bank services.
26. Analyze creditworthiness of obligators.
27. Supervise municipal finance activities, both public and private placements.
28. Participate in general loan policies of bank and large corporate financings through the Senior Loan Committee.
29. Participate in personnel allocations and benefits through the Personnel Committee.
30. Participate in planning through the Advanced Planning Committee.

31. Direct focus on bank capital needs and allocations through Capital Formation and Structure Subcommittee.
32. Participate in the day-to-day management of the bank, its capital, its personnel, and its facilities through the Senior Management Committee.
33. Participate in the bank's community involvement through the local charitable trust donations.
34. Work with the controller's office to maximize the tax posture of the bank and increase after-tax earnings.
35. Work on civic and community projects to further the goodwill of the bank and enhance image of bank and self.

ORGANIZATION

1. Initiate changes in the basic organization structure and complement of the planning function in order to accomplish the objectives as developed in concert with the Executive Vice President.
2. Activate new work procedures and systems to accomplish planning and bank development objectives more efficiently.

FINANCES

Prepare the annual budget for Investment Department, administering allotted funds in accordance with the budget and approved fiscal procedures; and, recommend capital expenditures for planning and bank development.

RELATIONSHIPS

1. Responsible to the Executive Vice President for the fulfillment of his or her functions, responsibilities, and authority and for their proper interpretation.
2. Will advise and assist department managers, officers, and staff in their respective functions associated with the areas for which he or she has direct responsibility.
3. Will have extensive contact with customers, the public and the community, and is to conduct relationships in a manner that will enhance the overall marketing effort of the bank.
4. Will be called upon from time to time to participate with community organizations and in community projects.

JOB DESCRIPTION: Secretary
DEPARTMENT/DIVISION: Investment
REPORTS TO: Senior Vice President — Investments
SUPERVISES: Has no supervisory responsibility.

JOB SUMMARY

General secretarial/clerical duties for Senior Vice President — Investments.

DUTIES

1. Collate and mail customer statements.
2. File loose-leaf services.
3. Prepare time cards weekly on staff employees.
4. File and maintain Investment Strategy and Portfolio Goals book.

Secretary (continued)

5. Arrange meetings and notify members of the Investment Committee.
6. Prepare pay for members of the Investment Committee.
7. Transcribe dictation and file administrative documentation for Senior Vice-President — Investments.
8. Transcribe monthly minutes of Investment Committee.
9. Insure completion of all initial documentation for new accounts opened by Senior Vice President — Investments.
10. Take offerings from brokers.
11. Report daily interest rates to Operations Department and New Accounts Department of the bank.
12. Open and distribute mail for Investments.
13. Contact various banks each Tuesday and Thursday to get rate information.
14. Telephone reception activities.
15. Clean Board of Director's room before and after meetings held by Senior Vice President — Investments.
16. Type letters and memos for Investment Division.
17. Prepare and coordinate all material needed by Senior Vice President — Investments for various committee activities.
18. Assist the Securities Clerk in all phases of work (general ledger, accruals, etc.), especially bidding of portfolio bonds and securities transactions.
19. General tidiness of Investment area, including desks, magazines and periodical areas (library materials).
20. Monitor and prepare subscriptions to investment periodicals.
21. Coordinate customer traffic to Investment Division and direct inquiries to proper person or area of the bank.

ORGANIZATION
Has an inherent duty and resonsibility to make recommendations to supervisvor concerning possible methods to improve department.

FINANCES
Has the responsibility to make recommendations to supervisor concerning the budgetary needs of the department.

RELATIONSHIPS
1. Responsible to the Senior Vice President — Investments for the fulfillment of functions, responsibilities, and authority and for their proper interpretation.
2. Will have extensive contact with customers and the public, and is to conduct relationships in a manner that will enhance the overall marketing effort of the bank.
3. Will be called upon from time to time to participate with community organizations and in community projects.

JOB DESCRIPTION: Securities Clerk
DEPARTMENT/DIVISION: Investment

REPORTS TO: Senior Vice President — Investments
SUPERVISES: Has no supervisory responsibility.

JOB SUMMARY

Monitor, check, and implement all bank security purchases and sales.

DUTIES

1. Send advices to safekeeping agents or give instruction by telephone for purchases and sales of securities.
2. Make all general ledger entries for investment portfolio.
3. Verify broker's figures on purchases and sales.
4. Maintain pledged security receipts and reports.
5. Computer maintenance of investment records.
6. Maintain files for portfolio.
7. Ship bonds and securities to safekeeping agents or to brokers or their agents.
8. Ship securities to transfer agents for transfer of registered securities to ensure that interest payments are received on a timely basis.
9. Reconcile all investment accounts on general ledger with computer balances and with manual balances.
10. Take offerings from brokers, execute, and confirm trades when directed.
11. Acquire bids from brokers for portfolio securities to be sold and calculate yields on these bids.
12. Calculate and prepare Treasury Bill Futures Report daily and circulate to Auditor and periodically to President of bank.
13. Calculate and prepare Treasury Bill Futures purchase and sales forms.
14. Prepare Board of Directors Report monthly which summarizes all activity of the portfolio for the month.
15. Prepare maturity distribution report which is sent to Secretary of Board of Directors monthly.
16. Prepare weekly Location of Governments report used by senior management to secure funds in repurchase agreements and various public deposits.
17. Balance Federal Reserve Bank weekly statement to book-entry (i.e. government) securities.
18. Prepare U.S. Government Treasury Department report monthly.
19. Deposit and withdraw securities from vault on purchases, sales, and maturities.
20. Receive, post, and balance interest received for all securities.
21. Clip coupons held in local vault and send for collection.
22. Prepare pricing report monthly and distribute to Controller for preparation of liquidity report.
23. Acquire current financial information on bonds and securities held in portfolio.
24. Check portfolio for called bonds and send for collection to trustee bank when affected.
25. Contact correspondent bankers by phone and by letter to coordinate bond closings and other correspondent bank needs.
26. Balance broker's statements monthly and maintain files.
27. Check security safekeeping statements.
28. Occasionally prepare trust checks for clients and take instructions from clients concerning their accounts.
29. Refer clients to trust services, financial services, or other area of bank, i.e. recognize services available through commercial banking, trust banking, and investment banking.
30. Participate in obtaining rates and other material needed by Funds Management Committee.

Securities Clerk (continued)

ORGANIZATION

Has an inherent duty and responsibility to make recommendations to supervisor concerning possible methods to improve department.

FINANCES

Has the responsibility to make recommendations to supervisor concerning the budgetary needs of the department.

RELATIONSHIPS

1. Responsible to the Senior Vice President — Investments for the fulfillment of functions, responsibilities, and authority and for their proper interpretation.
2. Will have extensive contact with customers and the public, and is to conduct relationships in a manner that will enhance the overall marketing effort of the bank.
3. Will be called upon from time to time to participate with community organizations and in community projects.

7

TRUST DEPARTMENT JOB DESCRIPTIONS

Trust departments handle the operations of trust accounts that have been established with the bank. Since the goal of most trust accounts is to preserve property so that the income from the property or the property itself passes on to an institution or individual and since all trust accounts have unique requirements and goals, the staff of a bank's trust department can be quite extensive.

The job descriptions which follow feature some of the key people who might be involved in trust work. All of the job descriptions describe jobs that share the goal of formulating, directing, and carrying out the investment needs and goals of the many trust accounts at the bank.

JOB DESCRIPTION: Trust Officer — Investment Department
DEPARTMENT/DIVISION: Trust Department
REPORTS TO: Senior Vice President and Trust Officer
SUPERVISES: Assistant Trust Officer
              Secretary III

JOB SUMMARY

To formulate, direct and carry out the investment needs and goals of the trust accounts as established by the responsibilities accepted by the Trust Department as trustee and each client's specific characteristics relative to the trust.

Trust Officer — Investment Department (continued)

DUTIES

1. Plan portfolio.
2. Select securities.
3. Evaluate alternative investments.
4. Buy and sell securities.
5. General customer transactions.
6. Account administration.
7. Account reviews.
8. Prepare and present reports.
9. Develop and retain records.
10. Trust administration investment results and goals to clients.
11. Communicate investment results and goals to clients.
12. Authorize securities involvement.
13. Sign checks and other forms.
14. Communicate investment position and changes to trust administrators.
15. Member of Trust Investment Committee, Trust Review Committee, and Trust Policy Committee.
16. Cash management.
17. Employee administration.
18. Be alert for and report any potential new business or potential business opportunities.
19. Participate in officer call program and complete reports on calls as required.

ORGANIZATION

1. Initiate changes in the basic organization structure and complement of the planning function in order to accomplish objectives as developed in concert with the Senior Vice President and Trust Officer — Trust Department.
2. Activate new work procedures and systems to accomplish planning and bank development objectives more efficiently.

FINANCES

Prepare the annual budget for Investment Department — Trust Department, administering allotted funds in accordance with the budget and approved fiscal procedures; and recommend capital expenditures for planning and bank development.

RELATIONSHIPS

1. Responsible to the Senior Vice President and Trust Officer for the fulfillment of his or her functions, responsibilities, and authority and for their proper interpretation.
2. Will advise and assist department managers, officers, and staff in their respective functions associated with the areas for which he or she has direct responsibility.
3. Will have extensive contact with customers, the public and the community, and is to conduct relationships in a manner that will enhance the overall marketing effort of the bank.
4. Will be called upon from time to time to participate with community organizations and in community projects.

JOB DESCRIPTION: Secretary III
DEPARTMENT/DIVISION: Trust Department

REPORTS TO: Trust Officer — Investment Department
SUPERVISES: Has no supervisory responsibility.

JOB SUMMARY

Performs secretarial duties for Trust Officer and Assistant Trust Officer.

DUTIES

1. Secretarial duties.
2. Filing in Moody Investors and Harris Bank Economics.
3. Prepare six reports for the minutes and Trust Policy meetings.
4. Call on government rates daily and distribute rates once a week.
5. Distribute general rates daily.
6. Do trades on securities with brokers for general customers.
7. Send general customers receipts.
8. Prepare a list of maturities on general customers once a month and send notices to customers of such maturities.
9. Keep copies of security order tickets, send tender and advices to the Federal Reserve.
10. Keep general customer files up-to-date and also corporate and municipal files.
11. Make sure all material required by federal regulations on securities is obtained.
12. Prepare direction advices on trust purchase and sale. Follow-up with 2nd notices if not timely returned.
13. Give bid list to brokers and get their reply.
14. Get estate evaluations from Data Services and send them adds and deletes on securities.
15. Pay monthly property taxes for 6 trust accounts and bill 3 for reimbursements.
16. Log proxies and mail them.
17. Be alert for and report any potential new business or potential business opportunities.

ORGANIZATION

Has an inherent duty and responsibility to make recommendations to supervisor concerning possible methods to improve department.

FINANCES

Has the responsibility to make recommendations to supervisor concerning the budgetary needs of the department.

RELATIONSHIPS

1. Responsible to the Trust Officer — Investment Department for the fulfillment of functions, responsibilities, and authority and for their proper interpretation.
2. Will have extensive contact with customers and the public, and is to conduct relationships in a manner that will enhance the overall marketing effort of the bank.
3. Will be called upon from time to time to participate with community organizations and in community projects.

JOB DESCRIPTION: Trust Officer
DEPARTMENT/DIVISION: Trust Department
REPORTS TO: Senior Vice President and Trust Officer
SUPERVISES: Secretary — Trust Department

Trust Officer (continued)

JOB SUMMARY

Administration of Personal Trust, Family Trust and Estates. Primary responsibility is to communicate with the customer, then relay this information to the various members of our staff.

DUTIES

1. Review account balance sheet and determine accounts that have received income or principal cash and invest these funds.
2. Review and process all incoming mail related to trust accounts.
3. Handle calls related to trust accounts.
4. Review monthly with the investment staff the accounts that have come up for their annual review and make recommended changes.
5. Review drafts of statements, make corrections, and mail the final completed statement to the customer along with a letter explaining the contents of the statement.
6. Make sure that all assets have been placed properly on the books.
7. Consult with the new accounts about purchases they are considering making.
8. Communicate with customers to find out their objectives.
9. Be alert for and report any potential new business or potential business opportunities.
10. Will participate in officer call program and complete reports on calls as required.

ORGANIZATION

1. Initiate changes in the basic organization structure and complement of the planning function in order to accomplish objectives as developed in concert with the Senior Vice President and Trust Officer.
2. Activate new work procedures and systems to accomplish planning and bank development objectives more efficiently.

FINANCES

Prepare the annual budget for Trust Department, administering allotted funds in accordance with the budget and approved fiscal procedures; and, recommend capital expenditures for planning and bank development.

RELATIONSHIPS

1. Responsible to the Senior Vice President and Trust Officer for the fulfillment of his or her functions, responsibilities, and authority and for their proper interpretation.
2. Will advise and assist department managers, officers, and staff in their respective functions associated with the areas for which he or she has direct responsibility.
3. Will have extensive contact with customers, the public and the community, and is to conduct relationships in a manner that will enhance the overall marketing effort of the bank.
4. Will be called upon from time to time to participate with community organizations and in community projects.

JOB DESCRIPTION: Secretary
DEPARTMENT/DIVISION: Trust Department
REPORTS TO: Trust Officer
SUPERVISES: Has no direct supervisory responsibility.

JOB SUMMARY

Secretary to Trust Officer specializing in estate settlement, receptionist duties to division; responsibility for coordinating preparation and filing of income tax returns on trust accounts; payment of real estate tax on property held in trust; responsibility for supplies and operation of copying machine; seasonal filing of clients' personal income tax returns, notary services.

DUTIES

1. Transcribe dictation.
2. File correspondence and mail statements to clients.
3. Receive clients and messages.
4. Handle routine procedures without instruction including monitoring checking accounts.
5. Transfer funds from checking accounts to trust accounts.
6. Make distributions from trust account to checking accounts.
7. Monitor conference room use.
8. Assist clients in accomplishing banking needs in other departments of the bank.
9. Assist in inventory or disposition of personal belongings of estate property.
10. Assist in the distribution of mail.
11. Notarize documents for the Trust Division and bond closings.
12. Coordinate tax returns for preparation and finally filing with appropriate tax authority.
13. Payment of real estate tax on property held in trust by deadline of December 31.
14. File and pay income tax due on income tax returns for trust accounts.
15. File and pay personal income tax from trust account funds for those clients who refer their returns to the Trust Division for this service.
16. Responsible for ordering supplies and accomplishing service on copy machine.
17. Receptionist duties for clients entering the Division as well as inquiries of new trust business.
18. Relief filing for Trust Operations when needed.
19. Maintain *Wall Street Journal* file in library.
20. Perform duties for all Trust Officers and the Division Head, not just immediate supervisor. (This includes substituting in the absence of their secretaries (lunch breaks and vacations) and assuming new duties to relieve a new employee until adjustment is made.)
21. Be alert for and report any potential new business or potential business opportunities.

ORGANIZATION

Has an inherent duty and responsibility to make recommendations to supervisor concerning possible methods to improve department.

FINANCES

Has the responsibility to make recommendations to supervisor concerning the budgetary needs of the department.

RELATIONSHIPS

1. Responsible to the Trust Officer for the fulfillment of functions, responsibilities, and authority and for their proper interpretation.
2. Will have extensive contact with customers and the public, and is to conduct relationships in a manner that will enhance the overall marketing effort of the bank.
3. Will be called upon from time to time to participate with community organizations and in community projects.

JOB DESCRIPTION: Secretary
DEPARTMENT/DIVISION: Trust Department
REPORTS TO: Senior Vice President and Trust Officer
SUPERVISES: Has no direct supervisory responsibility.

JOB SUMMARY

General secretarial duties for department head; handling all tapes; keeps calendar; answer telephone and announce callers; file all correspondence; arrange committee meetings each month
and type minutes; keeping minute book and the prearranging of all meetings; typing monthly
reports.

DUTIES

1. Handle all tape material for Department Head.
2. Keep calendar for Department Head.
3. Answer phone for Department Head.
4. File all correspondence in various areas of the department.
5. Arrange Trust Administration and Review Committee and Trust Policy Committee
    Meetings.
6. Compensate Board of Directors.
7. Type minutes and keep minute book.
8. Service customers.
9. Transcribe dictation.
10. Collate and mail statements to clients.
11. Make distributions from trust accounts to checking accounts and to customers.
12. Assist clients in accomplishing banking needs in other departments of the bank.
13. Assist in distribution of mail.
14. Assist in inventory or disposition of personal belongings of estate property.
15. Notarize documents for the trust division and bond closings.
16. Receptionist duties for clients entering the division as well as inquiries of miscellaneous
    nature.
17. Relief filing for trust operations when needed.
18. Provide secretarial services to other members of the staff when time permits and such services
    are required.
19. Prepare miscellaneous forms for entry into the data processing work such as address labels,
    ticklers, checks to be printed by the computer, and the changing of other data relating to the
    pending entry file or the account master.
20. Be alert for and report any potential new business or potential business opportunities.

ORGANIZATION

Has an inherent duty and responsibility to make recommendations to supervisor concerning possible methods to improve department.

FINANCES

Has the responsibility to make recommendations to supervisor concerning the budgetary needs of
the department.

RELATIONSHIPS

1. Responsible to the Senior Vice President and Trust Officer for the fulfillment of functions,
    responsibilities, and authority and for their proper interpretation.

2. Will have extensive contact with customers and the public, and is to conduct relationships in a manner that will enhance the overall marketing effort of the bank.
3. Will be called upon from time to time to participate with community organizations and in community projects.

JOB DESCRIPTION: Secretary
DEPARTMENT/DIVISION: Trust Department
REPORTS TO: Vice President and Trust Officer
SUPERVISES: Has no supervisory responsibility.

JOB SUMMARY

Performs secretarial duties. Also, makes distributions from trust accounts to checking accounts; receiving clients and messages; assists clients in accomplishing banking needs in other departments of the bank; receptionist duties for clients entering the division; relief filing for trust operations when needed.

DUTIES

1. Secretarial duties for Vice President and Trust Officer.
2. Collect mag cards and all materials for mag card typewriter.
3. All mag work for the department. (Summary Plan Descriptions, Hunting Leases, Co-Trustee Agreements, Release and Receipt, Powers for Executor and Trustee, etc.)
4. Mail monthly *Estate Planning Studies and Briefs.*
5. Filing in Prentice-Hall books.
6. Filing in Tax Management Portfolio.
7. Filing of *Estate Planning Studies and Briefs.*
8. Maintain will file system.
9. Maintain dry insurance trust files.
10. Monthly statements for the department—have all corrections keypunched, have corrected statements printed and distributed to each respective officer.
11. File monthly statements in red folder.
12. File monthly old statements in blue folder.
13. Put together and distribute summaries and review each month.
14. Open and distribute mail everyday.
15. Open all new trust accounts.
16. Straighten magazine rack and throw away old issues.
17. Responsible for Agency Agreements (corporate, individual & joint), Co-trustee Agreements, and Revocable Trust Agreements.
18. Be alert for and report any potential new business or potential business opportunities.

ORGANIZATION

Has an inherent duty and responsibility to make recommendations to supervisor concerning possible methods to improve department.

FINANCES

Has the responsibility to make recommendations to supervisor concerning the budgetary needs of the department.

Secretary (continued)

RELATIONSHIPS

1. Responsible to the Vice President and Trust Officer for the fulfillment of functions, responsibilities, and authority and for their proper interpretation.
2. Will have extensive contact with customers and the public, and is to conduct relationships in a manner that will enhance the overall marketing effort of the bank.
3. Will be called upon from time to time to participate with community organizations and in community projects.

JOB DESCRIPTION: Assistant Trust Officer
DEPARTMENT/DIVISION: Trust Department
REPORTS TO: Senior Vice President and Trust Officer
SUPERVISES: Secretary

JOB SUMMARY

Administration of Trust Accounts; support and input into investment process; completing agency transactions for nontrust customers.

DUTIES

1. Answer phone.
2. Review tax returns.
3. Coordinate and do rest of filing.
4. Coordinate and do quarterly valuations of common trust funds.
5. Write letters.
6. Execute purchases and sales for trust and nontrust customers.
7. Investment counseling to nontrust customers.
8. Fill in for Trust Officer.
9. Process mail.
10. Allocate securities purchased.
11. Account administration.
12. Meet with clients and officers.
13. Guarantee signatures; assist in transfer stocks for nontrust customers.
14. Read investment information and form opinions.
15. Prepare work to be processed by operations.
16. Supervise files related to closely held corps.
17. Account Reviews.
18. Attend Trust Asset and Review meetings.
19. Be alert for and report any potential new business or potential business opportunities.
20. Will participate in officer call program and complete reports on calls as required.

ORGANIZATION

1. Initiate changes in the basic organization structure and complement of the planning function in order to accomplish objectives as developed in concert with the Senior Vice President and Trust Officer.
2. Activate new work procedures and systems to accomplish planning and bank development objectives more efficiently.

FINANCES

Prepare the annual budget for Trust Department, administering allotted funds in accordance with the budget and approved fiscal procedures; and, recommend capital expenditures for planning and bank development.

RELATIONSHIPS

1. Responsible to the Senior Vice President and Trust Officer for the fulfillment of his or her functions, responsibilities, and authority and for their proper interpretation.
2. Will advise and assist department managers, officers, and staff in their respective functions associated with the areas for which he or she has direct responsibility.
3. Will have extensive contact with customers, the public and the community, and is to conduct relationships in a manner that will enhance the overall marketing effort of the bank.
4. Will be called upon from time to time to participate with community organizations and in community projects.

JOB DESCRIPTION: Secretary III
DEPARTMENT/DIVISION: Trust Department
REPORTS TO: Trust Officer and Assistant Trust Officer
SUPERVISES: Has no direct supervisory responsibility.

JOB SUMMARY

Performs basic secretarial duties for Trust Officer and Assistant Trust Officer.

DUTIES

1. File correspondence for Trust Officer and Assistant Trust Officer (usually no more than once a month).
2. Type any correspondence (daily).
3. Answer telephone.
4. Transfer money between accounts (when requested—not daily).
5. Some simple computer work, such as setting up address labels, ticklers and checks to be printed on computer (when requested, not daily).
6. Help with statements—statement corrections (first of each month).
7. Open and distribute mail (daily).
8. Type checks for customers or to wire funds (when requested).
9. Help with first of month filing in vault (by schedule—usually no more than once every three to four months).
10. Use dictaphone (daily).
11. Post bonds to be registered (fairly infrequently).
12. Look on the bank's telephone bill and find the charge per call to be charged back to an account. Also give each officer the form on which to list each call to be charged back. (Forms are given out on the 23rd of each month, telephone bill is received after the first of the month.)
13. Collect money from employees from other offices when they use our xerox machine and from employees in this office when the machine is used for other than bank business. Take money to teller downstairs and ask for a "to-from" ticket (infrequently).
14. Receive clients and messages.

Secretary III (continued)

15. Assist clients in accomplishing banking needs in other departments of the bank.
16. Assist in inventory or disposition of personal belongings of estate property.
17. Collate and prepare customer statements for mailing.
18. Prepare computer work for correcting statements.
19. Receptionist duties for clients entering the division.
20. Relief filing for trust operation when needed.
21. Be alert for and report any potential new business or potential business opportunities.

ORGANIZATION

Has an inherent duty and responsibility to make recommendations to supervisor concerning possible methods to improve department.

FINANCES

Has the responsibility to make recommendations to supervisor concerning the budgetary needs of the department.

RELATIONSHIPS

1. Responsible to the Trust Officer and Assistant Trust Officer for the fulfillment of functions, responsibilities, and authority and for their proper interpretation.
2. Will have extensive contact with customers and the public, and is to conduct relationships in a manner that will enhance the overall marketing effort of the bank.
3. Will be called upon from time to time to participate with community organizations and in community projects.

JOB DESCRIPTION: Assistant Trust Officer
DEPARTMENT/DIVISION: Trust Department
REPORTS TO: Senior Vice President and Trust Officer
SUPERVISES: Secretary
            Assistant Employee Benefit Administrator

JOB SUMMARY

Administration of Employee Benefit Accounts and supervision of other employees in retirement plan area.

DUTIES

1. Constant correspondence.
2. Preview accounts annually with clients.
3. File documents required on timely basis with the Department of Labor and Internal Revenue Service.
4. Provide assistance and guidance to clients in reference to provisions of retirement plan.
5. Advise employees under plans of options.
6. Answer questions employer and employees have with regulations and operations of plan.
7. Follow proposals for changes and/or new regulations.
8. Coordinate amendments to master plans as required.
9. Supervise to insure that work is accomplished in order of importance.

10. Frequently provide investment staff with updated list of cash to be invested in particular investments.
11. Make payments to retired and terminate participants.
12. Supervise reporting all taxable distributions to the Internal Revenue Service.
13. Be alert for and report any potential new business or potential business opportunities.
14. Will participate in officer call program and complete reports on calls as required.

ORGANIZATION

1. Initiate changes in the basic organization structure and complement of the planning function in order to accomplish objectives as developed in concert with the Senior Vice President and Trust Officer.
2. Activate new work procedures and systems to accomplish planning and bank development objectives more efficiently.

FINANCES

Prepare the annual budget for Trust Department, administering allotted funds in accordance with the budget and approved fiscal procedures; and, recommend capital expenditures for planning and bank development.

RELATIONSHIPS

1. Responsible to the Senior Vice President for the fulfillment of his or her functions, responsibilities, and authority and for their proper interpretation.
2. Will advise and assist department managers, officers, and staff in their respective functions associated with the areas for which he or she has direct responsibility.
3. Will have extensive contact with customers, the public and the community, and is to conduct relationships in a manner that will enhance the overall marketing effort of the bank.
4. Will be called upon from time to time to participate with community organizations and in community projects.

JOB DESCRIPTION: Assistant Employee Benefit Administrator
DEPARTMENT/DIVISION: Trust Department
REPORTS TO: Assistant Trust Officer
SUPERVISES: Has no supervisory responsibility.

JOB SUMMARY

Assists the Assistant Trust Officer in servicing and administration of Pension and Profit Sharing Plans.

DUTIES

1. Calculate contribution estimates.
2. Pay insurance premiums.
3. Calculate insurance amounts.
4. Deposit contribution checks.
5. Calculate and prepare loans to participants.
6. Handle monthly pension payments to retirees.
7. File new plans and amendments with the Internal Revenue Service.

Assistant Employee Benefit Administrator (continued)

8. Prepare and file annual returns/reports with the Internal Revenue Service.
9. Prepare drafts for Summary Annual Reports.
10. Maintain master list of activity needed on each of our employee benefit accounts.
11. Calculate vested benefits of termed participants.
12. Compile annual list of distributions from trusts taxable to participants.
13. Calculate capital gains and ordinary income portion of Lump Sum Distributions.
14. Computer service contact person—prepare plans for computer service.
15. Routine correspondence with customer.
16. Handle mergers of trust accounts.
17. Handle maintenance of pension plans on pending entry.
18. Reconcile trust earnings.
19. Allocate contributions, earnings and forfeitures on a portion of our accounts.
20. Verify employer contributions.
21. Plan Administrator ticklers.
22. Be alert for and report any potential new business or potential business opportunities.

ORGANIZATION
Has an inherent duty and responsibility to make recommendations to supervisor concerning possible methods to improve department.

FINANCES
Has the responsibility to make recommendations to supervisor concerning the budgetary needs of the department.

RELATIONSHIPS
1. Responsible to the Assistant Trust Officer for the fulfillment of functions, responsibilities, and authority and for their proper interpretation.
2. Will have extensive contact with customers and the public, and is to conduct relationships in a manner that will enhance the overall marketing effort of the bank.
3. Will be called upon from time to time to participate with community organizations and in community projects.

JOB DESCRIPTION: Secretary
DEPARTMENT/DIVISION: Employee Benefits/Trust Department
REPORTS TO: Assistant Trust Officer
SUPERVISES: Has no supervisory responsibility.

JOB SUMMARY
Secretary to Assistant Trust Officer and continual correspondence with clients in reference to their pension and profit sharing accounts.

DUTIES
I. Typing
    A. Duties performed with "Memory" typewriter
        1. All Summary Annual Reports and cover letters

      2. All Investment Analysis reports for individual accounts
      3. Participant statements for each participant under each account
      4. Miscellaneous form letters

  B. Other forms and reports to prepare:
      1. Monthly plan Administration Activity Report
      2. Plan Administration Activity Committee approval sheets
      3. Beneficiary Designation and Participation forms
      4. Investment Strategy and Portfolio goals
      5. Participant Directed Investment forms
      6. Investment Authorization forms
      7. Sample board minutes

  C. Other typing duties
      1. Dictation of letters, forms and reports
      2. Preparation of checks
      3. Preparation of fees
      4. Updating tax information lists
      5. Updating master plans and preparation of adoption agreements

II. Filing
  A. General correspondence
  B. Tax information
  C. Legal documents
  D. Rotation filing of transaction ledgers, asset and lot ledgers
  E. Gathering data for file check lists

III. Other Duties
  A. Gathering data for meetings with clients
  B. Updating master CCH Bulletin books
  C. Updating master lists
  D. Preparation of customer statements (making sure they are in balance before mailing to clients)
  E. Receptionist duties including answering telephone
  F. Be alert for and report any potential new business or potential business opportunities.

ORGANIZATION

Has an inherent duty and responsibility to make recommendations to supervisor concerning possible methods to improve department.

FINANCES

Has the responsibility to make recommendations to supervisor concerning the budgetary needs of the department.

RELATIONSHIPS

1. Responsible to the Assistant Trust Officer for the fulfillment of functions, responsibilities, and authority and for their proper interpretation.
2. Will have extensive contact with customers and the public, and is to conduct relationships in a manner that will enhance the overall marketing effort of the bank.
3. Will be called upon from time to time to participate with community organizations and in community projects.

JOB DESCRIPTION: Trust Officer — Personal Trust and Estate Administrator
DEPARTMENT/DIVISION: Trust Department
REPORTS TO: Senior Vice President and Trust Officer
SUPERVISES: Secretary

JOB SUMMARY

Estate and Trust Administrator.

DUTIES

1. Estate administration:
   a. Secure will and arrange for its probate.
   b. Generally supervise the probate process.
   c. Become acquainted with the terms of the will.
   d. Correspond with heirs and beneficiaries and become acquainted with those with whom you will work closely.
   e. Inventory estate, obtain appraisal of personal and real property, and insure all assets are on books and accounted for.
   f. Secure account or meet with family CPA and attorney to arrange for filing for all tax returns.
   g. Do tax planning for the estate.
   h. Arrange for the disposal or sale of personal and real property if appropriate or arrange for the transfer of the property to the beneficiaries.
   i. Maintain and oversee income producing properties in the estate.
   j. Insure all tax returns are timely filed, including fiduciary returns.
   k. Supervise the closing of the estate with probate court.
   l. Make sure all claims and charges against estate are paid.
   m. Insure all property is disposed of in accordance with terms of will.
2. Trust administration:
   a. Insure account is properly set up.
   b. Insure all assets of trust are on books and accounted for.
   c. Correspond with beneficiaries and become familiar with them.
   d. Insure all needed information regarding beneficiary is on file.
   e. Determine needs of beneficiaries and establish goals.
   f. Insure that funds are invested in accordance with goals.
   g. Become familiar with trust department and insure any required distributions are timely made to proper person.
   h. Manage and inspect all income producing properties, including farmland, timberland, minerals, etc.
   i. Periodically review investments to determine if still appropriate for account.
   j. Insure all tax returns are timely filed including quarterly estimates of beneficiaries if appropriate.
   k. Correspond with beneficiaries or make contact as frequently as possible.
3. Additional functions incidental to above duties:
   a. Income tax planning consultation with customer
   b. Family estate planning consultation with customer
   c. Investment consultation
   d. Financial planning
   e. Property management

4. Be alert for and report any potential new business or potential business opportunities.
5. Will participate in officer call program and complete reports on calls as required.

ORGANIZATION

1. Initiate changes in the basic organization structure and complement of the planning function in order to accomplish objectives as developed in concert with the Senior Vice President and Trust Officer.
2. Activate new work procedures and systems to accomplish planning and bank development objectives more efficiently.

FINANCES

Prepare the annual budget for Trust Department, administering allotted funds in accordance with the budget and approved fiscal procedures; and, recommend capital expenditures for planning and bank development.

RELATIONSHIPS

1. Responsible to the Senior Vice President and Trust Officer for the fulfillment of his or her functions, responsibilities, and authority and for their proper interpretation.
2. Will advise and assist department managers, officers, and staff in their respective functions associated with the areas for which he or she has direct responsibility.
3. Will have extensive contact with customers, the public and the community, and conduct relationships in a manner that will enhance the overall marketing effort of the bank.
4. Will be called upon from time to time to participate with community organizations and in community projects.

JOB DESCRIPTION: Assistant Trust Officer — Operations Manager and Corporate Trust
               Administrator
DEPARTMENT/DIVISION: Trust Department
REPORTS TO: Senior Vice President and Trust Officer
SUPERVISES: Senior Trust Clerk
            Secretary
            Receipts Clerk
            Balancing and Control Clerk
            Fees and Disbursement Clerk
            Security Settlement Clerk
            Cash Management and Filing Clerk

JOB SUMMARY

Corporate Trust Administrator and Trust Operations Manager.

DUTIES

1. Reviews lists of assigned accounts for excess cash/overdrafts and determines course of action.
2. Read mail/correspondence and respond accordingly.
3. Answer telephone inquiries about accounts.
4. Solve problems associated with department balancing/computer work.
5. Review outstanding check list monthly.

Assistant Trust Officer — Operations Manager and Corporate Trust Administrator (continued)

6. Review ticklers of things to do or monitor.
7. Prepare program change request forms for data processing.
8. Work closely with data processing department to get new programming implemented and tested.
9. Insure that real estate property owned by an account has insurance and taxes paid.
10. Insure that general maintenance associated with real property is performed.
11. Prepare vouchers for payments to beneficiaries, work orders, transfers among accounts.
12. Dictate correspondence to customers.
13. Perform necessary advance work associated with bond closings.
14. Attend bond closings, sign necessary documents and insure that our duties are reviewed and questions answered.
15. Prepare amortization schedules for bond trusteeships/corporate accounts.
16. Set up ticklers necessary for new and existing accounts.
17. Wire funds to other co-paying agents/banks on bond issues.
18. Solve various problems associated with accounts.
19. Dual control activities—remove/deposit securities in vault and remove checks—periodically.
20. Review and correct customer statements before mailing.
21. Attend various Trust Department meetings.
22. Prepare Trust Operations training sessions that are given every Wednesday morning.
23. Insure that the Trust Department computer operations manual is kept up-to-date.
24. Prepare and/or order new Trust Department forms.
25. Order various non-stocked items/materials for the Trust Department.
26. Request and review new prospective trust operations employees.
27. Coordinate training of new trust operations employees.
28. Solve problems associated with security settlements.
29. Insure that the filming of security transfer ledgers is done—every two years.
30. Monitor Trust Department profit and loss statement and expense items.
31. Supply financial information to accountants concerning corporate and personal customers.
32. Prepare account synopsis sheet for new accounts.
33. Transfer bonds from bearer to registered form or vice versa.
34. Monitor the balancing of paid bonds and/or coupons.
35. Monitor the monthly printing of trust department statements.
36. Dictate memos to Trust Department personnel on changes and/or new policies.
37. Attend various schools and conferences concerning trust operations or corporate trust.
38. Insure that securities registration tax is paid—annually.
3º Insure that corporate trust accounts have paid their semi-annual obligation on bonds outstanding.
40. Prepare and/or approve various fee billings.
41. Dictate letters to people who are late in paying their rent or mortgage.
42. Sign checks and charge tickets.
43. Be alert for and report any potential new business or potential business opportunities.
44. Will participate in officer call program and complete reports on calls as required.

ORGANIZATION
1. Initiate changes in the basic organization structure and complement of the planning function in order to accomplish objectives as developed in concert with the Senior Vice President and Trust Officer.

2. Activate new work procedures and systems to accomplish planning and bank development objectives more efficiently.

FINANCES

Prepare the annual budget for Trust Department, administering allotted funds in accordance with the budget and approved fiscal procedures; and, recommend capital expenditures for planning and bank development.

RELATIONSHIPS

1. Responsible to the Senior Vice President and Trust Officer for the fulfillment of his or her functions, responsibilities, and authority and for their proper interpretation.
2. Will advise and assist department managers, officers, and staff in their respective functions associated with the areas for which he or she has direct responsibility.
3. Will have extensive contact with customers, the public and the community, and is to conduct relationships in a manner that will enhance the overall marketing effort of the bank.
4. Will be called upon from time to time to participate with community organizations and in community projects.

JOB DESCRIPTION: Senior Trust Clerk
DEPARTMENT/DIVISION: Trust Department
REPORTS TO: Assistant Trust Officer
SUPERVISES: Has no direct supervisory responsibility.

JOB SUMMARY

Oversee work in operations and solve any problems which occur. When someone is out due to sickness or vacation, see that the work gets done.

DUTIES

1. Answer phone.
2. Balance Broker Statements (monthly).
3. Balance Chase Manhattan D.D.A. account (monthly).
4. Balance Chase Manhattan Securities statement (monthly).
5. Be able to get daily report from Chase.
6. Charge checking and savings accounts for contribution to trust.
7. Review account balances daily.
8. Cut checks for distributions upon request.
9. Send out Courtesy Notices to customers with Cash Management Accounts.
10. Contact Chase when any problem occurs.
11. Take in new securities for trusts to be inventoried and distributed to proper individuals for placement on the books.
12. Receive all new real estate into accounts.
13. Follow up work on Real Estate Check Off list with the officer of the account.
14. Do daily wires to Federated.
15. Balance TDOA and Federated ledgers daily.
16. Balance Revolving Note Journal the 1st working day of each month—interest for Federated and TDOA.

Senior Trust Clerk (continued)

17. Get daily factors for Federated.
18. Contact C.D. customers upon maturity for instructions on renewal.
19. Handle purchases and sales of gold and silver for street customers.
20. File reports with Securities Information Center, Inc. on new securities received into Trust.
21. Take all calls from Investment firms for U of A accounts on security transactions. Complete order tickets for same and give to securities clerk(s).
22. Balance Unallocated Collections Account (monthly).
23. Balance miscellaneous Cash Receipts Account (monthly).
24. Balance Securities Settlement Account (monthly).
25. Receive instructions from officers for transfer of assets from one account to another. See that transfers are completed.
26. Handle payment of Registration of Securities Tax each year.
27. Complete check off sheets for Common Trust Funds. Report any discrepancies to Senior Trust Officer.
28. Get supplies.
29. Keep up with monthly safekeeping account statements.
30. Do all free deliveries on C.D.E. system for securities being delivered out for customers.
31. Figure interest for accounts closing prior to the end of the month.
32. Furnish C.D. rates and other information for the TDOA rate change on the 1st and the 15th of each month.
33. Clean out 4th floor storage room periodically.
34. Box up closed account folders for storage.
35. Do PCR's (Program Change Request Forms) when necessary for computer changes.
36. Work with transfer agents on replacing lost securities.
37. Check account balances sheet of Operations Officer when he or she is out.
38. Be able to help the Operations Officer's customers when he or she is out.
39. Be alert for and report any potential new business or potential business opportunities.

Things done when someone is out
1. Take mortgage and rent payments.
2. Establish dividends.
3. Release dividends.
4. Release incoming cash on pending entry.
5. Balance pending entry batch.
6. Balance all daily work.
7. Make loans with commercial loan department and pay off same.
8. Close accounts.
9. Pay requisitions.
10. Pay bills.
11. Balance computer checks.
12. Distribute computer checks accordingly.
13. Cut miscellaneous checks.
14. Figure fees.
15. Send out fee billings.
16. Balance paid coupons and bonds.
17. Do daily deposits and withdrawals for Federated and TDOA.
18. Daily filing in red folders.

19. Daily filing in security ledgers.
20. Cut checks on coupons and bonds payable by us.
21. Handle stock and bond purchases and sales for trust.
22. Receive new securities and miscellaneous items into account.
23. Handle purchases and sales of government securities for street customers.
24. Clear up discrepancies on Federal Reserve statements.
25. File completed trade tickets.
26. Record stock transactions in black books.
27. Cover purchases daily by withdrawing funds.
28. Balance notes and mortgages monthly.
29. Work up dividend and interest claims received from brokers.
30. Request amortization schedules.
31. Send notices of purchases and sales to Federal Reserve.
32. Redeem Series H Bonds.
33. Send Securities Officer for transfer.
34. Do exchange of securities due to corporate reorganization.

ORGANIZATION

Has an inherent duty and responsibility to make recommendations to supervisor concerning possible methods to improve department.

FINANCES

Has the responsibility to make recommendations to supervisor concerning the budgetary needs of the department.

RELATIONSHIPS

1. Responsible to the Assistant Trust Officer for the fulfillment of functions, responsibilities, and authority and for their proper interpretation.
2. Will have extensive contact with customers and the public, and is to conduct relationships in a manner that will enhance the overall marketing effort of the bank.
3. Will be called upon from time to time to participate with community organizations and in community projects.

JOB DESCRIPTION: Disbursements Fee and Insurance Clerk
DEPARTMENT/DIVISION: Trust Department
REPORTS TO: Assistant Trust Officer
SUPERVISES: Has no supervisory responsibility.

JOB SUMMARY

Distributions to beneficiaries, payment of bills, keep record of insurance policies and figure FMV fees for trust accounts.

DUTIES

1. Distributions for trust accounts.
2. Balance computer checks weekly and monthly.
3. Check calendar daily for distribution.

Disbursements Fee and Insurance Clerk (continued)

4. Check pending entry file to make sure all distributions have been either updated or amounts changed.
5. Maintain regular bills set up on computer twice a month.
6. Verify checking account deposit slips on computer.
7. Pay other miscellaneous bills with manual check daily.
8. Keep record and file daily all maintenance forms for trust accounts.
9. Keep check vouchers for manual checks typed (daily).
10. Make transfers from one account to another.
11. Make wire transfers to other banks.
12. Maintain tickler file and insure a timely receipt policy which proves coverage of property owned by Trust Department.
13. Property covered by mortgages or bond trust indentures (keep filed).
14. Maintain and work with liability insurance coverage for property owned by trust department. Also commercial hazard blanket policy.
15. Maintain a tickler computation of fees due, figure accordingly with FMV as per fee schedule. Check with officer in charge of account for approval.
16. Maintain a record of fees deducted and file statements of fees paid.
17. Fees are either deducted or the company is billed.
18. Do a report for fees by capacity code report first of month. (This means different types of accounts.)
19. Account balance report for the end of month.
20. Help balancing clerk (when absent or as necessary).
21. Help collection clerk (when absent or as necessary).
22. Help filing clerk as necessary.
23. Go to supply room as necessary.
24. Be alert for and report any potential new business or potential business opportunities.

ORGANIZATION

Has an inherent duty and responsibility to make recommendations to supervisor concerning possible methods to improve department.

FINANCES

Has the responsibility to make recommendations to supervisor concerning the budgetary needs of the department.

RELATIONSHIPS

1. Responsible to the Assistant Trust Officer for the fulfillment of functions, responsibilities, and authority and for their proper interpretation.
2. Will have extensive contact with customers and the public, and is to conduct relationships in a manner that will enhance the overall marketing effort of the bank.
3. Will be called upon from time to time to participate with community organizations and in community projects.

JOB DESCRIPTION: Securities Settlement Clerk
DEPARTMENT/DIVISION: Trust Department

REPORTS TO: Assistant Trust Officer
SUPERVISES: Has no supervisory responsibility.

JOB SUMMARY

Daily stock settlement, splits, dividends, transfers, rights offering redemptions, receipts of new securities, distribution of securities and other miscellaneous transactions, update assets records for purchase and sales.

DUTIES

1. Daily stock settlement.
2. Assist in security transactions concerning liabilities.
3. Assist in completion of memo security transactions (receipt of new securities, distribution of securities, and miscellaneous transactions).
4. The security transaction part of paperwork concerned with the purchases and sales of units of the common trust funds.
5. Update account assets records and maintain file for mutual fund investments.
6. Verify and file securities in vault.
7. Monthly report of purchases/securities not received.
8. Monthly report of securities removed or pending deposit to vault for 30 days or longer.
9. Register securities.
10. Be alert for and report any potential new business or potential business opportunities.

ORGANIZATION

Has an inherent duty and responsibility to make recommendations to supervisor concerning possible methods to improve department.

FINANCES

Has the responsibility to make recommendations to supervisor concerning the budgetary needs of the department.

RELATIONSHIPS

1. Responsible to the Assistant Trust Officer for the fulfillment of functions, responsibilities, and authority and for their proper interpretation.
2. Will have extensive contact with customers and the public, and is to conduct relationships in a manner that will enhance the overall marketing effort of the bank.
3. Will be called upon from time to time to participate with community organizations and in community projects.

JOB DESCRIPTION: Securities Settlement Clerk
DEPARTMENT/DIVISION: Trust Department
REPORTS TO: Assistant Trust Officer
SUPERVISES: Has no supervisory responsibility.

JOB SUMMARY

Prepare the transactions needed for settlement of corporate bonds, municipal bonds, government securities, certificates of deposits, etc. for our trust accounts and general accounts.

Securities Settlement Clerk (continued)

DUTIES

1. File tickets of daily transactions.
2. Prepare daily balance of corresponding bank accounts used by department and give to bank's investors.
3. Record monthly, quarterly, or semiannual interest received on certificates of deposit and savings accounts for trust accounts.
4. Record monthly or semiannual interest on government securities, corporate bonds, and municipal bonds.
5. Perform transactions needed for sale of corporate bonds, municipal bonds and government securities.
6. Settle purchase of corporate bonds, municipal bonds, certificates of deposit, bankers acceptances, and government securities.
7. Answer telephone.
8. Call various banks for certificate of deposit market rates.
9. File advices of securities transactions from Federal Reserve for trust and general accounts.
10. Keep a list of purchase and sale of government securities for general customers.
11. Obtain a daily report from Chase Manhattan Bank Securities Department for daily transaction through the Federated Cash Management System.
12. Input data to Chase Manhattan Bank through the Federated Cash Management System.
13. Gather wire instruction for department.
14. Set up bulk purchase and sale tickets.
15. Redeem bonds.
16. Transfer securities from one trust to another trust account.
17. Have securities order tickets alphabetically and chronologically.
18. Clip coupons on bonds.
19. Be alert for and report any potential new business or potential business opportunities.

ORGANIZATION

Has an inherent duty and responsibility to make recommendations to supervisor concerning possible methods to improve department.

FINANCES

Has the responsibility to make recommendations to supervisor concerning the budgetary needs of the department.

RELATIONSHIPS

1. Responsible to the Assistant Trust Officer for the fulfillment of functions, responsibilities, and authority and for their proper interpretation.
2. Will have extensive contact with customers and the public, and is to conduct relationships in a manner that will enhance the overall marketing effort of the bank.
3. Will be called upon from time to time to participate with community organizations and in community projects.

JOB DESCRIPTION: Collection Clerk
DEPARTMENT/DIVISION: Trust Department

REPORTS TO: Assistant Trust Officer
SUPERVISES: Has no supervisory responsibility.

JOB SUMMARY

Collect money that comes into Trust Department, mainly rents, mortgages, royalties, etc.

DUTIES

1. Set up new mortgages, bond for titles and notes.
2. Collection for the above.
3. Late reports on 10th of each month.
4. Balance mortgages, bond for titles and notes.
5. Collect all pending entry items.
6. Set up and release dividends.
7. Pay bonds and coupons.
8. List coupons and bonds paid.
9. File and withdraw securities in vault.
10. Answer phone.
11. File miscellaneous papers.
12. Help balance coupons.
13. Balance pending entry batch in afternoon.
14. Amount of interest for the year on mortgages, bond for titles and notes for those who need it.
15. Do pending entry transaction report.
16. Set up and delete items on pending entry.
17. Be alert for and report any potential new business or potential business opportunities.

ORGANIZATION

Has an inherent duty and responsibility to make recommendations to supervisor concerning possible methods to improve department.

FINANCES

Has the responsibility to make recommendations to supervisor concerning the budgetary needs of the department.

RELATIONSHIPS

1. Responsible to the Assistant Trust Officer for the fulfillment of functions, responsibilities, and authority and for their proper interpretation.
2. Will have extensive contact with customers and the public, and is to conduct relationships in a manner that will enhance the overall marketing effort of the bank.
3. Will be called upon from time to time to participate with community organizations and in community projects.

JOB DESCRIPTION: Clerk II
DEPARTMENT/DIVISION: Trust Department
REPORTS TO: Assistant Trust Officer
SUPERVISES: Has no supervisory responsibility.

Clerk II (continued)

JOB SUMMARY

Filing, transfer of funds, coupons, filing of security ledgers, bonds, IDOA, FMMF, FUSTO, FTFT.

DUTIES

1. File red folders.
2. Deposit/withdrawals Federal Money Market, Federal U.S. Treasury, and Federal tax free trust daily and typing checks.
3. Transfer income/principal daily.
4. File security ledgers daily.
5. Data sheets.
6. Call in totals from IDOA.
7. Balance coupons monthly. Mail to appropriate people.
8. Maintain vault and red folders.
9. Answer phones.
10. Verify coupons and bonds that are sent from co-paying agent.
11. Get daily list from officers concerning their withdrawals, deposit, transfers to daily work.
12. Be alert for and report any potential new business or potential business opportunities.

ORGANIZATION

Has an inherent duty and responsibility to make recommendations to supervisor concerning possible methods to improve department.

FINANCES

Has the responsibility to make recommendations to supervisor concerning the budgetary needs of the department.

RELATIONSHIPS

1. Responsible to the Assistant Trust Officer for the fulfillment of functions, responsibilities, and authority and for their proper interpretation.
2. Will have extensive contact with customers and the public, and is to conduct relationships in a manner that will enhance the overall marketing effort of the bank.
3. Will be called upon from time to time to participate with community organizations and in community projects.

JOB DESCRIPTION: Tax Administrator and Trust Controller
DEPARTMENT/DIVISION: Trust Department
REPORTS TO: Senior Vice President and Trust Officer
SUPERVISES: Has no supervisory responsibility.

JOB SUMMARY

Responsible for preparing most of the fiduciary tax returns for the Trust Department. Also performs various accounting duties such as bank reconcilement analysis of accounts, trust statement of condition, and expense reports.

DUTIES

1. Statement of condition.
2. Trust Expense report.
3. Value and record keeping on Common Trust Funds.
4. Fiduciary tax returns.
5. Trust Bank reconcilements.
6. Quarterly employer tax returns.
7. Annual employees tax returns.
8. Profit/loss statements (real estate).
9. Cash flow reports.
10. Rental taxes.
11. FNB-T report.
12. Research on tax questions.
13. Project income and various accounts.
14. Be alert for and report any potential new business or potential business opportunities.

ORGANIZATION

Has an inherent duty and responsibility to make recommendations to supervisor concerning possible methods to improve department.

FINANCES

Has the responsibility to make recommendations to supervisor concerning the budgetary needs of the department.

RELATIONSHIPS

1. Responsible to the Senior Vice President and Trust Officer for the fulfillment of functions, responsibilities, and authority and for their proper interpretation.
2. Will have extensive contact with customers and the public, and is to conduct relationships in a manner that will enhance the overall marketing effort of the bank.
3. Will be called upon from time to time to participate with community organizations and in community projects.

JOB DESCRIPTION: Balancing Trust Control Clerk
DEPARTMENT/DIVISION: Trust
REPORTS TO: Assistant Trust Officer
SUPERVISES: Has no supervisory responsibility.

JOB SUMMARY

Prepare work for data processing and balance all work for the Trust Department.

DUTIES

1. Pick up Trust work in data processing.
2. Answer phone.
3. Close accounts.
4. Make tickets with Federal Reserve for federated work.

Balancing Trust Control Clerk (continued)

5. Send out principal and interest due notices—monthly.
6. Place incoming money for principal and interest in appropriate accounts.
7. Keep up with federal and state taxes due on accounts.
8. Pay interest on loans—monthly.
9. Type checks and make check vouchers.
10. Delete security ledgers with 0 balances.
11. Do next month's activity report.
12. Set up ticklers on leases.
13. Give each officer a list of leases for review.
14. Balance and make batch trailers for all trust work.
15. Take batches to data processing daily.
16. Write new security number in security master header.
17. List numbers of computer checks.
18. Type list of checks outstanding 90 days or more.
19. Call for general ledger balance.
20. Request checks.
21. File, get supplies.
22. Verify daily work on film.
23. Request cash equivalent report, special statements, security ledgers for loans, data sheets, pending entry, PE by function code, deposit slips, security ledgers on mortgages and special reports.
24. File computer checks and manual checks.
25. Be alert for and report any potential new business or potential business opportunities.

ORGANIZATION

Has an inherent duty and responsibility to make recommendations to supervisor concerning possible methods to improve department.

FINANCES

Has the responsibility to make recommendations to supervisor concerning the budgetary needs of the department.

RELATIONSHIPS

1. Responsible to the Assistant Trust Officer for the fulfillment of functions, responsibilities, and authority and for their proper interpretation.
2. Will have extensive contact with customers and the public, and is to conduct relationships in a manner that will enhance the overall marketing effort of the bank.
3. Will be called upon from time to time to participate with community organizations and in community projects.

JOB DESCRIPTION: Stock Transfer Clerk
DEPARTMENT/DIVISION: Trust — Corporate
REPORTS TO: Stock Transfer Supervisor
SUPERVISES: Has no direct supervisory responsibility.

JOB SUMMARY

Maintains records on stock transfer transactions.

DUTIES

1. Reviews stock certificates for transfer requirements.
2. Types new stock certificates.
3. Posts Stock Register sheets.
4. Transfers bonds per written instructions.
5. Maintains Bond Ledger for registered bond issues.
6. Calculates dividends and interest payable to holders.
7. Types and mails dividend and interest checks to customers.
8. Maintains records for registrar accounts.
9. Maintains record of outgoing insured mail.
10. Proves (periodic) Stockholder Ledgers.
11. Answers (phone) customer inquiries concerning date of purchase, dividends received, etc.
12. Accepts and Delivers securities (over the counter).
13. Maintains and Settles Corporate Trust Settlement Sheet.
14. Completes form to answer brokers confirmations.
15. Calculates annual tax forms.
16. Mails completed transfer forms to customers.
17. Assembles customers' stockholder list upon request.
18. Maintains records of stockholder tax identification numbers.
19. Maintains Stock Transfer files.

ORGANIZATION

Has an inherent duty and responsibility to make recommendations to supervisor concerning possible methods to improve department.

FINANCES

Has the responsibility to make recommendations to supervisor concerning the budgetary needs of the department.

RELATIONSHIPS

Some telephone and personal contact with customers and brokers.

8

COMMERCIAL CREDIT DEPARTMENT JOB DESCRIPTIONS

The job descriptions for the commercial credit department describe jobs which share the goal of smoothly furnishing credit to companies or organizations engaged in manufacture or distribution of commodities with the maximum profitability to the bank and the minimum amount of risk. These jobs are distinguished from the jobs in the commercial credit department which focus on lending to individuals.

JOB DESCRIPTION: Executive Secretary
DEPARTMENT/DIVISION: Commercial Credit
REPORTS TO: Executive Vice President and Senior Vice President and Senior Loan Officer
SUPERVISES: Has no supervisory responsibility.

JOB SUMMARY
Acts as receptionist. Highly skilled in taking dictation. Writes letters for top management officers. Handles confidential matters. May be responsible for some records of a highly confidential nature and may relieve executives of routine administration duties. Considerable tact and judgment essential.

DUTIES

1. Answer telephone.
2. Route mail.
3. Take and transcribe dictation (using shorthand and dictaphone).
4. Schedule appointments and meetings.
5. Set up and organize meetings.
6. Receptionist for second floor.
7. Deal with customers.
8. Handle interbank transfers and dealings via oral telephone communications from various customers.
9. Order supplies for Commercial Loan Officers and Executive Vice President.
10. File bankruptcy claims.
11. Assist in issuance of letters of credit, both foreign and domestic.
12. Handle requests for expense reimbursement.
13. On a daily basis, update *Interest Rate and Maturity Manual* and pass information on to other departments.
14. Keep files on various committees for both Executive Vice President and Senior Vice President.
15. Update and maintain various manuals and regulation booklets.

ORGANIZATION

Has an inherent duty and responsibility to make recommendations to supervisor concerning possible methods to improve department.

FINANCES

Has the responsibility to make recommendations to supervisor concerning the budgetary needs of the department.

RELATIONSHIPS

1. Responsible to the Executive Vice President and Senior Vice President and Senior Loan Officer for the fulfillment of functions, responsibilities, and authority and for their proper interpretation.
2. Will have extensive contact with customers and the public, and is to conduct relationships in a manner that will enhance the overall marketing effort of the bank.
3. Will be called upon from time to time to participate with community organizations and in community projects.

JOB DESCRIPTION: Senior Vice President — Commercial Loan Operations
DEPARTMENT/DIVISION: Commercial Credit
REPORTS TO: Executive Vice President
SUPERVISES: Assistant Vice President — Commercial Loan Operations
                    Commercial Loan Secretary

Senior Vice President — Commercial Loan Operations (continued)

JOB SUMMARY

Indirect supervision of the Commercial Loan Operations area. To develop and manage commercial loan accounts which meet established lending requirements and which provide maximum profitability to the bank with a minimum of risk.

DUTIES

1. Interviews loan applicants and collects and analyzes financial and related data in order to determine the general creditworthiness of the prospect and the merits of the specific loan request.
2. Establishes, and negotiates where necessary the terms under which credit will be extended, including the costs, repayment method and schedule and collateral requirements.
3. Approves Class II loans up to $50,000 and serves as a Contact Officer on loans above this limit. In general, handles the more complex and substantial loans of the Department.
4. Collects and analyzes information which reflects the current creditworthiness of customers and the current merits of existing loans. Information may be obtained by direct inspection of the applicant's business and/or collateral, review of interim financial reports, personal interview, etc.
5. Monitors loan repayment activities and takes necessary action to collect from past-due accounts.
6. Advises customers, where possible, on business management and financial matters.
7. Develops new business by contacting prospects and customers. Also cross-sells bank services.
8. Serves as member of Loan Committee which makes preliminary evaluations of loan requests.
9. Develops material for and makes loan presentations to the Executive Committee where required.
10. Participates in community affairs to increase the Bank's visibility and to enhance new business opportunities.
11. Serves as a contact officer for non-borrowing accounts and loan customers for matters relating to other bank services.
12. Counsels with and assists in the training and development of Commercial Loan Officers.
13. Undertakes special projects relating to departmental services.
14. Ensure the protection of the bank's interests in matters of adequate documentation and adherence to bank policy and the various laws and regulations applicable to department operations, as well as the exercise of sound credit decisions in the commercial credit area.
15. Ensure a competent, motivated staff through training, counseling, supervision, and review of department activity and results.
16. Handle difficult or complex problems, transactions, computations and servicing of credits of a difficult nature.
17. Keep abreast of new developments in the field of commercial loans and changing government regulations, ensuring that the staff is kept informed.
18. Ensure the maintenance of good customer and/or dealer relations in cases involving improperly completed legal forms, collection problems, credit decisions and servicing operations in general.

ORGANIZATION

1. Initiate changes in the basic organizational structure and complement of the planning func-

tion in order to accomplish objectives as developed in concert with the Executive Vice President.
2. Activate new work procedures and systems to accomplish planning and bank development objectives more efficiently.

FINANCES

Prepare the annual budget for commercial credit, administering allotted funds in accordance with the budget and approved fiscal procedures; and, recommend capital expenditures for planning and bank development.

RELATIONSHIPS

1. Responsible to the Executive Vice President for the fulfillment of his or her functions, responsibilities, and authority and for their proper interpretation.
2. Will advise and assist department managers, officers, and staff in their respective functions associated with the areas for which he or she has direct responsibility.
3. Will have extensive contact with customers, the public and the community, and is to conduct relationships in a manner that will enhance the overall marketing effort of the bank.
4. Will be called upon from time to time to participate with community organizations and in community projects.

JOB DESCRIPTION: Secretary
DEPARTMENT/DIVISION: Commercial Credit
REPORTS TO: Senior Vice President — Commercial Loan Operations
SUPERVISES: Has no supervsiory responsibility.

JOB SUMMARY

Acts as a receptionist. Types letters, documents and reports required by department. Handles some confidential records for department. Prepares loan papers, notes, mortgages, etc., for Commercial Loan Officers. Checks accuracy of loan papers. Prepares checks for pay-outs on loans. Must be able to figure notes, interest charges, etc. Relieves other secretaries in the Commercial Loan Division when necessary. Assists window personnel when needed. Exercises independent judgment under moderate supervision.

DUTIES

1. Greet customers.
2. Answer telephone.
3. Type letters, reports, and documents.
4. Prepare loan papers, notes, mortgages, etc.
5. Handle some confidential records for department.
6. Check accuracy of loan papers.
7. Relieve other secretaries in division.
8. Assist Loan Tellers when needed.
9. Is alert for and reports any potential new business or potential business opportunities.

ORGANIZATION

Has an inherent duty and responsibility to make recommendations to supervisor concerning possible methods to improve department.

Secretary (continued)

FINANCES
Has the responsibility to make recommendations to supervisor concerning the budgetary needs of the department.

RELATIONSHIPS
1. Responsible to the Senior Vice President — Commercial Loans for the fulfillment of functions, responsibilities, and authority and for their proper interpretation.
2. Will have extensive contact with customers and the public, and is to conduct relationships in a manner that will enhance the overall marketing effort of the bank.
3. Will be called upon from time to time to participate with community organizations and in community projects.

JOB DESCRIPTION: Assistant Vice President
DEPARTMENT/DIVISION: Commercial Credit
REPORTS TO: Senior Vice President — Commercial Loan Operations
SUPERVISES: Loan Teller I
             Loan Teller II
             Loan Teller III

JOB SUMMARY
Commercial Loan Operations Officer with limited lending authority. This includes supervision of all daily activities of the department and to represent the bank in a manner beneficial to the bank.

DUTIES
1. Pick up computer work daily.
2. Pick up mail in mail room for department and other officers on second floor daily.
3. Check computer work and distribute to personnel responsible for proofing of work daily.
4. Sort department and branch mail and have ready for personnel who work up the mail daily.
5. Check new branch notes that come from branch the previous day and give to computer input person daily.
6. Distribute officer notifications daily.
7. Interview loan customers, approve or disapprove loan, and fill out loan approval daily.
8. Approve renewal of loans daily.
9. When necessary, type loans and other documents.
10. Help other officers with their customers daily.
11. Call on returned checks.
12. Work past due accounts.
13. Check to see if computer work balances with general ledger daily.
14. Answer questions and help loan tellers with any problems they have in their daily work.
15. Maintain dual control of negotiable collateral.
16. Notarize documents for customers, but not for the bank.
17. Distribute past due reports to officers — weekly.
18. Make adjustments on loans that have paid out and have a small debit or credit balance — weekly.

19. Put loans on zero accrual that are beyond ninety days past due — weekly.
20. Responsible for all reports that come from the department whether on a scheduled basis or a special report requested by an officer.
21. Get together all reports that are needed by the bank examiners.
22. Get information together for commercial part of call report and past due report — quarterly.
23. Sign all charges for monthly payments that have been authorized by customers.
24. Sign officers' checks for loan proceeds daily.
25. Prepare all general ledger tickets for letters of credit.
26. Keep a tickler system for expiration dates of letters of credit.
27. Make sure that letters of credit are not on computer balance — monthly.
28. Send in credit life insurance report — monthly.
29. Handle large participations (this includes making sure notices that go to customers are correct).
30. Sign all general ledger tickets on participation loans and check to see that they have been prepared correctly.
31. Help customers who have questions regarding loans. (This includes getting customers to the right person or department when they have a question regarding a bank service.)
32. Handle correspondence on secured loans.
33. Keep department manuals up to date.
34. Keep up with prime rate and put on computer each day.

ORGANIZATION

1. Initiate changes in the basic organization structure and complement of the planning function in order to accomplish objectives as developed in concert with the Senior Vice President — Commercial Loan Operations.
2. Activate new work procedures and systems to accomplish planning and bank development objectives more efficiently.

FINANCES

Prepare the annual budget for Commercial Credit, administering allotted funds in accordance with the budget and approved fiscal procedures; and, recommend capital expenditures for planning and bank development.

RELATIONSHIPS

1. Responsible to the Senior Vice President — Commercial Loan Operations for the Fulfillment of his or her functions, responsibilities, and authority and for their proper interpretation.
2. Will advise and assist department managers, officers, and staff in their respective functions associated with the areas for which he or she has direct responsibility.
3. Will have extensive contact with customers, the public and the community, and is to conduct relationships in a manner that will enhance the overall marketing effort of the bank.
4. Will be called upon from time to time to participate with community organizations and in community projects.

JOB DESCRIPTION: Secretary
DEPARTMENT/DIVISION: Commercial Credit
REPORTS TO: Assistant Vice President — Commercial Loans
SUPERVISES: Has no supervisory responsibility.

Secretary (continued)

JOB SUMMARY

Acts as receptionist. Types letters, documents and reports required by department. Handles some confidential records for department. Prepares loan papers, notes, mortgages, etc., for Commercial Loan officers. Checks accuracy of loan papers. Prepares checks for pay-outs on loans. Must be able to figure notes, interest charges, etc. Relieves other secretaries in the Commercial Loan Division when necessary. Assists window personnel when needed. Exercises independent judgment under moderate supervision.

DUTIES

1. Greet customers.
2. Answer telephone.
3. Type letters, reports, and documents.
4. Prepare loan papers, notes, mortgages, etc.
5. Handle some confidential records for department.
6. Check accuracy of loan papers.
7. Relieve other secretaries in division.
8. Assist Loan Tellers when needed.

ORGANIZATION

Has an inherent duty and responsibility to make recommendations to supervisor concerning possible methods to improve department.

FINANCES

Has the responsibility to make recommendations to supervisor concerning the budgetary needs of the department.

RELATIONSHIPS

1. Responsible to the Assistant Vice President — Commercial Loans for the fulfillment of functions, responsibilities, and authority and for their proper interpretation.
2. Will have extensive contact with customers and the public, and is to conduct relationships in a manner that will enhance the overall marketing effort of the bank.
3. Will be called upon from time to time to participate with community organizations and in community projects.

JOB DESCRIPTION: Collateral Insurance and Documentation Clerk
DEPARTMENT/DIVISION: Commercial Credit
REPORTS TO: Assistant Vice President
SUPERVISES: Has no supervisory responsibility.

JOB SUMMARY

Job is primarily one of processing the approved new loans and renewals. This would include typing the various notes and related documents disbursing proceeds, establishing necessary collateral files and other clerical duties.

DUTIES

1. Pull notes from file in order to work daily mail.
2. Sort incoming mail for our department.
3. Type renewal notes and new notes with all related documents that can be prepared in department.
4. Prepare mortgage releases, payment extensions, remittance reports for SBA participation loan and prepare file cards for assigned life insurance policies.
5. Keep updated Mortgage Insurance card file.
6. Keep file of satisfied mortgage slips.
7. Check for and file UCC's and motor vehicle titles.
8. Have access to dual control collateral vault for depositing and withdrawing negotiable collateral.
9. Wait on customers at window.
10. Answer telephone inquiries from general public, customers and other bank personnel.
11. Take payments, payoffs, deposits and cash checks.
12. File commercial notes.
13. Balance daily work.
14. Send forms for recordance with county or state.
15. Send out mail.
16. Perform notary work.
17. Perform various types of correspondence for collateral assignments.
18. Receive and return cash for day's business.
19. Limited supervisory duties when immediate supervisor is out of bank.

ORGANIZATION

Has an inherent duty and responsibility to make recommendations to supervisor concerning possible methods to improve department.

FINANCES

Has the responsibility to make recommendations to supervisor concerning the budgetary needs of the department.

RELATIONSHIPS

1. Responsible to the Assistant Vice President for the fulfillment of functions, responsibilities, and authority and for their proper interpretation.
2. Will have extensive contact with customers and the public and is to conduct relationships in a manner that will enhance the overall marketing effort of the bank.
3. Will be called upon from time to time to participate with community organizations and in community projects.

JOB DESCRIPTION: Document Preparation and Filing Clerk
DEPARTMENT/DIVISION: Commercial Credit
REPORTS TO: Assistant Vice President — Commercial Credit
SUPERVISES: Has no supervisory responsibility.

Document Preparation and Filing Clerk (continued)

JOB SUMMARY

May be accountable for a cash drawer. Accepts payment on loans. Keeps records of all transactions. Makes checks on loans as instructed by lending officer. Checks accuracy of loan papers. Responsible for proper filing of notes, mortgages, insurance files and related loan papers. Prepares reports for the department. Figures discounts and payoffs. Must be able to figure notes, interest, charges, etc. Handles negotiable securities in vault. Keeps files on wholesale checking reports. Prepares floor plan interest statements. Trains new personnel. Takes on responsibilities of supervisor when necessary. Reasonable amount of judgment required with moderate supervision.

DUTIES

1. Operate cash drawer.
2. Accept payment on loans.
3. Prepare loan papers, notes, mortgages, etc.
4. Check accuracy of loan papers.
5. Figure discounts, pay-offs, and insurance rates.
6. Verify interest and charges.
7. Prepare checks for payouts on loans.
8. Keep security files and wholesale checking report files.
9. Keep negotiable stocks in vault.
10. Prepare floor plan interest statements.
11. Work up morning mail.

ORGANIZATION

Has an inherent duty and responsibility to make recommendations to supervisor concerning possible methods to improve department.

FINANCES

Has the responsibility to make recommendations to supervisor concerning the budgetary needs of the department.

RELATIONSHIPS

1. Responsible to the Assistant Vice President — Commercial Credit for the fulfillment of functions, responsibilities, and authority and for their proper interpretation.
2. Will have extensive contact with customers and the public, and is to conduct relationships in a manner that will enhance the overall marketing effort of the bank.
3. Will be called upon from time to time to participate with community organizations and in community projects.

JOB DESCRIPTION: Data Entry Clerk
DEPARTMENT/DIVISION: Commercial Credit
REPORTS TO: Assistant Vice President — Commercial Credit
SUPERVISES: Has no supervisory responsibility.

JOB SUMMARY

Convert the manual operations of Commercial Loans (payments, loans, renewals) onto paper and then keypunch that data into the computer.

DUTIES

1. Type lists of new loans.
2. Separate various forms and pass them out to loan officers.
3. Fill out general ledger tickets.
4. Go through previous day's new loans and put any endorses for these loans on computer.
5. Write up previous day's new branch notes on input sheets and totals.
6. Balance Commercial Loan accounts with general ledger.
7. Write up all new loans, renewals, and payments on assorted input sheets.
8. Keypunch all data into the computer.
9. Make all adjustments, corrections, and changes on any loan.
10. Clean out files once a month.
11. Throw away old computer printouts. Responsible for keeping printouts from the last day of every month in a separate file.
12. Check all new loans once a week to make sure payment schedules are correctly entered into the computer.
13. Answer phone.
14. Type loans and take customer's payments.
15. When prime rate changes, separate and alphabetize triplicate notices which are put out by the computer. Pull all loans whose interest rate is to change with the prime and check each notice with each loan for the correct rate. Mail each customer the notice of the change. Give each loan officer the duplicate copy of his or her customers' notices. Check previous day's loans and interest disclosures statements for correct dates and amounts. See that a letter is written to any customer informing him or her of errors.
16. Order computer reports from data processing.
17. Write all new reports requested.
18. Punch computer cards on Univac 1700.

ORGANIZATION

Has an inherent duty and responsibility to make recommendations to supervisor concerning possible methods to improve department.

FINANCES

Has the responsibility to make recommendations to supervisor concerning the budgetary needs of the department.

RELATIONSHIPS

1. Responsible to the Assistant Vice President — Commercial Credit for the fulfillment of functions, responsibilities and authority and for their proper interpretation.
2. Will have extensive contact with customers and the public, and is to conduct relationships in a manner that will enhance the overall marketing effort of the bank.
3. Will be called upon from time to time to participate with community organizations and in community projects.

JOB DESCRIPTION: Senior Vice President and Senior Loan Officer
DEPARTMENT/DIVISION: Commercial Credit
REPORTS TO: Executive Vice President
SUPERVISES: Senior Vice President — Commercial Lending
               Vice President — Commercial Lending
               Commercial Credit Department Manager
               Executive Secretary

JOB SUMMARY

Administer the Commercial Loan function in accordance with the policies of the bank under direction of the Executive Vice President. Make loans and assist in the general management of the bank as chairman of the Senior Loan Committee and as a member of the Senior Management, Personnel, Data Processing, Trust Administration and Review, and Asset/Liability Committees.

DUTIES

1. Make loans.
2. Assist other loan personnel in loan matters.
3. Solicit new loan business.
4. Monitor compliance with loan policy and appropriate regulations.
5. Structure and complete various documents used in lending process, e.g. loan agreements.
6. Collect loans.
7. Monitor overall performance of loan officers.
8. Provide training for commercial loan personnel.
9. Handle some bank related customer matters or inquiries not necessarily involving the lending function.
10. Participate in overall bank management through committee assignments.
11. Maintain relationships with correspondent banks relative to the sale and purchase of loan participations.
12. Provide executive management with reports and loan information as required.

ORGANIZATION

1. Initiate changes in the basic organization structures and complement of the planning function in order to accomplish objectives as developed in concert with the Executive Vice President.
2. Activate new work procedures and systems to accomplish planning and bank development objectives more efficiently.

FINANCES

Prepare the annual budget for Commercial Credit, administering allotted funds in accordance with the budget and approved fiscal procedures; and, recommend capital expenditures for planning and bank development.

RELATIONSHIPS

1. Responsible to the Executive Vice President for the fulfillment of his or her functions, responsibilities, and authority and for their proper interpretation.
2. Will advise and assist department managers, officers, and staff in their respective functions associated with the areas for which he or she has direct responsibility.

3. Will have extensive contact with customers, the public and the community, and is to conduct relationships in a manner that will enhance the overall marketing effort of the bank.
4. Will be called upon from time to time to participate with community organizations and in community projects.

JOB DESCRIPTION: Vice President — Commercial Lending
DEPARTMENT/DIVISION: Commercial Credit
REPORTS TO: Senior Vice President and Senior Loan Officer
SUPERVISES: Secretary

JOB SUMMARY

To develop and manage commercial loan accounts which meet established lending requirements and which provide maximum profitability to the bank with a minimum of risk.

DUTIES

1. Interview loan applicants and collect and analyze financial and related data in order to determine the general creditworthiness of the prospect and the merits of the specific loan request.
2. Establish, and negotiate where necessary the terms under which credit will be extended, including the costs, repayment method and schedule and collateral requirements.
3. Approve Class II loans up to $50,000 and serve as a Contact Officer on loans above this limit. In general, handle the more complex and substantial loans of the department.
4. Collect and analyze information which reflects the current creditworthiness of customers and the current merits of existing loans. Information may be obtained by direct inspection of the applicant's business and/or collateral, review of interim financial reports, personal interview, etc.
5. Monitor loan repayment activities and take necessary action to collect from past due accounts.
6. Advise customers, where possible, on business management and financial matters.
7. Develop new business by contacting prospects and customers. Also cross-sells bank services.
8. Serve as member of Loan Committee which makes preliminary evaluations of loan requests.
9. Develop material for and make loan presentations to the Executive Committee where required.
10. Participate in community affairs to increase the bank's visibility and to enhance new business opportunities.
11. Serve as a contact officer for non-borrowing accounts and loan customers for matters relating to other bank services.
12. Counsel with and assist in the training and development of Commercial Loan Officers.
13. Undertake special projects relating to departmental services.

ORGANIZATION

1. Initiate changes in the basic organization structure and complement of the planning function in order to accomplish objectives as developed in concert with the Senior Vice President and Senior Loan Officer.
2. Activate new work procedures and systems to accomplish planning and bank development objectives more efficiently.

Vice President — Commercial Lending (continued)

FINANCES

Prepare the annual budget for Commercial Credit, administering allotted funds in accordance with the budget and approved fiscal procedures; and, recommend capital expenditures for planning and bank development.

RELATIONSHIPS

1. Responsible to the Senior Vice President and Senior Loan Officer for the fulfillment of his or her functions, responsibilities, and authority and for their proper interpretation.
2. Will advise and assist department managers, officers, and staff in their respective functions associated with the areas for which he or she has direct responsibility.
3. Will have extensive contact with customers, the public and the community, and is to conduct relationships in a manner that will enhance the overall marketing effort of the bank.
4. Will be called upon from time to time to participate with community organizations and in community projects.

JOB DESCRIPTION: Commercial Credit Department Manager
DEPARTMENT/DIVISION: Commercial Credit
REPORTS TO: Senior Vice President and Senior Loan Officer — Commercial Lending
SUPERVISES: Administrative Assistant — Financial and Credit Information
　　　　　　　Secretary — Loan/Preparation/Review
　　　　　　　Filing Clerk

JOB SUMMARY

Under the charge of the Senior Vice President and Senior Loan Officer, this position is largely concerned with the supervision and control of a wide variety of duties as found in the Commercial Credit Department.

DUTIES

1. Analyze financial statements.
2. Structure loans.
3. Administer loan agreements.
4. Generate quarterly and monthly interest rate and problem loan reports.
5. Assist loan officers in structuring credits.
6. Establish commercial credit department policy.
7. Manage commercial credit department.
8. Prepare applications for the Senior Loan Committee.
9. Function as secretary to the Senior Loan Committee.
10. Sit on the Loan Review Committee.
11. Prepare commercial loan advances.
12. Review new commercial loans for adherence to loan policy.

ORGANIZATION

1. Initiate changes in the basic organization structures and complement of the planning function in order to accomplish objectives as developed in concert with the Senior Vice President and Senior Loan Officer — Commercial Lending.

2. Activate new work procedures and systems to accomplish planning and bank development objectives more efficiently.

FINANCES

Prepare the annual budget for Commercial Credit, administering allotted funds in accordance with the budget and approved fiscal procedures; and, recommend capital expenditures for planning and bank development.

RELATIONSHIPS

1. Responsible to the Senior Vice President and Senior Loan Officer — Commercial Lending for the fulfillment of his or her functions, responsibilities, and authority and for their proper interpretation.
2. Will advise and assist department managers, officers, and staff in their respective functions associated with the areas for which he or she has direct responsibility.
3. Will have extensive contact with customers, the public and the community, and is to conduct relationships in a manner that will enhance the overall marketing effort of the bank.
4. Will be called upon from time to time to participate with community organizations and in community projects.

JOB DESCRIPTION: Administrative Assistant — Financial and Credit Information
DEPARTMENT/DIVISION: Commercial Credit
REPORTS TO: Commercial Credit Department Manager
SUPERVISES: Has no supervisory responsibility.

JOB SUMMARY

Handle oral and written inquiries, check credit and in-house information for lending officers and for other purposes regarding customers and employees and handle correspondence as requested by branches and officers. Work with lending officers in maintaining current financial statements necessary to loans and helping customers fill out financial statements when requested by lending officer. Work with credit files necessary to properly maintain them.

DUTIES

1. Filing.
2. Letter writing.
3. Telephoning.
4. Checking in-house information and credit.
5. Providing credit information.
6. Serve with others in department as dual control for safe deposit and check savings bonds quarterly for security purposes.
7. Any other activity necessary in the day-to-day operation of the department.

ORGANIZATION

Has an inherent duty and responsibility to make recommendations to supervisor concerning possible methods to improve department.

Administrative Assistant — Financial and Credit Information (continued)

FINANCES

Has the responsibility to make recommendations to supervisor concerning the budgetary needs of the department.

RELATIONSHIPS

1. Responsible to the Commercial Credit Department Manager for the fulfillment of functions, responsibilities, and authority and for their proper interpretation.
2. Will have extensive contact with customers and the public, and is to conduct relationships in a manner that will enhance the overall marketing effort of the bank.
3. Will be called upon from time to time to participate with community organizations and in community projects.

JOB DESCRIPTION: Secretary — Loan/Preparation/Review
DEPARTMENT/DIVISION: Commercial Credit
REPORTS TO: Commercial Credit Department Manager
SUPERVISES: Has no supervisory responsibility.

JOB SUMMARY

Job involves maintaining large volume of credit file records. Monitors the bank's National Lines of Credit. Requires some independent judgment under moderate supervision. Relieves management of some routine detail work. Has access to confidential records. Work requires use of office machines such as typewriter and calculator. Work involves handling somewhat complex operations.

DUTIES

1. Answer telephone.
2. Knowledge such as credit and accounting.
3. Monitor the bank's National Lines of Credit.
4. Prepare applications for the Senior Loan Committee.
5. Handle some complex credit lines.
6. Has the responsibility of advising when Director's statements are needed.
7. Is proficient on calculator and typewriter.
8. Take shorthand.

ORGANIZATION

Has an inherent duty and responsibility to make recommendations to supervisor concerning possible methods to improve department.

FINANCES

Has the responsibility to make recommendations to supervsior concerning the budgetary needs of the department.

RELATIONSHIPS

1. Responsible to the Commercial Credit Department Manager for the fulfillment of functions, responsibilities, and authority and for their proper interpretation.

2. Will have extensive contact with customers and the public, and is to conduct relationships in a manner that will enhance the overall marketing effort of the bank.
3. Will be called upon from time to time to participate with community organizations and in community projects.

JOB DESCRIPTION: Commercial Credit Clerk
DEPARTMENT/DIVISION: Commercial Credit
REPORTS TO: Commercial Credit Department Manager
SUPERVISES: Has no supervisory responsibility.

JOB SUMMARY

Maintain credit file involving a large volume of records. Accumulate credit information on various individuals and businesses. Report credit information to authorized persons and businesses. File various items. Relieve management of some routine detail work. Has access to confidential records. Reasonable amount of on-the-job training required to perform certain procedures. Moderate amount of individual judgment required under moderate supervision.

DUTIES

1. Obtain credit reports from various agencies.
2. Give credit information to authorized persons.
3. File letters, records, reports, etc.
4. Maintain records and files.
5. Handle routine correspondence regarding credit.

ORGANIZATION

Has an inherent duty and responsibility to make recommendations to supervisor concerning possible methods to improve department.

FINANCES

Has the responsibility to make recommendations to supervisor concerning the budgetary needs of the department.

RELATIONSHIPS

1. Responsible to the Commercial Credit Department Manager for the fulfillment of functions, responsibilities, and authority and for their proper interpretation.
2. Will have extensive contact with customers and the public, and is to conduct relationships in a manner that will enhance the overall marketing effort of the bank.
3. Will be called upon from time to time to participate with community organizations and in community projects.

9

CONSUMER CREDIT DEPARTMENT JOB DESCRIPTIONS

The consumer credit department job descriptions which we include in *Job Descriptions in Banking* are quite extensive. Banks do a significant amount of business with individuals who need to borrow money in one form or another, whether it's for an automobile, education, or credit purchases.

Since the jobs in a consumer credit department can be quite diverse, we have broken them down into four categories: Operations, Adjustment, Credit Card, and Installment Loans. The specifics of the jobs in these various categories differ, but they all focus on the central goal of making the consumer credit department of a bank run smoothly and profitably.

JOB DESCRIPTION: Senior Vice President
DEPARTMENT/DIVISION: Consumer Credit
REPORTS TO: Executive Vice President
SUPERVISES: Consumer Loan Operations Department
               Loan Servicing Department
               Dealer Department
               Credit Card Department

JOB SUMMARY

Overall responsibility for all aspects of the operations of the Consumer Loan Division.

DUTIES

1. Overall responsibility and supervision of the consumer loan division
2. Coordinate activities of the departments in the division.
3. Interview, approve or decline consumer loan requests.
4. Approve or decline VISA requests.
5. Approve or decline some loans made through the commercial loan department.
6. Member of senior loan committee to review all loans in excess of loan officer's lending authority bankwide.
7. Review and receive requests for dealer loans and lines of credit. If amount of request exceeds my loan authority, it must be taken to senior loan committee for presentation and a vote of the committee.
8. Responsible for policy and procedures of the division and for making recommendations to the board for any changes.
9. Responsible for establishing and reviewing job duties of Consumer Loan Operations Department members.
10. Approval of expenses.
11. Bank compliance officer; responsible for establishing bankwide policy and coordinating activities of other divisions to insure that policy is being carried out. Responsible for training programs as necessary to insure compliance with regulations.
12. Community Reinvestment Act officer. Chairman of CRA committee to insure the bank's involvement in various activities, both banking and non-banking, comply with the spirit of the act.
13. Member of senior management committee.
14. 19XX Chairman of Advance Planning Committee to set goals.
15. Responsible for employee evaluations that are done directly by department manager. They are approved by me prior to going back to personnel.
16. Chairman of facilities committee to look at both long- and short-range needs.
17. CIF committee member. Establishing timetable for bank systems to be on CIF.
18. Hold staff meeting monthly or sooner if necessary to coordinate activities of the division.
19. Approve hiring of employees in the division. (Department manager actually does the interviewing and hiring; Senior Vice President approves the filling of the position.)
20. Responsible for dealer call program and dealer development. Schedule activities and monitor expenses and calls made by other officers.
21. Work with marketing department on advertising programs.
22. Approve any business with dealers (new business).
23. Evaluate charge offs monthly and request for charge off.
24. Notify loan officers and their supervisors of charge off status.
25. Member of asset/liability management committee. Set rates paid by bank on various department instruments. Set the consumer prime rate for variable rate consumer loans.
26. Review problem loan listing each month with loan servicing department manager.
27. Continuously study and review and form committees to study new programs to offer.
28. Currently studying variable rate consumer loans to begin in September. Currently studying open-ended revolving credit lines.
29. Continuously study ways to better organize the division to be more efficient. Currently studying the Credit Card department.

Senior Vice President (continued)

30. Evaluate officer performance and recommend salary increase. Counsel with officers and employees when necessary.
31. Approve vacation schedule of officers in the division.
32. Monitor monthly rates charged by other banks in the area on installment loans.
33. Set discount rates on retail contracts purchased from bank dealers.
34. Continuous communications with data processing in correcting automated systems problems and enhancing the systems to better benefit the bank and serve the customer.
35. Review all departmental reports monthly.
36. Review and approve division monthly report before its distribution.

ORGANIZATION

1. Initiate changes in the basic organization structure and complement of the planning function in order to accomplish objectives as developed in concert with the Executive Vice President.
2. Activate new work procedures and systems to accomplish planning and bank development objectives more efficiently.

FINANCES

Prepare the annual budget for Consumer Credit, administering allotted funds in accordance with the budget and approved fiscal procedures; and, recommend capital expenditures for planning and bank development.

RELATIONSHIPS

1. Responsible to the Executive Vice President for the fulfillment of his or her functions, responsibilities, and authority and for their proper interpretation.
2. Will advise and assist department managers, officers, and staff in their respective functions associated with the areas for which he or she has direct responsibility.
3. Will have extensive contact with customers, the public and the community, and will conduct relationships in a manner that will enhance the overall marketing effort of the bank.
4. Will be called upon from time to time to participate with community organizations and in community projects.

JOB DESCRIPTION: Secretary
DEPARTMENT/DIVISION: Consumer Credit
REPORTS TO: Senior Vice President — Consumer Credit
SUPERVISES: Has no supervisory responsibility.

JOB SUMMARY

Perform Secretarial duties, process loans, perform some data processing duties tied to installment loans.

DUTIES

1. Answer phone.
2. Process loans, changes of collateral, and transfers of equity.
3. Figure and type extensions.
4. File report bulletins, repair bills, charges and deposits to dealer reserve accounts.

5. Order title applications and remittance forms and record their distribution.
6. Maintain a form book. Be sure that updated forms are sent to other individuals responsible for form books.
7. Collect long distance call sheets on first of the month.
8. On first of the month, separate reports and make necessary copies to distribute.
9. Type monthly loan item count report, mobile home reports and departmental monthly reports.
10. Pay repossession expenses on the first of the month.
11. Distribute used car guide books, truck guide book, NADA books, and microfiche.
12. Reconcile department VISA statement.
13. Prepare charge-off tickets, stamp paid out card and index cards. Place paid out cards in the collateral file and make necessary copies of charge-off reports and distribute them.
14. Compile quarterly charge-off reports.
15. Prepare the ICS monthly report and pay premium.
16. Type annual reports.
17. Prepare Home Mortgage Disclosure Report.
18. Responsible for setting up branch and type records on computer system for installment loans.
19. Backup for Floor Plan clerk while he or she is on vacation.

ORGANIZATION
Has an inherent duty and responsibility to make recommendations to supervisor concerning possible methods to improve department.

FINANCES
Has the responsibility to make recommendations to supervisor concerning the budgetary needs of the department.

RELATIONSHIPS
1. Responsible to the Senior Vice President — Consumer Credit for the fulfillment of functions, responsibilities, and authority and for their proper interpretation.
2. Will have extensive contact with customers and the public, and is to conduct relationships in a manner that will enhance the overall marketing effort of the bank.
3. Will be called upon from time to time to participate with community organizations and in community projects.

Consumer Loan Operations Divisions

JOB DESCRIPTION: Assistant Vice Presidenteand Department Manager — Consumer Loan
                 Operations
DEPARTMENT/DIVISION: Consumer Loan Operations
REPORTS TO: Senior Vice President — Consumer Credit Division
SUPERVISES: Operations Supervisor

JOB SUMMARY
Exercise sound judgment in loanmaking process and insure accurate recording and timely servicing and precise termination of bank's installment loans and guarantee student loans.

Assistant Vice President and Department Manager — Consumer Loan Operations (continued)

DUTIES

1. Monitor daily activity in Installment Loan Operations.
2. Complete loan applications.
3. Prepare necessary reports.
4. Evaluate credit.
5. Approve and reject direct loans.
6. Close loans.
7. Generate memorandums as they apply to area of responsibility.
8. Contact person for the bank with Insured Credit Services of Chicago, who insures our home equity and property improvement loans.
9. Monitor filing of UCC-1 and UCC-3 forms for collateral recording.
10. Loan review and documentation.
11. Assist in filing of bankruptcy claims.
12. Assist in filing of non-filing and VSI claims.
13. Spot check APR for compliance purposes.
14. Verify: Extension Report, Charge Off/Repossession Report and loans with $25 or less payoff. Take appropriate action in each case.
15. Employee reviews for evaluation and raise in pay.
16. Assist in other departments when necessary.

ORGANIZATION

1. Initiate changes in the basic organization structure and complement of the planning function in order to accomplish objectives as developed in concert with the Senior Vice President — Consumer Credit Division.
2. Activate new work procedures and systems to accomplish planning and bank development objectives more efficiently.

FINANCES

Prepare the annual budget for Consumer Loan Operations, administering allotted funds in accordance with the budget and approved fiscal procedures; and, recommend capital expenditures for planning and bank development.

RELATIONSHIPS

1. Responsible to the Senior Vice President — Consumer Credit Division for the fulfillment of his or her functions, responsibilities, and authority and for their proper interpretation.
2. Will advise and assist department managers, officers, and staff in their respective functions associated with the areas for which he or she has direct responsibility.
3. Will have extensive contact with customers, the public and the community, and is to conduct relationships in a manner that will enhance the overall marketing effort of the bank.
4. Will be called upon from time to time to participate with community organizations and in community projects.

JOB DESCRIPTION: Operations Supervisor — Consumer Credit
DEPARTMENT/DIVISION: Consumer Loan Operations

REPORTS TO: Assistant Vice President and Department Manager — Consumer Loan
Operations
SUPERVISES: Credit Clerk
File Maintenance Clerk
Senior Operations Clerk

JOB SUMMARY

Supervise personnel in the Operations Section of the Consumer Credit Division. Balance Bank
Activity Recap daily and transfer of funds through general ledger. Prepare monthly reports, quarterly reports and annual reports for Consumer Credit Division.

DUTIES

1. Supervise personnel in the Operations Section of the Consumer Credit Division.
2. Balance Bank Activity Recap daily with general ledger.
3. Transfer rebates, interest, credit life interest, late fees, simple interest.
4. Check closed accounts for correct rebating and also checking accounts at random to see if computer is figuring interest correctly by the rule of 78s.
5. Handle problem accounts that cannot be handled by operations clerks.
6. Handle Special Issue Insurance.
7. Certificate of Deposit control.
8. Handle Credit Life Exception.
9. Prepare required monthly reports.
10. Prepare Bankers Credit Life report.
11. Prepare monthly billing for coupon books.
12. Prepare Controller's Department Memorandum — loan item count.
13. Prepare Quarterly Reports. (We receive worksheets from the Controllers.)
14. Prepare Annual Reports for department.
15. Release CD holds.
16. Pick up time cards each week and give to supervisor.
17. Help out in Operations Department when someone is out sick or on vacation.
18. Check accounts when late fee waived to make sure it goes on account correctly.

ORGANIZATION

1. Initiate changes in the basic organization structure and complement of the planning function in order to accomplish objectives as developed in concert with the Assistant Vice President and Department Manager — Consumer Loan Operations.
2. Activate new work procedures and systems to accomplish planning and bank development objectives more efficiently.

FINANCES

Prepare the annual budget for Consumer Loan Operations, administering allotted funds in accordance with the budget and approved fiscal procedures. Recommend capital expenditures for planning and bank development.

RELATIONSHIPS

1. Responsible to the Assistant Vice President and Department Manager — Consumer Loan Operations for the fulfillment of his or her functions, responsibilities, and authority and for their proper interpretation.

Operations Supervisor — Consumer Credit (continued)

2. Will advise and assist department managers, officers, and staff in their respective functions associated with the areas for which he or she has direct responsibility.
3. Will have extensive contact with customers, the public and the community, and is to conduct relationships in a manner that will enhance the overall marketing effort of the bank.
4. Will be called upon from time to time to participate with community organizations and in community projects.

JOB DESCRIPTION: Credit Clerk
DEPARTMENT/DIVISION: Consumer Loan Operations
REPORTS TO: Operations Supervisor — Consumer Credit
SUPERVISES: Has no supervisory responsibility.

JOB SUMMARY

General preparation and review of loan applicants' credit history. Also performs clerical/secretarial duties related to consumer loan operations.

DUTIES

1. Credit investigation for Loan Officer.
2. Credit investigation follow-up.
3. Handle inquiries.
4. Film and file credit information.
5. Maintain and control credit files.
6. Stay current with state and federal regulations.
7. Report information to credit bureau.

ORGANIZATION

Has an inherent duty and responsibility to make recommendations to supervisor concerning possible methods to improve department.

FINANCES

Has the responsibility to make recommendations to supervisor concerning the budgetary needs of the department.

RELATIONSHIPS

1. Responsible to the Operations Supervisor — Consumer Credit for the fulfillment of functions, responsibilities, and authority and for their proper interpretation.
2. Will have extensive contact with customers and the public, and is to conduct relationships in a manner that will enhance the overall marketing effort of the bank.
3. Will be called upon from time to time to participate with community organizations and in community projects.

JOB DESCRIPTION: File Maintenance Clerk
DEPARTMENT/DIVISION: Consumer Loan Operations

REPORTS TO: Operations Supervisor — Consumer Credit
SUPERVISES: Has no supervisory responsibility.

JOB SUMMARY

Perform file maintenance responsibilities for installment loan department. Also answer incoming calls from customers asking for information on their loans.

DUTIES

1. Go through the stack of paid out cards.
2. Answer telephone. Give pay offs information concerning loans.
3. Correct address when changed.
4. Fill out data form to data processing to be keypunched.
5. Check information on loans and compare to bank's Activity Recap sheet.
6. Fill out credit ticket to Consumer Loan Income for the interest.
7. Handle all consumer loan return mail.
8. Fill in for vacations and sick leave.
9. Send paid out papers when the clerk is out on vacation.

ORGANIZATION

Has an inherent duty and responsibility to make recommendations to supervisor concerning possible methods to improve department.

FINANCES

Has the responsibility to make recommendations to supervisor concerning the budgetary needs of the department.

RELATIONSHIPS

1. Responsible to the Operations Supervisor — Consumer Credit for the fulfillment of functions, responsibilities, and authority and for their proper interpretation.
2. Will have extensive contact with customers and the public, and is to conduct relationships in a manner that will enhance the overall marketing effort of the bank.
3. Will be called upon from time to time to participate with community organizations and in community projects.

JOB DESCRIPTION: Senior Operations Clerk
DEPARTMENT/DIVISION: Consumer Loan Operations
REPORTS TO: Operations Supervisor
SUPERVISES: Has no supervisory responsibility.

JOB SUMMARY

Daily balance and assignment of new numbers to all new consumer loans.

DUTIES

1. Pick up and separate daily work for the department.
2. Assign new account numbers.
3. Occasionally figure daily pro-rata, regular pro-rata and rule of 78s payoffs.

Senior Operations Clerk (continued)

4. Help with other office work such as phone calls, taking payments, prepare titles for release, etc.
5. Alphabetize all contracts and loan documents.
6. Check all contracts for credit life limit, bank drafts, etc.
7. Fold all contracts for weekly meetings.
8. Keep up-to-date journal on UCC's, mortgages and second mortgage correspondence.
9. Check all extensions to see that they are up-dated properly.
10. Rework all unposted transactions.
11. Assist Supervisor.
12. Balance Bank Activity Recap daily with general ledger.
13. Transfer rebates, earnings, and late charges to appropriate account.
14. Check closed accounts for correct rebating.
15. Check loan prepaid six months in advance.

ORGANIZATION

Has an inherent duty and responsibility to make recommendations to supervisor concerning possible methods to improve department.

FINANCES

Has the responsibility to make recommendations to supervisor concerning the budgetary needs of the department.

RELATIONSHIPS

1. Responsible to the Operations Supervisor for the fulfillment of functions, responsibilities, and authority and for their proper interpretation.
2. Will have extensive contact with customers and the public, and is to conduct relationships in a manner that will enhance the overall marketing effort of the bank.
3. Will be called upon from time to time to participate with community organizations and in community projects.

JOB DESCRIPTION: Data Entry Clerk
DEPARTMENT/DIVISION: Consumer Loan Operations
REPORTS TO: Senior Operations Clerk
SUPERVISES: Has no supervisory responsibility.

JOB SUMMARY

The purpose of this job is to enter data into the CIF computer system, mail out customer's loan papers and act as receptionist.

DUTIES

1. Key punch: loans, relationship ties; loan maintenance; dealer transactions, additions, dealer maintenance and purges; transfer of equities; request history cards, file cards, labels and coupon books.
2. Record coupon book requests on ledger.
3. Pull customer files for removal of paid out loans.

4. Process paid out papers and mail to customers.
5. Type and send prepaid letters to customers paid in advance.
6. Send official check letters for overpayment refunds.
7. Investigate customer inquiries pertaining to account problems.
8. Quote payoffs: 78s, regular and pro rata.
9. Order supplies.
10. Film loan contracts, coupons, maintenance and dealer transactions on film machine.
11. Type letters or reports occasionally.
12. Take payments and payoffs, then process papers.
13. Assist customers.
14. Telephone receptionist.
15. Periodic manual revision.

ORGANIZATION

Has an inherent duty and responsibility to make recommendations to supervisor concerning possible methods to improve department.

FINANCES

Has the responsibility to make recommendations to supervisor concerning the budgetary needs of the department.

RELATIONSHIPS

1. Responsible to the Senior Operations Clerk for the fulfillment of functions, responsibilities, and authority and for their proper interpretation.
2. Will have extensive contact with customers and the public, and is to conduct relationships in a manner that will enhance the overall marketing effort of the bank.
3. Will be called upon from time to time to participate with community organizations and in community projects.

JOB DESCRIPTION: Insurance and Collateral Clerk
DEPARTMENT/DIVISION: Consumer Loan Operations
REPORTS TO: Senior Operations Clerk
SUPERVISES: Has no supervisory responsibility.

JOB SUMMARY

Insure that all collateral requiring insurance has proper coverage. Also maintains collateral files in the vault.

DUTIES

1. Open insurance mail.
2. Alphabetize insurance.
3. File insurance on data input form using microfiche.
4. Debit loans for single interest insurance.
5. Credit loans for single interest insurance cancellations.
6. Status loans for insurance cancellations when loans pay off.
7. Change payment schedules on loans when adding and cancelling single interest insurance.

Insurance and Collateral Clerk (continued)

8. Credit general ledger account and single interest DDA account when insurance is added.
9. Debit general ledger account and single interest DDA account when insurance is cancelled.
10. Mail notices and policies regarding single interest insurance.
11. Answer phones.
12. Maintain the collateral vault. Check collateral files out and in.
13. Balance single interest insurance DDA account monthly.
14. Serve as back-up title clerk: Release titles; File titles; File new loans and documents; Make new files for new loans; Answer phones; Title inquiries about lost titles; Mail letters to customer regarding titles; Paid off loans, customer moved out of state.
15. Serve as back-up CIF Clerk: Keypunch — new loans, dealer transactions, maintenance, extensions.

ORGANIZATION

Has an inherent duty and responsibility to make recommendations to supervisor concerning possible methods to improve department.

FINANCES

Has the responsibility to make recommendations to supervisor concerning the budgetary needs of the department.

RELATIONSHIPS

1. Responsible to the Senior Operations Clerk for the fulfillment of functions, responsibilities, and authority and for their proper interpretation.
2. Will have extensive contact with customers and the public, and is to conduct relationships in a manner that will enhance the overall marketing effort of the bank.
3. Will be called upon from time to time to participate with community organizations and in community projects.

JOB DESCRIPTION: Title Clerk
DEPARTMENT/DIVISION: Consumer Loan Operations
REPORTS TO: Senior Operations Clerk — Consumer Credit
SUPERVISES: Has no supervisory responsibility.

JOB SUMMARY

Maintain an accurate record and accounting on all incoming car titles, filing each with appropriate loan. Release and record the disbursement of each title on paid out loans sending information to credit for filing. Make all collateral files and file all related papers, mortgages, and titles with proper loan.

DUTIES

1. Open and check all titles received, verifying bank as lienholder.
2. Make a copy of each title for credit files.
3. Make a copy of all title applications that are returned from state for corrections, filing copy in

collateral file and sending application to proper loan officer or branch to correct and return to state.

4. Record the returns on Title Print Out, when returned for corrections and date.
5. File titles with proper loan in person's collateral file, making a list of loan numbers that titles were received for.
6. Mark off each loan number and name from the Installment Loan Title follow up report indicating title and date.
7. Report to Department Manager any delinquent titles over three months past due and notations about any correspondence since loan was made.
8. Title follow up is done continuously until title is received or until 90 days passes.
9. Letters typed to all customers whose loans have paid out having a car title as to the disbursement of title, or current status of vehicle. This is done daily.
10. Answer phone calls concerning titles (for any reason) and assist customers applying for lost titles.
11. Make new collateral files on all loans. Put sticker with name on file.
12. File all contracts, mortgages, lease agreements in customer's file, on all Consumer Loans for bank.
13. Give Loan Officers information needed from the collateral file.
14. Relieve Insurance clerk for breaks and lunch and vacation. Try to keep up with all changes and special instructions.
15. Release titles to state daily on routine schedule, 15 days from date of letter inquiring current status. (Send titles to state to have our lien released.)
16. Comply with each state's request for a title when a customer has moved out of state and has applied for title in state he or she is now residing. Keep an accurate accounting of each and send information to credit.
17. Inform customers of *their liability* of transferring title when they move to another state. Send letter (form letter) to customer explaining the need for retitling vehicle in new state.
18. Notarize various papers: Release of Liens, Bill of Sales, etc.
19. Comply with branch officers' requests for titles being sent to branches due to C/S requesting a trade on car or sell, etc.
20. Assist on phones when possible with customers, branches, tellers, and dealers.

ORGANIZATION

Has an inherent duty and responsibility to make recommendations to supervisor concerning possible methods to improve department.

FINANCES

Has the responsibility to make recommendations to supervisor concerning the budgetary needs of the department.

RELATIONSHIPS

1. Responsible to the Senior Operations Clerk — Consumer Credit for the fulfillment of functions, responsibilities, and authority and for their proper interpretation.
2. Will have extensive contact with customers and the public, and conduct relationships in a manner that will enhance the overall marketing effort of the bank.
3. Will be called upon from time to time to participate with community organizations and in community projects.

JOB DESCRIPTION: Operations Clerk
DEPARTMENT/DIVISION: Consumer Loan Operations
REPORTS TO: Senior Operations Clerk — Consumer Credit
SUPERVISES: Has no supervisory responsibility.

JOB SUMMARY

Performs clerical responsibilities as necessary.

DUTIES

1. Mail payments (add and balance).
2. File new index cards (new loans maintenance).
3. Return checks.
4. Mail inquiries.
5. Receive telephone inquiries.
6. Accident and health checks.
7. Receive interest request for income tax purposes.
8. Prepare drafts to payoff loans.
9. Assist walk-in customers.

ORGANIZATION

Has an inherent duty and responsibility to make recommendations to supervisor concerning possible methods to improve department.

FINANCES

Has the responsibility to make recommendations to supervisor concerning the budgetary needs of the department.

RELATIONSHIPS

1. Responsible to the Senior Operations Clerk — Consumer Credit for the fulfillment of functions, responsibilities, and authority and for their proper interpretation.
2. Will have extensive contact with customers and the public, and is to conduct relationships in a manner that will enhance the overall marketing effort of the bank.
3. Will be called upon from time to time to participate with community organizations and in community projects.

JOB DESCRIPTION: Documentation Clerk
DEPARTMENT/DIVISION: Consumer Loan Operations
REPORTS TO: Senior Operations Clerk — Consumer Credit
SUPERVISES: Has no supervisory responsibility.

JOB SUMMARY

To check each loan that is made in the consumer loan department to be sure all documentation is done and all forms filled out correctly. Also handle recoveries and credit the money to the correct account.

DUTIES

1. Type loans (new loans as needed).
2. Check loans for documentation and compliance errors.
3. Give loan values to customers who make inquiries.
4. Answer telephone.
5. Recoveries — process payments and keep records on charged off accounts.

ORGANIZATION

Has an inherent duty and responsibility to make recommendations to supervisor concerning possible methods to improve department.

FINANCES

Has the responsibility to make recommendations to supervisor concerning the budgetary needs of the department.

RELATIONSHIPS

1. Responsible to the Senior Operations Clerk — Consumer Credit for the fulfillment of functions, responsibilities, and authority and for their proper interpretation.
2. Will have extensive contact with customers and the public, and is to conduct relationships in a manner that will enhance the overall marketing effort of the bank.
3. Will be called upon from time to time to participate with community organizations and in community projects.

Adjustment Division

JOB DESCRIPTION: Department Manager — Adjustment
DEPARTMENT/DIVISION: Adjustment
REPORTS TO: Senior Vice President — Consumer Credit
SUPERVISES: Secretary
Adjustment Supervisor

JOB SUMMARY

Supervise the credit, adjustment (collection) sections, and the loan documentation and review functions. Also handle direct lending, in part.

DUTIES

1. Primary responsibility is for the Supervision of Adjustment section. Must insure that employees are handling responsibilities so that functions of department are completed.
2. File nonfiling and VSI claims — consists of preparing and filing of claims as necessary.
3. Maintain repossession files — Once a repossession file is set up, it is maintained until the collateral is sold, money disbursed, and appropriate action taken.
4. Charge Offs — At the end of each month, the "Uncollectable Accounts" are compiled and set up for charge-off. After investigation of account is done, they are submitted to the Consumer Credit Division Manager for his or her approval.
5. Employee Review — An evaluation of employees performance for pay increase purposes.

Department Manager — Adjustment (continued)

6. Will make direct loans as necessary.
7. Responsible for necessary action on bankruptcy claims.

ORGANIZATION

1. Initiate changes in the basic organization structure and complement of the planning function in order to accomplish objectives as developed in concert with the Senior Vice President — Consumer Credit.
2. Activate new work procedures and systems to accomplish planning and bank development objectives more efficiently.

FINANCES

Prepare the annual budget for Adjustment, administering allotted funds in accordance with the budget and approved fiscal procedures; and, recommend capital expenditures for planning and bank development.

RELATIONSHIPS

1. Responsible to the Senior Vice President — Consumer Credit for the fulfillment of his or her functions, responsibilities, and authority and for their proper interpretation.
2. Will advise and assist department managers, officers, and staff in their respective functions associated with the areas for which he or she has direct responsibility.
3. Will have extensive contact with customers, the public and the community, and is to conduct relationships in a manner that will enhance the overall marketing effort of the bank.
4. Will be called upon from time to time to participate with community organizations and in community projects.

JOB DESCRIPTION: Secretary — Receptionist
DEPARTMENT/DIVISION: Adjustment
REPORTS TO: Department Manager — Adjustment
SUPERVISES: Has no supervisory responsibility.

JOB SUMMARY

Handles all typing duties for Adjustment Supervisor. Types letters for all adjusters. Handles return checks on loan accounts. Maintains supply cabinet for department. Answers phones in absence of adjusters and supervsior. Types debtor's court, bankruptcy and various insurance claims. Maintains records on debtor's court accounts to include posting payments and disbursing monies from the court. Also directs customer traffic. Job involves considerable typing.

DUTIES

1. Answer phones.
2. Type collection letters.
3. Mail past due notices (5 day and 10 day notices).
4. Keep needed work supplies available.
5. Write to customers regarding return checks on loan payments.
6. Transcribe dictation or speedwriting.
7. Type letters and gather necessary information for accounts given to attorney.

8. Type bankruptcy and insurance claims. Gather other needed information to accompany claims (copies of notes, titles, etc.).
9. Maintain and post debtor's court payments and disburse monies from court.

ORGANIZATION

Has an inherent duty and responsibility to make recommendations to supervisor concerning possible methods to improve department.

FINANCES

Has the responsibility to make recommendations to supervisor concerning the budgetary needs of the department.

RELATIONSHIPS

1. Responsible to the Department Manager — Adjustment for the fulfillment of functions, responsibilities, and authority and for their proper interpretation.
2. Will have extensive contact with customers and the public, and is to conduct relationships in a manner that will enhance the overall marketing effort of the bank.
3. Will be called upon from time to time to participate with community organizations and in community projects.

JOB DESCRIPTION: Adjustment Supervisor
DEPARTMENT/DIVISION: Adjustment
REPORTS TO: Department Manager — Adjustment
SUPERVISES: Recovery Clerk
                 Field Representative
                 Inside Adjuster
                 Collection Clerk
                 Permanent Hourly Collection Clerk

JOB SUMMARY

Supervises loan adjuster and field representative in their duties. Is responsible for the overall collection efforts on delinquent consumer installment loans. Works some past due installment loans by telephone and letter. Works out repayment plan with past due customers in order to get accounts current. Extends loan payments when necessary. Makes own decisions about what actions to take in adjusting consumer loan accounts. May attend bankruptcy and debtor's court hearings. Considerable judgment and tact required. Works with minimal supervision.

DUTIES

1. Supervise and coordinate all activities of the Adjustment department.
2. Make sure all employee duties are being carried out according to bank policy.
3. Assist adjusters with any problems that might arise in daily work.
4. Make the final decision on all Adjustment department repossessions.
5. If an account is up for repossession and is out of state or is located too far away to send our outside representative, Adjustment Supervisor makes the decision as to whether the account will be turned over to another bank or collection agency. Personally makes contact with the bank or recovery agency or assigns the adjuster working the account to do so.

Adjustment Supervisor (continued)

6. If necessary, assists the outside representative in the repossession of our security, or will assign another inside adjuster to do so.
7. Assists in the repossession of commercial loan notes, if necessary.
8. Compiles the end-of-the-month delinquency reports giving the necessary information to analyze our effectiveness in our collection efforts.
9. Personally handles the collection of all indirect dealer loans and student loans guaranteed by the government.
10. After determining that all collection efforts on an account have been made and the customer has ignored all efforts, makes the decision whether to take legal action or not. If an attorney suit is necessary, has all the paper work prepared and signs all the necessary documents and forwards them to the attorney.
11. At the end of the month reviews all direct loans which are up for charge off with the adjuster working the account. Once it has been determined all efforts have been exhausted in collecting the account, submits the necessary forms to the Department Manager for charge off.
12. Same as No. 11, only for VISA accounts.
13. Renew accounts if to the benefit of the customer and the bank.
14. Try to help all adjusters with accounts they are having difficulty with and try to make personal contact with the customer.
15. Processes all the necessary paper work needed to file pre-claims assistance and any claims made on our student loans.
16. Assistance given to the Department Manager whenever needed.

ORGANIZATION

1. Initiate changes in the basic organization structure and complement of the planning function in order to accomplish objectives as developed in concert with the Department Manager — Adjustment.
2. Activate new work procedures and systems to accomplish planning and bank development objectives more efficiently.

FINANCES

Prepare the annual budget for Adjustment, administering allotted funds in accordance with the budget and approved fiscal procedures. Recommend capital expenditures for planning and bank development.

RELATIONSHIPS

1. Responsible to the Department Manager — Adjustment for the fulfillment of his or her functions, responsibilities, and authority and for their proper interpretation.
2. Will advise and assist department managers, officers, and staff in their respective functions associated with the areas for which he or she has direct responsibility.
3. Will have extensive contact with customers, the public and the community, and is to conduct relationships in a manner that will enhance the overall marketing effort of the bank.
4. Will be called upon from time to time to participate with community organizations and in community projects.

JOB DESCRIPTION: Recovery Clerk
DEPARTMENT/DIVISION: Adjustment

REPORTS TO: Adjustment Supervisor
SUPERVISES: Has no supervisory responsibility.

JOB SUMMARY

Responsible for the recovery efforts for Consumer Installment, Credit Card, and some Commercial Loan Department accounts. Handles the collection of all Consumer Installment loan charge offs, and some Commercial Loan accounts. Performs collection efforts by telephone and letters. Has authority to turn P&L accounts over to attorneys. Keeps files and follow-ups with attorney on all accounts. Job requires judgment, tact, and perseverance. Job is performed under minimum supervision.

DUTIES

1. Telephone customers on charged-off accounts to make arrangements for repayment.
2. Send letters to customers when applicable.
3. Turn accounts over to attorney when other collection means are exhausted. Also meet with attorneys as necessary to adjust or liquidate accounts.
4. Maintain charge-off files and attorney account files. Responsible for setting up and maintaining record keeping system.

ORGANIZATION

Has an inherent duty and responsibility to make recommendations to supervisor concerning possible methods to improve department.

FINANCES

Has the responsibility to make recommendations to supervisor concerning the budgetary needs of the department.

RELATIONSHIPS

1. Responsible to the Adjustment Supervisor for the fulfillment of functions, responsibilities, and authority and for their proper interpretation.
2. Will have extensive contact with customers and the public, and is to conduct relationships in a manner that will enhance the overall marketing effort of the bank.
3. Will be called upon from time to time to participate with community organizations and in community projects.

JOB DESCRIPTION: Field Representative
DEPARTMENT/DIVISION: Adjustment
REPORTS TO: Adjustment Supervisor
SUPERVISES: Has no supervisory responsibility.

JOB SUMMARY

Makes personal contact with customers at residence. Works out payment plans to help get past due accounts current. Repossesses collateral when necessary. Checks dealer's floor plan inventory. Considerable judgment and tact required. Works under close supervision.

DUTIES

1. Call on past due customers at their residences.
2. Work out a repayment plan compatible with the customer and the bank.

Field Representative (continued)

3. Repossess collateral on past due accounts when necessary.
4. Fill out necessary repossession reports.
5. Keep a list of all accounts he or she calls on in person.
6. Check dealer's floor plan inventory.

ORGANIZATION

Has an inherent duty and responsibility to make recommendations to supervisor concerning possible methods to improve department.

FINANCES

Has the responsibility to make recommendations to supervisor concerning the budgetary needs of the department.

RELATIONSHIPS

1. Responsible to the Adjustment Supervisor for the fulfillment of functions, responsibilities, and authority and for their proper interpretation.
2. Will have extensive contact with customers and the public, and is to conduct relationships in a manner that will enhance the overall marketing effort of the bank.
3. Will be called upon from time to time to participate with community organizations and in community projects.

JOB DESCRIPTION: Inside Adjuster
DEPARTMENT/DIVISION: Adjustment
REPORTS TO: Adjustment Supervisor
SUPERVISES: Has no supervisory responsibility.

JOB SUMMARY

Handles past due direct loans. Makes contact by phone with customers. Writes necessary collection letters. Works out payment plan to help get past due accounts current. Makes decisions on what action to take on collecting past due accounts. Checks dealer's floor plan inventory. Considerable judgment and tact required. Works under close supervision.

DUTIES

1. Telephone past due customers.
2. Try to work out a repayment plan satisfactory to both the customer and the bank.
3. Send collection letters to past due customers.
4. Skip traces.
5. May extend loan payments on past due customers.
6. Check dealer's floor plan inventory.

ORGANIZATION

Has an inherent duty and responsibility to make recommendations to supervisor concerning possible methods to improve department.

FINANCES

Has the responsibility to make recommendations to supervisor concerning the budgetary needs of the department.

RELATIONSHIPS

1. Responsible to the Adjustment Supervisor for the fulfillment of functions, responsibilities, and authority and for their proper interpretation.
2. Will have extensive contact with customers and the public, and is to conduct relationships in a manner that will enhance the overall marketing effort of the bank.
3. Will be called upon from time to time to participate with community organizations and in community projects.

JOB DESCRIPTION: VISA Collection Clerk
DEPARTMENT/DIVISION: Adjustment
REPORTS TO: Adjustment Supervisor
SUPERVISES: Has no supervisory responsibility.

JOB SUMMARY

Screens accounts for past due payments, making personal contact by phone, retrieves Visa cards when necessary by asking customer to return card. May handle Visa or Consumer Loan accounts. Job involves considerable phone usage. Considerable tact and judgment is needed. Job requires moderate supervision.

DUTIES

1. Contact customer by phone for payment.
2. Send letters to past due customers.
3. Skip traces.
4. Maintain files on past due accounts.

ORGANIZATION

Has an inherent duty and responsibility to make recommendations to supervisor concerning possible methods to improve department.

FINANCES

Has the responsibility to make recommendations to supervisor concerning the budgetary needs of the department.

RELATIONSHIPS

1. Responsible to the Adjustment Supervisor for the fulfillment of functions, responsibilities, and authority and for their proper interpretation.
2. Will have extensive contact with customers and the public, and is to conduct relationships in a manner that will enhance the overall marketing effort of the bank.
3. Will be called upon from time to time to participate with community organizations and in community projects.

JOB DESCRIPTION: Permanent Hourly Collection Clerk
DEPARTMENT/DIVISION: Adjustment
REPORTS TO: Adjustment Supervisor
SUPERVISES: Has no supervisory responsibility.

JOB SUMMARY

Contacts customers regarding delinquent Visa accounts. Arranges a repayment schedule with customers. Sends letters when unable to reach customers by telephone. Assists in other areas during vacation season, as needed. Job involves considerable tact and judgment and can be accomplished with moderate supervision.

DUTIES

1. Telephone customers concerning delinquent accounts.
2. Assist in other areas of adjustment section when needed.
3. Send letters on delinquent accounts.
4. Maintain files on certain delinquent accounts.

ORGANIZATION

Has an inherent duty and responsibility to make recommendations to supervisor concerning possible methods to improve department.

FINANCES

Has the responsibility to make recommendations to supervisor concerning the budgetary needs of the department.

RELATIONSHIPS

1. Responsible to the Adjustment Supervisor for the fulfillment of functions, responsibilities, and authority and for their proper interpretation.
2. Will have extensive contact with customers and the public, and is to conduct relationships in a manner that will enhance the overall marketing effort of the bank.
3. Will be called upon from time to time to participate with community organizations and in community projects.

Credit Card Division

JOB DESCRIPTION: Vice President and Department Manager
DEPARTMENT/DIVISION: Credit Card Department
REPORTS TO: Senior Vice President — Consumer Credit Division
SUPERVISES: Office Manager
            Secretary

JOB SUMMARY

To form policies and procedures to be followed to insure the development and maintenance of an effective Bankcard operation in compliance with credit card operating regulations and bank policies.

DUTIES

1. Determines, usually on own initiative, procedures to be followed to insure the development and maintenance of effective center operations in compliance with credit card operating regulations and bank policies.
    a. Sees to maintenance of proper records and safeguards, compiling of necessary reports, and audit of plastics, sales draft purchases, merchant data recorders and other assets and liabilities of the center.
    b. Coordinates and expedites flow of work through the department, reassigns staff to distribute work loads.
    c. Spot checks sub-sections to insure operational conformance with credit card and the bank's policies and regulations.
    d. Interprets credit card regulations and revisions; determines procedure to be taken in unusual or non-standard cases.
    e. Answers Audit inspection reports to Division Head; sees to corrections of exceptions and criticized practices.
2. Supervises center operations to assure adequate, efficient and courteous service to center's customers.
    a. Recommends to Division Manager any changes needed in authorized staff.
    b. Initiates and conducts training programs for orientation of new employees and for continued development of all center staff.
    c. Keeps informed of current bank policies, goals and practices, and conversant with all bank services and their application; sets up proper procedure to assure that center staff are adequately informed on such matters.
    d. Makes certain that center and interior work spaces are kept neat and orderly, in order to provide an inviting atmosphere for center staff and visitors.
    e. Personally discusses customer problems and complaints with customers referred by other officers and staff.
3. Supervises staff.
    a. Discusses with officers and employees such matters as division of work, working conditions and hours, time off, leaves of absence, vacations, salary advances, complaints, benefits, performance reports and any operations problems that may arise from time to time.
    b. Counsels with employees to assist them with their personal problems and to help them improve in performance of their duties.
    c. Recommends salary adjustments in accordance with existing policy for all non-officer employees and for designated officer(s) assigned to the credit card Center.
    d. Recommends promotions, transfers or dismissals for non-officer employees, with concurrence of Division Manager.
    e. Performs several, or all, of the following duties:
        I. Holds periodic staff meetings to keep staff informed of new procedures.
        II. Handles correspondence relating to personnel and operating matters.
        III. Prepares, or sees to the preparation of, the quarterly credit card reports.
        IV. Discusses monthly employee overlimit and past due accounts with the employee's supervisor.
4. Supervises Bankcard Merchant Representative program to plan and coordinate activities in areas of new Merchant Members acquisition and call-back programs.
    a. Maintains contacts and liaison through Division Manager with the Consumer Loan De-

Vice President and Department Manager (continued)

   partment, Business Development, Branch Operations, and other Administration Departments to effect coordination of planning and efforts in promotion of the Bankcard program.
   b. Visits branches and discusses various Bankcard matters with officers and staff: outlines
      changes in plan or interpretation of policy; conducts periodic staff meetings to promote
      better branch comprehension of procedures and indoctrinates new employees in Bankcard
      procedures. Resolves disputes or differences of interpretations between branches and major
      Merchant Members or certain Bankcard holders.
5. Visits major business establishments to develop new Bankcard Merchant Memberships.
   a. Prior to visit consults all available sources of information to develop data on company such
      as general condition, previous attitudes towards plan, and principal bank contacts.
   b. Explains plan to officers of business and answers questions regarding deposit arrangements,
      sales draft procedures, discount rates, and general operational matters.
   c. Arranges, as necessary, for co-visitation by a representative of the Business Development
      Section or the closest Branch Manager to further establish other bank services.
   d. When business expresses desire to participate in plan, sees to the completion of Bankcard
      Member Agreement and necessary supporting documents. Obtain necessary signatures
      and signs acceptance of agreement on behalf of the bank. Considers and negotiates with
      Division Head any concessions or deviations from conventional relationships necessary to
      establish membership. Arrange for issue of credit cards to company officers, if desired.
   e. Works with store managers or personnel officer in establishing and conducting employee
      classes and demonstrations in use of Bankcard sales draft and credit voucher procedures
      and dispatch of deposit envelopes to bank. May assist the business in preparation of written
      procedures.
   f. Visits major Merchant Members' business establishments in interest of goodwill, business
      extension, and maintenance of business; discusses promotion of plan to increase Bankcard
      usage and addresses employee groups to keep them informed of latest developments; dis-
      cusses with owners and managers individual and area trends, suggestions for use of other
      bank services, and resolution of Bankcard operational problems; answers questions, makes
      suggestions, and gives advice relating to bank policy, loans, deposit accounts, and other
      services.
   g. Answers mail and telephone inquiries from Merchant Members, potential members and
      Bankcard holders relating to services offered, theory of plan, and specific complaints; when
      necessary, talks to irate callers and explains bank's position.
   h. Supervises adjustments involving merchant problems and customer complaints; reviews
      fraudulent sales drafts to determine possible Merchant Member involvement.
   i. Verifies such details as reputability of prospective member, acceptability of products sold,
      conformance of plan to established policy, and accuracy of discount rate established.
6. Participates in and attends activities of civic, service, and fraternal organizations for development of contacts and promotion of good will for the bank. Attends other functions such as
   openings of new businesses or new bank branches, conventions, merchant or trade association
   meetings, and exhibitions.
7. Conducts tours of Bankcard Center for visiting bankers and representatives of commerce and
   industry.
8. Reviews various publications and business journals to keep abreast of general economics, mer-
   chandising, sales and Bankcard trends.

ORGANIZATION

1. Initiate changes in the basic organization structure and complement of the planning function in order to accomplish objectives as developed in concert with the Senior Vice President — Consumer Credit Division.
2. Activate new work procedures and systems to accomplish planning and bank development objectives more efficiently.

FINANCES

Prepare the annual budget for Credit Card Department, administering allotted funds in accordance with the budget and approved fiscal procedures; and, recommend capital expenditures for planning and bank development.

RELATIONSHIPS

1. Responsible to the Senior Vice President — Consumer Credit Division for the fulfillment of his or her functions, responsibilities, and authority and for their proper interpretation.
2. Will advise and assist department managers, officers, and staff in their respective functions associated with the area for which he or she has direct responsibility.
3. Will have extensive contact with customers, the public and the community, and is to conduct relationships in a manner that will enhance the overall marketing effort of the bank.
4. Will be called upon from time to time to participate with community organizations and in community projects.

JOB DESCRIPTION: Secretary
DEPARTMENT/DIVISION: Credit Card Department
REPORTS TO: Vice President and Department Manager
SUPERVISES: Has no supervisory responsibility.

JOB SUMMARY

Performs such secretarial duties as typing, receptionist work and answering the telephone. Handles most of the typing and correspondence for management. Uses own judgment in some instances. Requires moderate supervision. An extensive amount of on-the-job training is required.

DUTIES

1. Able to take shorthand and/or use dictating equipment.
2. Customer service — in person and by telephone. Requires a stable temperament.
3. Researches problem statements.
4. Handles termination notices and changes file records of ex-employees.
5. Assist with preparation and typing of quarterly reports.
6. Maintains current and past years' departmental reports and files.
7. Maintains National and International Operating Regulations Manuals.
8. Handles credit balance statements — either refund or send out.
9. Handles request for tickets and helps with charge-backs.
10. Sets up Cycle 9 (business) accounts and maintains the accounts as requested by the customer. (For example, adding and deleting people from the account as employee turnover occurs.)

Secretary (continued)

11. Gives authorization codes for cash advances to the tellers.
12. Gives credit references for in-house checks and other banks.
13. Checks Request Confirm Report daily.

ORGANIZATION

Has an inherent duty and responsibility to make recommendations to supervisor concerning possible methods to improve department.

FINANCES

Has the responsibility to make recommendations to supervisor concerning the budgetary needs of the department.

RELATIONSHIPS

1. Responsible to the Vice President and Department Manager for the fulfillment of functions, responsibilities, and authority and for their proper interpretation.
2. Will have extensive contact with customers and the public, and is to conduct relationships in a manner that will enhance the overall marketing effort of the bank.
3. Will be called upon from time to time to participate with community organizations and in community projects.

JOB DESCRIPTION: Office Manager
DEPARTMENT/DIVISION: Credit Card Department
REPORTS TO: Vice President and Department Manager
SUPERVISES: Operations Supervisor
                    Over Limit Clerk
                    Processing Clerk

JOB SUMMARY

Reviews accounts, raises limits, reissues cards and checking tickets, checking new applications for accounts, and reviews overlimit accounts.

DUTIES

1. Reissues cards — monthly by cycles (Feb. through Oct.).
2. Reviews accounts for limit raise.
3. Reviews accounts for card reissue.
4. Reviews accounts that are over limit.
5. Reviews exception file print-out.
6. Authorizes general ledger tickets to proof department.
7. Responsible for day-to-day card issuance.
8. Balances card safe (not cash).
9. Reviews new application for cards or loan.
10. Reviews possible fraud on an account.
11. Reviews any adjustment or change made on an account.
12. Cross-trains for other jobs in department.

ORGANIZATION

1. Initiate changes in the basic organization structure and complement of the planning function in order to accomplish objectives as developed in concert with the Vice President and Department Manager.
2. Activate new work procedures and systems to accomplish planning and bank development objectives more efficiently.

FINANCES

Prepare the annual budget for Credit Card Department, administering allotted funds in accordance with the budget and approved fiscal procedures; and, recommend capital expenditures for planning and bank development.

RELATIONSHIPS

1. Responsible to the Vice President and Department Manager for the fulfillment of his or her functions, responsibilities, and authority and for their proper interpretation.
2. Will advise and assist department managers, officers, and staff in their respective functions associated with the areas for which he or she has direct responsibility.
3. Will have extensive contact with customers, the public and the community, and is to conduct relationships in a manner that will enhance the overall marketing effort of the bank.
4. Will be called upon from time to time to participate with community organizations and in community projects.

JOB DESCRIPTION: Operations Supervisor
DEPARTMENT/DIVISION: Credit Card Department
REPORTS TO: Office Manager
SUPERVISES: Mail Clerk
             File Clerk
             Data Entry Clerk

JOB SUMMARY

Keypunching, balancing to general ledger and general bookkeeping.

DUTIES

1. Work up, microfilm, key and balance credit card payments, cash advances, and sales drafts.
2. Responsible for wire of net settlement.
3. Correct merchant errors in deposits.
4. Work up Master Charge payments, cash advances, and sales drafts, writing appropriate tickets and forms to send to corresponding bank.
5. Post and balance credit card income account daily.
6. Balance Credit Card Interbank Clearing account daily.
7. Balance Credit Card Loan account daily.
8. Handle all requests for ticket copies and confirmations.
9. Write general ledger tickets for finance charges and cardholder fees.
10. Write tickets for reconciliation of general ledger accounts.
11. Handle charge backs, representations, fee collections, and reversals.

Operations Supervisor (continued)

12. Handle mail received (deposits, advice from corresponding bank, charge back documentation).
13. Handle phone problems (customers and merchants).
14. Separate and distribute computer print-outs.
15. Post Forgery, Fraud and Miscellaneous account.
16. Post and check talley sheet.
17. Responsible for Weekly Progress Report to officers.
18. Responsible for Loan Account Report (1st and 15th).
19. Responsible for Income Report (monthly).
20. Posts P&L charge-offs, payments, and maintenance.
21. Balances P&L with controllers.
22. Balance and bill merchants for discount (monthly).
23. Figure rebate to Agent banks (quarterly).
24. Responsible for quarterly report.
25. Assists with reissue of cards.

ORGANIZATION

1. Initiate changes in the basic organization structure and complement of the planning function in order to accomplish objectives as developed in concert with the Office Manager — VISA.
2. Activate new work procedures and systems to accomplish planning and bank development objectives more efficiently.

FINANCES

Prepare the annual budget for Credit Card Department, administering allotted funds in accordance with the budget and approved fiscal procedures; and, recommend capital expenditures for planning and bank development.

RELATIONSHIPS

1. Responsible to the Office Manager for the fulfillment of his or her functions, responsibilities, and authority and for their proper interpretation.
2. Will advise and assist department managers, officers, and staff in their respective functions associated with the areas for which he or she has direct responsibility.
3. Will have extensive contact with customers, the public and the community, and is to conduct relationships in a manner that will enhance the overall marketing effort of the bank.
4. Will be called upon from time to time to participate with community organizations and in community projects.

JOB DESCRIPTION: File Clerk
DEPARTMENT/DIVISION: Credit Card Department
REPORTS TO: Operations Supervisor
SUPERVISES: Has no supervisory responsibility.

JOB SUMMARY

Investigation of customer credit through the use of bank and department credit files. Assist merchants with transition from local in-house authorization to the NDC system (temporary). Assist customers with any type of problems. Prepare and deliver merchant supplies. Keep inventory of merchant and department supplies in storage areas. Handle account folder filing and assist everyone in the office with everyday tasks. Prepare credit card statements (microfilm, pull statements, fold, insert and run postage). Credit card work is prepared nightly. Type and mail the new credit cards daily. Load microfilm into cartridges, check and label. Assist in cycle reissue of credit cards. Close office at night. Perform manual tasks of other departments. One clerk is primarily responsible for the charge-off of accounts and the subsequent posting of P & L payments to their respective accounts. This clerk corresponds with the Credit Department and collectors to obtain cards on delinquent accounts and assists them in locating "skips." This clerk is also responsible for the preparation of the Functional Cost and Charge-off Analyses at the end of the calendar year.

A reasonable amount of on-the-job training is required to perform certain tasks. The job requires a moderate amount of independent judgment and supervision.

DUTIES
1. Answer the phone.
2. Prepare credit card work nightly.
3. Prepare credit card statements.
4. Prepare supplies and deliver to merchants.
5. Emboss new account cards and assist in cycle reissue.
6. Handle account folder filing.
7. Provide assistance to anyone who needs it.
8. Give credit reports.
9. Load and mark film cartridges.

ORGANIZATION
Has an inherent duty and responsibility to make recommendations to supervisor concerning possible methods to improve department.

FINANCES
Has the responsibility to make recommendations to supervisor concerning the budgetary needs of the department.

RELATIONSHIPS
1. Responsible to the Operations Supervisor for the fulfillment of functions, responsibilities, and authority and for their proper interpretation.
2. Will have extensive contact with customers and the public, and is to conduct relationships in a manner that will enhance the overall marketing effort of the bank.
3. Will be called upon from time to time to participate with community organizations and in community projects.

JOB DESCRIPTION: Mail Clerk
DEPARTMENT/DIVISION: Credit Card Department
REPORTS TO: Operations Supervisor
SUPERVISES: Has no supervisory responsibility.

Mail Clerk (continued)

JOB SUMMARY

Responsibilities are to answer the telephones for card authorizations when necessary. To assist customers who may call with any problems or complaints. Pick up and process mail payments daily. Receives telephone calls regarding lost, stolen, or destroyed cards, and prepares and files temporary blocks against accounts.

DUTIES

1. Receptionist.
2. Cash advances from loan officers.
3. Handle mail problems.
4. Check maintenance against printouts and file.
5. Name and address changes.
6. Handle all return statements, cards and checks.
7. Charge checking accounts for credit card payments.
8. Assist with reissue of cards.
9. Film payments and envelopes.
10. Give credit references to other banks and other departments in bank.
11. Mail out applications to update our files.

ORGANIZATION

Has an inherent duty and responsibility to make recommendations to supervisor concerning possible methods to improve department.

FINANCES

Has the responsibility to make recommendations to supervisor concerning the budgetary needs of the department.

RELATIONSHIPS

1. Responsible to the Operations Supervisor for the fulfillment of functions, responsibilities, and authority and for their proper interpretation.
2. Will have extensive contact with customers and the public, and is to conduct relationships in a manner that will enhance the overall marketing effort of the bank.
3. Will be called upon from time to time to participate with community organizations and in community projects.

JOB DESCRIPTION: Data Entry Clerk
DEPARTMENT/DIVISION: Credit Card Department
REPORTS TO: Operations Supervisor
SUPERVISES: Has no supervisory responsibility.

JOB SUMMARY

Control and balancing of general books in the Credit Card Department. Operates IBM 3278 CRT Data Entry Machine; transcribes information from various documents to on-line disk for computer input. Assists with balancing and control work. Exercises maximum independent judgment under minimum supervision.

RESPONSIBILITY AND AUTHORITY

Within the limits of approved bank policies and procedures, the Data Entry Clerk is responsible for and has commensurate authority to accomplish the fulfillment of the duties stated below.

DUTIES

1. Work up, microfilm, key and balance credit card payments, cash advances, and sales drafts.
2. Responsible for wire of net settlement.
3. Correct merchant errors in deposits.
4. Work up credit card payments, cash advances, and sales drafts, writing appropriate tickets and forms to send to corresponding bank.
5. Post and balance credit card income account daily.
6. Balance Credit Card Interbank Clearing account daily.
7. Balance Credit Card Loan account daily.
8. Handle all requests for ticket copies and confirmations.
9. Write general ledger tickets for finance charges and cardholder fees.
10. Write tickets for reconciliation of general ledger accounts.
11. Handle charge backs, representations, fee collections, and reversals.
12. Handle mail received (deposits, advice from corresponding bank, charge back documentation).
13. Handle phone problems (customers and merchants).
14. Separate and distribute computer print-outs.
15. Post Forgery, Fraud and Miscellaneous account.
16. Post and check talley sheet.
17. Responsible for Weekly Progress Report to officers.
18. Responsible for Loan Account Report (1st and 15th).
19. Responsible for Income Report (monthly).
20. Posts P&L charge-offs, payments, and maintenance.
21. Balances P&L with controllers.
22. Balance and bill merchants for discount (monthly).
23. Figure Rebate to agent banks (quarterly).
24. Responsible for quarterly report.
25. Assists with reissue of cards.

ORGANIZATION

Has an inherent duty and responsibility to make recommendations to supervisor concerning possible methods to improve department.

FINANCES

Has the responsibility to make recommendations to supervisor concerning the budgetary needs of the department.

RELATIONSHIPS

1. Responsible to the Operations Supervisor for the fulfillment of functions, responsibilities, and authority and for their proper interpretation.
2. Will have extensive contact with customers and the public, and is to conduct relationships in a manner that will enhance the overall marketing effort of the bank.
3. Will be called upon from time to time to participate with community organizations and in community projects.

JOB DESCRIPTION: Over Limit Clerk
DEPARTMENT/DIVISION: Credit Card Department
REPORTS TO: Office Manager
SUPERVISES: Has no supervisory responsibility.

JOB SUMMARY

To be able to assist credit card customers to the best of my ability in answering questions, correcting errors and solving problems. To assist customers in maintaining their accounts in the proper manner. This includes reviewing all over-the-limit/past due accounts to decide on the proper action for the account. Should have knowledge of Base I and II systems in order to maintain and update the lost/stolen card files. Handle correspondence from National Data Corporation concerning statused accounts (our card holders) in their system. Correct all entries appearing on Non-Posted Exceptions. Be able to review accounts appearing on General Exceptions.

DUTIES

1. Review over-the-limit accounts. The accounts are either watched, letters sent out, cards pulled or the file reviewed for a limit raise.
2. Maintain the lost/stolen card file.
3. Verify that the lost/stolen card numbers appear on the National Data Corporation and Base II exception files.
4. Answer the telephone and provide the proper assistance or information to the customer.
5. Handle mail problems sent to my attention.
6. Maintain the Non-Posted exception printouts.
7. Maintain the General Exception printouts.
8. Give out Cash Advance authorization codes.
9. Give out National Data Corporation referral authorization codes.
10. Provide assistance to merchants ordering supplies, who are having problems obtaining authorization codes or other problems.
11. Be able to set up cash advance account when loan officers call up.
12. Be able to answer questions concerning chargebacks and prepare the chargeback documentation.
13. Give out credit references to the proper sources.
14. Prepare maintenance for credit card account.
15. Provide assistance to customers who visit the credit card office.
16. Maintain 1 of 2 keys to the credit card vault.
17. Send out charge privilege discontinued letters via certified mail.
18. Type over-the-limit letters on the memory typewriter.

ORGANIZATION

Has an inherent duty and responsibility to make recommendations to supervisor concerning possible methods to improve department.

FINANCES

Has the responsibility to make recommendations to supervisor concerning the budgetary needs of the department.

RELATIONSHIPS

1. Responsible to the Office Manager for the fulfillment of functions, responsibilities, and authority and for their proper interpretation.

2. Will have extensive contact with customers and the public, and is to conduct relationships in a manner that will enhance the overall marketing effort of the bank.
3. Will be called upon from time to time to participate with community organizations and in community projects.

JOB DESCRIPTION: Processing Clerk
DEPARTMENT/DIVISION: Credit Card Department
REPORTS TO: Office Manager
SUPERVISES: Has no supervisory responsibility.

JOB SUMMARY

Answer the phone, new account and turn downs.

DUTIES

1. New accounts.
2. Turn downs.
3. Answer the telephones.
4. Pull credit reports daily and weekly and reconcile monthly.
5. Take care of the customers that come in.
6. Help the part-time employees pre-sort the cycle for mailing.
7. Requisition department supplies from bank supply room.
8. Back-up for the bookkeepers.
9. Check checking accounts.
10. Check savings accounts.
11. Give authorization.
12. File customers' folders.
13. New cash advance accounts from loan officers.
14. Charge checking accounts.
15. Charge offs.
16. P & L payments.
17. Setting up credit card merchants.
18. Credit card monthly settlements.
19. Non-posted exception report.
20. Credit balances and issuance of cashier checks with management approval.
21. Requested tickets.
22. Assist with reissue of cards.
23. Name and address changes (maintenance).
24. Handle all return statements, cards, and checks.
25. Checking maintenance against printouts and file.
26. Film payments, envelopes, new accounts and turn downs.
27. Type and mail counter proposals.
28. Handle mail problems.

ORGANIZATION

Has an inherent duty and responsibility to make recommendations to supervisor concerning possible methods to improve department.

Processing Clerk (continued)

FINANCES

Has the responsibility to make recommendations to supervisor concerning the budgetary needs of the department.

RELATIONSHIPS

1. Responsible to the Office Manager for the fulfillment of functions, responsibilities, and authority and for their proper interpretation.
2. Will have extensive contact with customers and the public, and is to conduct relationships in a manner that will enhance the overall marketing effort of the bank.
3. Will be called upon from time to time to participate with community organizations and in community projects.

Installment Loans Division

JOB DESCRIPTION: Assistant Vice President and Department Manager — Installment Loans
DEPARTMENT/DIVISION: Installment Loans
REPORTS TO: Senior Vice President — Consumer Credit Division
SUPERVISES: Retail Loan Supervisor and Loan Officer

JOB SUMMARY

Supervision of the Installment Loan Department, which consists of the retail and wholesale areas of Direct Loans and Student Loans. Also handles direct loan requests.

DUTIES

1. Supervises the following functional areas: Retail Loans, Wholesale Credit (floor plan), Dealer Leases, Student Loans, and Direct Loans (downtown).
2. Reviews credit application denials which are denied by the loan officers in the Dealer Division to insure that the application was checked and handled properly and the necessary turn-down procedures were followed.
3. Reviews contracts and applications on loans made by Dealer Division Officers to insure that they do comply with bank policy, and are loans which were handled properly for the appropriate dealer.
4. Insures that contracts are discounted as soon as possible once they are received from the dealers and also that these contracts are discounted accurately.
5. Reviews the Dealer Posting Journal to determine what each dealer's reserve account balance is.
6. Insures that the Posting Journal balances daily with the appropriate general ledger Account.
7. Periodically makes personal visits to dealerships in order to stay in contact with the dealers and deal with any problems which they may have and try to generate as much business as possible.
8. Reviews Dealer Floor Plan balances to insure that dealers do not exceed their approved credit line.
9. Insures that the Floor Plan balances are reconciled each day with the appropriate accounts.
10. Reviews and initials all notes which are made on orders to floor plan units.

11. Insures that used automobiles being floor planned are in line with reasonable wholesale values.
12. Constantly reviews each Floor Plan Dealer to insure that necessary documentation is in file.
13. Insures that all Dealer Floor Plans are checked on a regular basis and reviews these verification checks to insure that they are properly handled.
14. Reviews all lease lines to insure that they are handled properly.
15. Insures that all lease dealers do not exceed their approved credit line.
16. Reviews the day-to-day operation of the student loan area.
17. Periodically sells student loans to the Student Loan Marketing Association (Sallie Mae).

ORGANIZATION

1. Initiate changes in the basic organization structure and complement of the planning function in order to accomplish objectives as developed in concert with the Senior Vice President — Consumer Credit Division.
2. Activate new work procedures and systems to accomplish planning and bank development objectives more efficiently.

FINANCES

Prepare the annual budget for Installment Loans Department, administering allotted funds in accordance with the budget and approved fiscal procedures; and, recommend capital expenditures for planning and bank development.

RELATIONSHIPS

1. Responsible to the Senior Vice President — Consumer Credit Division for the fulfillment of his or her functions, responsibilities, and authority and for their proper interpretation.
2. Will advise and assist department managers, officers, and staff in their respective functions associated with the areas for which he or she has direct responsibility.
3. Will have extensive contact with customers, the public and the community, and is to conduct relationships in a manner that will enhance the overall marketing effort of the bank.
4. Will be called upon from time to time to participate with community organizations and in community projects.

JOB DESCRIPTION: Retail Loan Supervisor and Loan Officer
DEPARTMENT/DIVISION: Installment Loans
REPORTS TO: Assistant Vice President and Department Manager — Installment Loans
SUPERVISES: Direct Loan Officer
　　　　　　　Retail Loan Officer
　　　　　　　Wholesale Clerk
　　　　　　　Student Loan Clerk

JOB SUMMARY

The Retail Loan Supervisor has all the duties of the other loan officer. In addition to these duties, the Retail Loan Supervisor is responsible for the overall operation of the department. Any problems with contracts to be discounted are brought to his or her attention. On any contract that has to be returned to a dealer, the Retail Loan Supervisor must be advised and his or her approval given before the contract is returned to the dealer.

Retail Loan Supervisor and Loan Officer (continued)

DUTIES

1. Take applications for loan and process.
2. Make loan decisions.
3. Prepare credit denial letters.
4. Process and check loan documents.
5. Balance loans.
6. Audit loans.
7. Approve extensions.
8. Transfer loans.
9. Approve general ledger tickets.
10. Authorize dealer reserve transfer.
11. Supervise employees in department.
12. Prepare end-of-month reports.
13. Distribute dealer past due printout.
14. Follow up dealer past dues.
15. Maintain repossession record.
16. Make dealer calls.
17. Distribute sales contracts and applications.
18. Audit monthly dealer statements.
19. Locate real estate section on Flood Zone map for mobile home loans.
20. Send past due letters.
21. Follow up dealers and maintain current financial statements.

ORGANIZATION

1. Initiate changes in the basic organization structure and complement of the planning function in order to accomplish objectives as developed in concert with the Assistant Vice President and Department Manager — Installment Loans.
2. Activate new work procedures and systems to accomplish planning and bank development objectives more efficiently.

FINANCES

Prepare the annual budget for Installment Loans Department, administering allotted funds in accordance with the budget and approved fiscal procedures; and, recommend capital expenditures for planning and bank development.

RELATIONSHIPS

1. Responsible to the Assistant Vice President and Department Manager — Installment Loans for the fulfillment of his or her functions, responsibilities, and authority and for their proper interpretation.
2. Will advise and assist department managers, officers, and staff in their respective functions associated with the areas for which he or she has direct responsibility.
3. Will have extensive contact with customers, the public and the community, and is to conduct relationships in a manner that will enhance the overall marketing effort of the bank.
4. Will be called upon from time to time to participate with community organizations and in community projects.

JOB DESCRIPTION: Direct Loan Officer
DEPARTMENT/DIVISION: Installment Loans
REPORTS TO: Retail Loan Supervisor and Loan Officer
SUPERVISES: Has no supervisory responsibility.

JOB SUMMARY

Interviews and evaluates loan requests for purpose of making direct loans. Takes appropriate action on these requests. Makes dealer wholesale inventory verifications. Responsible for recording mortgages and UCC's at probate office.

DUTIES

1. Interviews direct loan applicants.
2. Evaluates loan applicants and takes appropriate action.
3. Makes dealer wholesale inventory verifications.
4. Carries mortgages and UCC recordings to county courthouse to be recorded in Probate judge's office.

ORGANIZATION

Has an inherent duty and responsibility to make recommendations to supervisor concerning possible methods to improve department.

FINANCES

Has the responsibility to make recommendations to supervisor concerning the budgetary needs of the department.

RELATIONSHIPS

1. Responsible to the Retail Loan Supervisor and Loan Officer for the fulfillment of functions, responsibilities, and authority and for their proper interpretation.
2. Will have extensive contact with customers and the public, and is to conduct relationships in a manner that will enhance the overall marketing effort of the bank.
3. Will be called upon from time to time to participate with community organizations and in community projects.

JOB DESCRIPTION: Retail Loan Officer
DEPARTMENT/DIVISION: Installment Loans
REPORTS TO: Retail Loan Supervisor and Loan Officer
SUPERVISES: Has no supervisory responsibility.

JOB SUMMARY

Installment loan officer in the dealer loan department making dealer loans.

DUTIES

1. Take credit application from the dealer.
2. Pull credit files on the customer.
3. Check customer credit.

Retail Loan Officer (continued)

4. Evaluate credit of the customer.
5. Approve or turn down customer to the dealer.
6. Check contracts for accuracy.
7. Balance the daily posting journal with general ledger.

ORGANIZATION

Has an inherent duty and responsibility to make recommendations to supervisor concerning possible methods to improve department.

FINANCES

Has the responsibility to make recommendations to supervisor concerning the budgetary needs of the department.

RELATIONSHIPS

1. Responsible to the Retail Loan Supervisor and Loan Officer for the fulfillment of functions, responsibilities, and authority and for their proper interpretation.
2. Will have extensive contact with customers and the public, and is to conduct relationships in a manner that will enhance the overall marketing effort of the bank.
3. Will be called upon from time to time to participate with community organizations and in community projects.

JOB DESCRIPTION: Wholesale Clerk (A)
DEPARTMENT/DIVISION: Installment Loans
REPORTS TO: Retail Loan Supervisor and Loan Officer
SUPERVISES: Has no supervisory responsibility.

JOB SUMMARY

Responsible for discounting and disbursing sales contracts and other designated secretarial/clerical duties.

DUTIES

1. Responsible for answering phones and taking applications.
2. Discounting and disbursing sales contracts.
3. Loan officer correspondence.
4. Mail reserve statements.
5. Keep check on deposit books and reorder before we run out.
6. Type extensions.
7. Type adverse action and counter-office letters.
8. Balance loans discounted that day.
9. Keep dealer books updated.
10. Fill out UCC-1 financing statements.
11. Handle contracts when they are received in Dealer Section.
12. Follow-up list.
13. Reimburse dealer for money held in reserve account on contracts.

14. Responsible for filing tickets.
15. Type Repossession letters.

ORGANIZATION

Has an inherent duty and responsibility to make recommendations to supervisor concerning possible methods to improve department.

FINANCES

Has the responsibility to make recommendations to supervisor concerning the budgetary needs of the department.

RELATIONSHIPS

1. Responsible to the Retail Loan Supervisor and Loan Officer for the fulfillment of functions, responsibilities, and authority and for their proper interpretation.
2. Will have extensive contact with customers and the public, and is to conduct relationships in a manner that will enhance the overall marketing effort of the bank.
3. Will be called upon from time to time to participate with community organizations and in community projects.

JOB DESCRIPTION: Wholesale Clerk (B)
DEPARTMENT/DIVISION: Installment Loans
REPORTS TO: Retail Loan Supervisor and Loan Officer
SUPERVISES: Has no supervisory responsibility.

JOB SUMMARY

Responsible for discounting retail installment contracts and disbursing proceeds to dealer. Also performs designated secretarial/clerical tasks.

DUTIES

1. Responsible for answering phones and taking applications.
2. Discounting and disbursing sales contracts.
3. Loan officer correspondence.
4. Mail reserve statements.
5. Keep check on deposit books and reorder before we run out.
6. Type extensions.
7. Type adverse action and counter-offer letters.
8. Balance loans discounted that day.
9. Keep dealer books updated.
10. Fill out UCC-1 financing statements.
11. Handle contracts when they are received in dealer section.
12. Follow-up list.
13. Reimburse dealer for money held in reserve account on contracts.
14. Responsible for filing tickets.
15. Type Repossession letters.
16. Mail "Monthly Dealer Past Due Report" to dealers each Thursday.

Wholesale Clerk (B) (continued)

17. Mail "Past Due Payment Report" to Full Recourse Dealers each day.
18. Type Change of Collateral for dealers.
19. Process Change of Collateral after it is returned from dealer.
20. Type Transfer of Equity.
21. Process Transfer of Equity when it is returned from dealer.
22. Obtain supplies from the supply room.

ORGANIZATION

Has an inherent duty and responsibility to make recommendations to supervisor concerning possible methods to improve department.

FINANCES

Has the responsibility to make recommendations to supervisor concerning the budgetary needs of the department.

RELATIONSHIPS

1. Responsible to the Retail Loan Supervisor and Loan Officer for the fulfillment of functions, responsibilities, and authority and for their proper interpretation.
2. Will have extensive contact with customers and the public, and is to conduct relationships in a manner that will enhance the overall marketing effort of the bank.
3. Will be called upon from time to time to participate with community organizations and in community projects.

JOB DESCRIPTION: Student Loan Secretary/Clerk
DEPARTMENT/DIVISION: Installment Loans
REPORTS TO: Retail Loan Supervisor and Loan Officer
SUPERVISES: Has no supervisory responsibility.

JOB SUMMARY

Interview students and process student loans.

DUTIES

1. Interview students both over the phone and in person.
2. Check over applications that students have turned in to be sure all sections are complete and correct.
3. Have credit department check students' credit.
4. Make files for all approved loans.
5. Maintain a list of all rejected applicants.
6. Type up necessary papers and get students' signatures.
7. Mail checks to the appropriate schools attached to a copy of the student's application. Log all student loan disbursements.
8. Keypunch to get the new student loans on computer.
9. When billed monthly by the state or government, be sure the amount billed is correct and submit a check.

10. Prepare annual report. Prepare interest and special allowance report quarterly.
11. Mail out computer notices to students.
12. Type past due letters.
13. Calculate repayment schedules and type repayment notes. Have student sign after going over it.
14. Keep up with when these students need to be put on repayment schedule.
15. Take all student loans to Operations to be entered on the books.
16. File claims, if any, and type deferments.
17. Prepare monthly reports.
18. Transfer interest each month by doing general ledger tickets.
19. Fill out Federal Loan Transaction Statement each month, listing all loans disbursed, loans put in repayment, and all loans paid off.
20. Film the files that were completed at the end of the month for that month.
21. Do insurance assignment releases by typing up Assignment Release Forms and sending to insurance company.
22. Type state Protective Services loans.
23. Type loans. Go over loans with customers. Type Insurance Cards and Credit Life Certificates. Cut checks. Do title work when necessary. Complete computer sheets on loans. Answer phones, take dictation, and make copies on xerox, and other general secretarial/clerical responsibilities.

ORGANIZATION

Has an inherent duty and responsibility to make recommendations to supervisor concerning possible methods to improve department.

FINANCES

Has the responsibility to make recommendations to supervisor concerning the budgetary needs of the department.

RELATIONSHIPS

1. Responsible to the Retail Loan Supervisor and Loan Officer for the fulfillment of functions, responsibilities, and authority and for their proper interpretation.
2. Will have extensive contact with customers and the public, and is to conduct relationships in a manner that will enhance the overall marketing effort of the bank.
3. Will be called upon from time to time to participate with community organizations and in community projects.

JOB DESCRIPTION: Floor Plan Clerk
DEPARTMENT/DIVISION: Installment Loans
REPORTS TO: Retail Loan Supervisor and Loan Officer
SUPERVISES: Has no supervisory responsibility.

JOB SUMMARY

Oversee and perform day-to-day clerical operations of the floor plan function.

Floor Plan Clerk (continued)

DUTIES

Monthly
1. Generate required reports.
2. Mail notes.
3. Post and transfer funds to general ledger accounts.
4. Balance accounts (general ledger).

Yearly
5. Request financial information.
6. Secure and maintain information files.

Daily
7. File invoices.
8. Post charges.
9. Post payments.
10. Make deposits.
11. Collect overdrafts (call dealers).
12. Balance general ledger and subsidiary ledgers.
13. Film and file notes.
14. Loan documentation.
15. Receive payments.
16. Loan disbursements.
17. Distribute reports (weekly).
18. Credit and debit adjustments to subsidiary balances (investigate and resolve) when necessary.
19. Oversee day-to-day operation of automated system which manages floor plan accounts.
20. Perform maintenance, if necessary, to unit information.
21. Any other tasks assigned by Department Manager relating to Dealer Retail Section.
22. Audit dealer paper.
23. On occasion, give direction to Dealer Section employees in Department Manager's absence.
24. User consultation — Student Loans D.P. System.
25. Handle leases under current lease program.

ORGANIZATION

Has an inherent duty and responsibility to make recommendations to supervisor concerning possible methods to improve department.

FINANCES

Has the responsibility to make recommendations to supervisor concerning the budgetary needs of the department.

RELATIONSHIPS

1. Responsible to the Retail Loan Supervisor and Loan Officer for the fulfillment of functions, responsibilities, and authority and for their proper interpretation.
2. Will have extensive contact with customers and the public, and is to conduct relationships in a manner that will enhance the overall marketing effort of the bank.
3. Will be called upon from time to time to participate with community organizations and in community projects.

JOB DESCRIPTION: Consumer Loan Secretary
DEPARTMENT/DIVISION: Installment Loans
REPORTS TO: Retail Loan Supervisor and Loan Officer
SUPERVISES: Has no supervisory responsibility.

JOB SUMMARY

To act as a secretary-receptionist for the Installment Loan Department.

DUTIES

1. Serve as a receptionist, which includes: answering directory for department, directing customers to proper department and loan officer, and assisting with gathering general information for customers.
2. Type notes.
3. Type adverse action letters.
4. Type counter offer letters.
5. Process death claims.
6. Type director loans.
7. Type extensions.
8. Type due date changes.
9. Type title release.

ORGANIZATION

Has an inherent duty and responsibility to make recommendations to supervisor concerning possible methods to improve department.

FINANCES

Has the responsibility to make recommendations to supervisor concerning the budgetary needs of the department.

RELATIONSHIPS

1. Responsible to the Retail Loan Supervisor and Loan Officer for the fulfillment of functions, responsibilities, and authority and for their proper interpretation.
2. Will have extensive contact with customers and the public, and is to conduct relationships in a manner that will enhance the overall marketing effort of the bank.
3. Will be called upon from time to time to participate with community organizations and in community projects.

10

HUMAN RESOURCES AND CUSTOMER SERVICES DEPARTMENT JOB DESCRIPTIONS

The human resources and customer services department of a bank is responsible for hiring and training personnel and maintaining good relations with customers. Some banks will have separate departments for these functions, but the smaller bank should have little problem combining the two.

The proper performance of the duties and responsibilities described in the job descriptions which follow should result in smooth relationships among employees and customers.

JOB DESCRIPTION: Senior Vice President — Human Resources and Customer Services
DEPARTMENT/DIVISION: Human Resources and Customer Services
REPORTS TO: Executive Vice President
SUPERVISES: Vice President and Branch Administrator
 Division Secretary

ATM Coordinator and H.R.C.S. Officer
Director, Personnel and Training
Assistant Vice President and Coordinator of Special Services

JOB SUMMARY

To supervise, plan and coordinate the activities of the Human Resources and Customer Services Division as well as assist the Executive Vice President, Chairman, and CEO on special projects or other functions as they may deem necessary.

DUTIES

1. Supervise Division subordinates.
2. Plan and carry out advertising campaigns.
3. Consult with Personnel Director on employee problems, dismissals and benefits.
4. Be available and report to Executive Vice President when needed.
5. Serve on different management committees:
    a. Personnel
    b. Pricing
    c. Senior Management
    d. Welfare
    e. Charitable Trust
    f. Committee for Better Government
    g. Cash Management (Plan bank customer parties)
6. Plan all employee receptions.
7. Bank Advisor to FEW Committee.
8. Attend functions that Executive Vice President, Chairman and CEO are unable to attend.
9. Attend funerals as the bank representative.
10. Attend many social functions as the bank representative.
11. Manage customer complaints.
12. Manage bank advertising.
13. Review new account and closed account list daily.
14. Participate in officer call program.
15. Responsible for bank football orders and distribution; baseball and basketball also.
16. Responsible for bank Annual Report Prints of Covers.
17. Responsible for business development and retention of customer business.
18. Responsible for marketing research.
19. Available to coordinate activities that affect Human Resources and Customer Services Division.
20. Review all employees' performance evaluations in connection with supervision of the Personnel Director.

ORGANIZATION

1. Initiate changes in the basic organization structure and complement of the planning function in order to accomplish objectives as developed in concert with the Executive Vice President.
2. Activate new work procedures and systems to accomplish planning and bank development objectives more efficiently.

Senior Vice President — Human Resources and Customer Services (continued)

FINANCES

Prepare the annual budget for Human Resources and Customer Services, administering allotted funds in accordance with the budget and approved fiscal procedures; and, recommend capital expenditures for planning and bank development.

RELATIONSHIPS

1. Responsible to the Executive Vice President for the fulfillment of his or her functions, responsibilities, and authority and for their proper interpretation.
2. Will advise and assist department managers, officers, and staff in their respective functions associated with the areas for which he or she has direct responsibility.
3. Will have extensive contact with customers, the public and the community, and is to conduct relationships in a manner that will enhance the overall marketing effort of the bank.
4. Will be called upon from time to time to participate with community organizations and in community projects.

JOB DESCRIPTION: Salary & Benefits Administrator
DEPARTMENT/DIVISION: Human Resources and Customer Service
REPORTS TO: Personnel Officers
SUPERVISES: Has no direct supervisory responsibility.

JOB SUMMARY

Responsible for bank's salary administration and benefits administration programs.

DUTIES

1. Analyzes and writes employee job descriptions.
2. Interviews employees and officers for same.
3. Determines position dimensions, responsibilities, accountabilities, and knowledge requirements.
4. Heads Job Evaluation Committee involved in evaluating and rating job positions.
5. Computes (monthly) premium payments and coverage adjustments for Medical, Group Life and Long Term Disability insurances.
6. Reviews and processes major medical and death insurance claims.
7. Answers (by phone, mail, and in person) inquiries from employees, officers, and pensioners regarding medical coverage, life insurance, disability insurance, and profit sharing.
8. Advises personnel on medical coverage, deductions, enrollments, and distributions.
9. Advises officers on salary administration policy and benefit interpretation.
10. Answers officer inquiries regarding job descriptions, grades, evaluations, etc.
11. Maintains (monthly) employee performance reports, confirmations and computer runs.
12. Settles same.
13. Computes divisional wage and salary controls from same.
14. Participates in employee and officer salary surveys and comparisons.
15. Analyzes same in relation to other area banks and industries.
16. Recommends adjustments regarding problem areas, policy changes, grades, market prices, etc.

17. Keypunches officer position evaluations.
18. Represents bank at various salary and benefit meetings and conferences.
19. Compiles special projects and reports as necessary.
20. Administers bank's exempt status program.
21. Determines and Advises Division Heads as to eligibility for exempt status.

ORGANIZATION
Has an inherent duty and responsibility to make recommendations to supervisor concerning possible methods to improve department.

FINANCES
Has the responsibility to make recommendations to supervisor concerning the budgetary needs of the department.

RELATIONSHIPS
Considerable personal, telephone and mail contact with other banks, area industries, federal agencies, educational institutions, insurance representatives, and bank personnel.

JOB DESCRIPTION: Division Secretary
DEPARTMENT/DIVISION: Human Resources and Customer Services
REPORTS TO: Senior Vice President — Human Resources and Customer Services
SUPERVISES: Has no supervisory responsibility.

JOB SUMMARY
To perform secretarial as well as other assigned duties for the Senior Vice President and Division. To assist in all phases of the Division and be available and willing to do necessary tasks for any bank employee.

DUTIES
1. Maintain Senior Vice President — Human Resources and Customer Services' desk.
2. Distribute Division mail.
3. Distribute bank information — closed accounts, statement of condition, daily reporter.
4. Distribute memos, notices, bank policies throughout the Division.
5. Send out laminated public relation news clippings.
6. Send out newcomer kits and be in charge of the storage cabinet as well as keep the cabinet stocked.
7. Type the Downtown Unlimited minutes and xerox.
8. Do DTU monthly notices of meetings on the MAG machine and mail out monthly.
9. Type the Committee for Better Government's minutes.
10. Maintain personal files on bank officers.
11. Assist in doing First United Methodist Church Offering deposits.
12. Assist organizations that use bank for fund raising displays.
13. Maintain funds collected for American Cancer Society, Heart Fund, Jump Rope for Life.
14. Keep Senior Vice President's calendar up-to-date.
15. Order and distribute supplies for the Human Resources and Customer Services Division.

Division Secretary (continued)

16. Keep bank scrapbooks.
17. Keep the Book of Golden Deeds, Exchange Club, up-to-date.
18. Assist with the bank Golf Tournament and write letters to people who helped with tournament. Handle all the money and keep good records.
19. Order bank football tickets yearly.
20. Type and issue memos sent out by Senior Vice President.
21. Distribute Annual Reports.
22. Maintain accurate file on bank policies and procedures.
23. Keep Senior Vice President's politics file.
24. Give out applications for personnel and explain to applicants.
25. Maintain Advertising file and make general ledger deposits for Ad Agency.
26. Maintain Bankers Association File.
27. Maintain Bank Marketing Association File.
28. Maintain bank PAC file.
29. Maintain bank clock information in file and distribute keys.
30. Maintain all the keys to Division facilities.
31. Maintain supply cabinet.
32. Sign all new accounts and savings and closed accounts letters daily.
33. File all returned account correspondence.
34. File daily reporters, condition of reports, and statement of condition daily.
35. Type and mail newcomer letters.
36. Provide secretarial assistance to all Division staff.
37. Act as receptionist for the Division.
38. Book the board room for all bank and community functions.

ORGANIZATION

Has an inherent duty and responsibility to make recommendations to supervisor concerning possible methods to improve department.

FINANCES

Has the responsibility to make recommendations to supervisor concerning the budgetary needs of the department.

RELATIONSHIPS

1. Responsible to the Senior Vice President — Human Resources and Customer Services Division for the fulfillment of functions, responsibilities, and authority and for their proper interpretation.
2. Will have extensive contact with customers and the public, and is to conduct relationships in a manner that will enhance the overall marketing effort of the bank.
3. Will be called upon from time to time to participate with community organizations and in community projects.

JOB DESCRIPTION: Senior Payroll Clerk
DEPARTMENT/DIVISION: Personnel

REPORTS TO: Vice President
SUPERVISES: Payroll Clerk

JOB SUMMARY

Responsible for Payroll function pertaining to preparation of bi-weekly officer and employee payroll.

DUTIES

1. Maintains separate controls on employee status and salary information, pensioners, medical insurance, United Fund, savings bonds, stock purchase, statement savings certificates, employee loans, government deductions, etc.
2. Posts changes to controls for payroll deductions.
3. Keypunches payroll data for computer entry.
4. Settles computer pay journal versus controls.
5. Posts adjustments on settlement sheet.
6. Types adjusted pay statements, special pension checks, and off payroll list as necessary.
7. Distributes (by mail) pay statements, W-2 forms, bonds, stock, etc. to employees.
8. Maintains list of bonds and saving certificates issued each pay period.
9. Forwards same to Time Deposit and Addressograph.
10. Calculates and compiles (bi-weekly) Gross Payroll by department run for Cost & Budget.
11. Settles same with payroll distribution for regular, part-time, officer, and overtime salaries.
12. Settles quarterly and annual cost reports from computer with General Accounting.
13. Calculates and compiles payroll tax returns monthly and quarterly including city wage, state, federal, and county.
14. Settles same with General Accounting.
15. Settles and forwards (quarterly) United Fund payments pledged by employees.
16. Receives (by mail) and maintains quarterly employee time records.
17. Receives (by phone) part-time and overtime hours from departments and branches (bi-weekly).
18. Answers (by phone) inquiries from bank personnel and departments concerning taxes, pay statements, cost run settlement, etc.
19. Assists Assistant Comptroller in settling and distributing profit sharing payments to employees.
20. Recommends performance evaluations on Payroll Clerk to Assistant Comptroller
21. Performs duties of Payroll Clerk as necessary.

ORGANIZATION

Has an inherent duty and responsibility to make recommendations to supervisor concerning possible methods to improve department.

FINANCES

Has the responsibility to make recommendations to supervisor concerning the budgetary needs of the department.

RELATIONSHIPS

Frequent telephone and mail contact with bank personnel.

JOB DESCRIPTION: Payroll Clerk
DEPARTMENT/DIVISION: Personnel
REPORTS TO: Senior Payroll Clerk
SUPERVISES: Has no direct supervisory responsibility.

JOB SUMMARY

Prepares bi-weekly officer and employee payroll.

DUTIES

1. Maintains separate controls on employee status and salary information, pensioners, medical insurance, United Fund, savings bonds, stock purchase, saving certificates, employee loans, government deductions, etc.
2. Posts changes to controls for payroll deductions.
3. Keypunches payroll data for computer entry.
4. Settles computer pay journal versus controls.
5. Posts adjustments on settlement sheet.
6. Types adjusted pay statements, special pension checks, and off payroll list as necessary.
7. Distributes (by mail) pay statements, W-2 forms, bonds, stocks, etc. to employees.
8. Maintains list of bonds and saving certificates issued each pay period.
9. Forwards same to Time Deposit and Addressograph.
10. Calculates and compiles (bi-weekly) Gross Payroll by department run for Cost & Budget.
11. Settles same with payroll distribution for regular, part-time, officer, and overtime salaries.
12. Settles quarterly and annual cost reports from computer with General Accounting.
13. Calculates and compiles payroll tax returns monthly and quarterly including city wage, state, federal, and county.
14. Settles same with General Accounting.
15. Settles and forwards (quarterly) United Fund payments pledged by employees.
16. Receives (by mail) and maintains quarterly employee time records.
17. Receives (by phone) part-time and overtime hours from departments and branches (bi-weekly).
18. Answers (by phone) inquiries from bank personnel and departments concerning taxes, pay statements, cost run settlement, etc.
19. Assists Assistant Comptroller and Senior Payroll Clerk in settling and distributing profit sharing payments to employees.
20. Performs duties of Senior Payroll Clerk as necessary.

ORGANIZATION

Has an inherent duty and responsibility to make recommendations to supervisor concerning possible methods to improve department.

FINANCES

Has the responsibility to make recommendations to supervisor concerning the budgetary needs of the department.

RELATIONSHIPS

Frequent telephone and mail contact with bank personnel.

JOB DESCRIPTION: ATM Coordinator and H.R.C.S. Officer
DEPARTMENT/DIVISION: Human Resources and Customer Services
REPORTS TO: Senior Vice President — Human Resources and Customer Services
SUPERVISES: Hourly Employees
               ATM Function — Babysitters
               Other Administrative Functions

JOB SUMMARY

Responsible for the daily and long term operation of the ATM "PAT" system. Makes procedural changes and recommendations to Senior Management offering direction for the system's development. Responsible for assuring that the system is properly maintained. Coordination and good rapport with Data Processing, IBM representatives, branches, New Accounts, and Bookkeeping is required. Supervises ATM babysitting program. Assists in customer service. May assist in various Marketing functions. Knowledge of bank operations and thorough understanding of bank services are necessary. Daily decisions require a good deal of independent judgment under minimum supervision. Long term decisions require input from divisions affected.

DUTIES

1. Machine service.
2. Employee and customer training on ATM use and maintenance.
3. Daily close out and resupply.
4. Performs balancing procedures and assistance.
5. Service coordination with IBM.
6. Lost and stolen card procedures.
7. Fraud control.
8. Handles customer complaints and inquiries.
9. Handles PIN requests and issues and audit control.
10. Handles new and replacement card requests.
11. Maintains PAT account records.
12. Destruction of void or unwanted PAT cards.
13. Maintains PAT babysitting schedules.
14. Provides monthly reports to management.

ORGANIZATION

1. Initiate changes in the basic organization structure and complement of the planning function in order to accomplish objectives as developed in concert with the Senior Vice President — Human Resources and Customer Services.
2. Activate new work procedures and systems to accomplish planning and bank development objectives more efficiently.

FINANCES

Prepare the annual budget for Human Resources and Customer Services, administering allotted funds in accordance with the budget and approved fiscal procedures; and, recommend capital expenditures for planning and bank development.

ATM Coordinator and H.R.C.S. Officer (continued)

RELATIONSHIPS

1. Responsible to the Senior Vice President — Human Resources and Customer Services for the fulfillment of his or her functions, responsibilities, and authority and for their proper interpretation.
2. Will advise and assist department managers, officers, and staff in their respective functions associated with the areas for which he or she has direct responsibility.
3. Will have extensive contact with customers, the public and the community, and is to conduct relationships in a manner that will enhance the overall marketing effort of the bank.
4. Will be called upon from time to time to participate with community organizations and in community projects.

JOB DESCRIPTION: Hourly Clerk
DEPARTMENT/DIVISION: Human Resources and Customer Service
REPORTS TO: ATM Coordinator and H.R.C.S. Officer
SUPERVISES: Has no supervisory responsibility.

JOB SUMMARY

To perform the paperwork maintenance necessary for PAT customers, cut and mail out all PAT cards, answer the phone for Division, and generally assist the PAT coordinator.

DUTIES

1. Write letters to PAT customers (type two times a month).
2. Cut new and duplicate PAT cards and mail them out (weekly).
3. File paperwork for new PAT cards (daily).
4. File duplicate card requests (daily).
5. Hot card PAT cards in the event of loss (daily).
6. Help customers with problems (deposits, withdrawals) look up transactions on microfiche (daily).
7. Fill out general ledger tickets and deposits to pay babysitters mileage expense (monthly).
8. Buy liquor and mixers for the bank and keep the liquor closet in order (monthly).
9. Copy and distribute PAT monthly report (monthly).
10. Open and close PAT machines as necessary (daily).
11. Answer the phone for the PAT department; act as a receptionist (daily).
12. Occasional hauling and lifting for marketing and other departments (weekly).
13. Act as Editor of the bank newsletter — i.e. contact civic organizations, Parks Department, and university and get current events for the coming month — contact our coupon merchants for their coupon changes for the coming month — take the typed copy to the printer (monthly).
14. Buy groceries, etc. for bank sponsored parties (monthly).
15. File computer printouts (daily).
16. Write collection letters in PAT fraud cases (monthly).
17. Make monthly calendar for PAT babysitters and distribute (monthly).
18. Make phone list changes for PAT babysitters and distribute (as needed).
19. Make trips to all branches to distribute PAT materials and supplies (as needed).
20. Send new card address changes to Auditing Department (daily).

ORGANIZATION

Has an inherent duty and responsibility to make recommendations to supervisor concerning possible methods to improve department.

FINANCES

Has the responsibility to make recommendations to supervisor concerning the budgetary needs of the department.

RELATIONSHIPS

1. Responsible to the ATM Coordinator and H.R.C.S. Officer for the fulfillment of functions, responsibilities, and authority and for their proper interpretation.
2. Will have extensive contact with customers and the public, and is to conduct relationships in a manner that will enhance the overall marketing effort of the bank.
3. Will be called upon from time to time to participate with community organizations and in community projects.

JOB DESCRIPTION: Director of Personnel and Training
DEPARTMENT/DIVISION: Human Resources and Customer Services
REPORTS TO: Senior Vice President — Human Resources and Customer Services
SUPERVISES: Human Resources Assistant
                        Teller Training Officer

JOB SUMMARY

Interview and screen job applicants. Coordinate selection, placement, inducting, transferring, promotion, discipline and termination of employees. Administer all employee benefits including wages and salaries. Advise employees on personnel policies, procedures and employment laws.

DUTIES

1. Employment:
    a. Interview job applicants.
    b. Recommend candidates for openings.
    c. Run credit and employment checks on serious candidates.
    d. Coordinate hiring.
    e. Indoctrinate new employees on benefits package.
    f. Conduct official new employee orientation.
    g. Coordinate transferring, promotion, discipline and termination.
    h. Counsel employees on personal problems, conflicts with other employees and use of benefits.
    i. Advise employees on personnel policies and procedures.
    j. Advise supervisors on laws regarding all phases of personnel administration.
    k. Maintain officers' personnel files.
    l. Recommend changes in training and development.
2. Government Reports:
    a. Prepare IRS form 5500 on benefits plans yearly.
    b. Prepare PBGC report for pension plan yearly.
    c. Prepare and maintain Affirmative Action plan. Do EEO-1 report yearly.

Director of Personnel and Training (continued)

   d. Prepare and distribute Summary Annual Reports and Summary Plan Descriptions as needed (ERLSA requirements).
   e. Prepare Schedule E on bank officer salaries yearly.
   f. Prepare OSHA reports yearly. Keep up with OSHA cases as they occur.
   g. Prepare Table I tax 1099 form for officers' insurance and bank automobiles and airplane.
3. Wage and Salary Administration:
   a. Prepare and maintain monthly payroll.
   b. Oversee assistant on biweekly payroll.
   c. Oversee assistant on all government payroll requirements.
   d. Prepare records for cash bonus.
   e. Oversee statewide salary survey.
   f. Advise employees on W-4 tax forms.
   g. Attend personnel committee meeting; advise members on personnel policies, salary ranges, absenteeism, wage and hour laws, etc.
4. Benefit Administration:
   a. Maintain all benefit plans.
      (1) Health Insurance
         (a) Oversee assistant in payment of premium.
         (b) Enroll employees in plan.
         (c) Advise employees in using plan.
         (d) Help employees with problems with plan.
         (e) Prepare IRS form 5500.
      (2) Life Insurance
         (a) Oversee assistant in payment of premium.
         (b) Fill out necessary paperwork in case of death or dismemberment.
         (c) Prepare IRS form 5500.
      (3) Pension Plan and L.T.D.
         (a) Oversee assistant in payment of plan premium.
         (b) Enroll new members.
         (c) Do necessary paperwork if plan is used.
         (d) Prepare IRS form 5500.
         (e) Act as secretary for Pension Review Committee.
      (4) Profit Sharing Plan
         (a) Enroll new members in plan.
         (b) Maintain profit sharing ledger.
         (c) Post yearly contribution, quarterly earnings, and forfeitures.
         (d) Post employee withdrawals.
         (e) Provide salary information for yearly contribution.
         (f) Prepare IRS form 5500.
         (g) Act as secretary for Benefit Review Committee.

ORGANIZATION

1. Initiate changes in the basic organization structure and complement of the planning function in order to accomplish objectives as developed in concert with the Senior Vice President — Human Resources and Customer Services.
2. Activate new work procedures and systems to accomplish planning and bank development objectives more efficiently.

FINANCES

Prepare the annual budget for Human Resources and Customer Services, administering allotted funds in accordance with the budget and approved fiscal procedures; and recommend capital expenditures for planning and bank development.

RELATIONSHIPS

1. Responsible to the Senior Vice President — Human Resources and Customer Services for the fulfillment of his or her functions, responsibilities, and authority and for their proper interpretation.
2. Will advise and assist department managers, officers, and staff in their respective functions associated with the areas for which he or she has direct responsibility.
3. Will have extensive contact with customers, the public and the community, and is to conduct relationships in a manner that will enhance the overall marketing effort of the bank.
4. Will be called upon from time to time to participate with community organizations and in community projects.

JOB DESCRIPTION: Human Resources Assistant
DEPARTMENT/DIVISION: Human Resources and Customer Services
REPORTS TO: Director, Personnel and Training
SUPERVISES: Has no supervisory responsibility.

JOB SUMMARY

Maintain personnel files, employees benefit records, state and federal tax reports, payroll records, insurance files, and other secretarial/clerical responsibilities.

DUTIES

1. Post and balance regular hours worked, overtime hours, proof work lates and PAT sitting on payroll transmittal sheet.
2. Make changes to payroll master records.
3. Prepare and balance general ledger tickets.
4. Stuff in envelopes and distribute pay statement.
5. Record hours worked on time card report.
6. Record overtime hours.
7. Record absences.
8. Prepare salary reviews.
9. Prepare benefit statements.
10. Prepare rating forms.
11. Record salary increases.
12. Adjust benefits.
13. Prepare salaries by department report.
14. Prepare overtime paid report.
15. Pay state and federal taxes.
16. File quarterly state and federal tax returns.
17. Balance invoices and pay premium for employee insurance.
18. Pay insurance premiums.
19. Check new accounts opened and make any corrections necessary.

Human Resources Assistant (continued)

20. Mail Welcome Letter, insurance policy and membership card.
21. Send letter to remind customers when they are approaching age 65.
22. Purge file of closed accounts.
23. Set up file for new employees.
24. Prepare probationary rating forms.
25. Add to insurance, etc.
26. Add to payroll.
27. Send out termination notices and final evaluation forms on terminated employees.
28. Figure final pay for payroll.
29. Make necessary changes and adjustments to payroll.
30. Maintain ledger of Directors' fees paid and prepare 1099s at end of year.
31. Prepare employee telephone directory.
32. Prepare employee addition and termination report.
33. Prepare progress report.
34. Add employees to benefits as they become eligible.
35. Prepare forms necessary for actuary to figure retirement benefits.
36. Prepare salary survey.
37. Type letters and reports.
38. Answer employee questions on benefits and policies.
39. Verify base salary for bonus and profit sharing.
40. Prepare name tags for meat boxes.
41. Handle inquiries from state Unemployment Agency.
42. Order supplies for department.

ORGANIZATION

Has an inherent duty and responsibility to make recommendations to supervisor concerning possible methods to improve department.

FINANCES

Has the responsibility to make recommendations to supervisor concerning the budgetary needs of the department.

RELATIONSHIPS

1. Responsible to the Director, Personnel and Training for the fulfillment of functions, responsibilities, and authority and for their proper interpretation.
2. Will have extensive contact with customers and the public, and is to conduct relationships in a manner that will enhance the overall marketing effort of the bank.
3. Will be called upon from time to time to participate with community organizations and in community projects.

JOB DESCRIPTION: Assistant Vice President and Coordinator of Special Services
DEPARTMENT/DIVISION: Human Resources and Customer Services
REPORTS TO: Senior Vice President — Human Resources and Customer Services
SUPERVISES: Cafeteria Attendants

JOB SUMMARY

To assist in Division duties, handle the Cash Management program for the bank and manage the bank's employee cafeteria.

DUTIES

1. Handle all aspects of Cash Management Program through Federated Asset Management Corp.
2. Contact customers and send brochures and other information to them.
3. Talk to customers and prospective customers who call or come to office.
4. Open accounts. Distribute deposits, new account forms, signature cards, etc. to various departments/divisions of the bank.
5. Check computer print-out each morning for transactions to be carried out that day, calling Federated to give purchase or redemption order and having money wired to State Bank & Trust Co.
6. Transfer money to and from various customer accounts for investment purposes.
7. On 13 column accountant's work sheet, keep record of daily interest factor and accrued interest as well as bank's servicing fee factor for each account, so as to be able to determine monthly fee to be redeemed for bank.

Cafeteria management duties:

8. Manage money — take cash box to cafeteria each morning and pick it up after lunch is served. Count money and make deposits.
9. Instruct and supervise two cafeteria attendants, discuss menus, plan menus weekly, and distribute copies to all bank departments.
10. Pay bills and balance bank statements.
11. At 5:00 p.m. each day, lock outside cafeteria doors and cut off coffee machine.
12. Call for maintenance service when needed.
13. Buy equipment and other supplies.

Personnel duties:

14. In absence of Personnel Payroll Clerk, make bi-weekly payroll.
15. Fill-in person for Teller Orientation, when necessary.

Marketing duties:

16. Cut out ads, pictures, etc. from daily paper, laminate for scrapbook. Send pictures and clippings to customers.
17. Clip obituaries from paper and send sympathy cards to survivors.
18. Daily check board room book to see what meetings will be held and determine if they need cokes or coffee served.
19. Help with anniversary parties, luncheons, cocktail parties, as needed.
20. Help count church money each Monday morning.
21. Conduct training programs for new bank services (IRA, Direct Deposit, etc.).
22. Any other Marketing duties as necessary. Answer phone for PAT Department.

ORGANIZATION

1. Initiate changes in the basic organization structure and complement of the planning function in order to accomplish objectives as developed in concert with the Senior Vice President — Human Resources and Customer Services.
2. Activate new work procedures and systems to accomplish planning and bank development objectives more efficiently.

Assistant Vice President and Coordinator of Special Services (continued)

FINANCES

Prepare the annual budget for Human Resources and Customer Services, administering allotted funds in accordance with the budget and approved fiscal procedures; and recommend capital expenditures for planning and bank development.

RELATIONSHIPS

1. Responsible to the Senior Vice President — Human Resources and Customer Services for the fulfillment of his or her functions, responsibilities, and authority and for their proper interpretation.
2. Will advise and assist department managers, officers, and staff in their respective functions associated with the areas for which he or she has direct responsibility.
3. Will have extensive contact with customers, the public and the community, and is to conduct relationships in a manner that will enhance the overall marketing effort of the bank.
4. Will be called upon from time to time to participate with community organizations and in community projects.

JOB DESCRIPTION: Cafeteria Attendant
DEPARTMENT/DIVISION: Human Resources and Customer Services
REPORTS TO: Coordinator of Special Services
SUPERVISES: Has no supervisory responsibility.

JOB SUMMARY

Orders, prepares and serves food in the cafeteria; also responsible for maintenance of the service counter and cleanliness of the cafeteria. Performs routine duties under close supervision of the cafeteria supervisor.

DUTIES

1. Orders food to be served each day.
2. Prepares and serves food.
3. Collects charges for food.
4. Keeps stove, refrigerator, ice-machine, food counter and utensils clean.
5. Keeps tables and cafeteria clean.

ORGANIZATION

Has an inherent duty and responsibility to make recommendations to supervisor concerning possible methods to improve department.

FINANCES

Has the responsibility to make recommendations to supervisor concerning the budgetary needs of the department.

RELATIONSHIPS

Will observe and conduct the following listed relationships:
1. Responsible to the Coordinator of Special Services for the fulfillment of functions, responsibilities, and authority and for their proper interpretation.

2. Will have extensive contact with customers and the public, and is to conduct relationships in a manner that will enhance the overall marketing effort of the bank.
3. Will be called upon from time to time to participate with community organizations and in community projects.

JOB DESCRIPTION: Teller Training Officer
DEPARTMENT/DIVISION: Personnel and Training
REPORTS TO: Director, Personnel and Training
SUPERVISES: Teller Trainees

JOB SUMMARY
Teaches Teller Trainees their duties at the teller window. Assists in placement of new tellers. May relieve in other positions within the bank (i.e. teller, rover, safe deposit) as needed. Thorough knowledge of teller operations required. Exercises reasonable amount of independent judgment under minimal supervision.

DUTIES
1. Instructs Teller Trainees in their duties at the teller window.
2. Assists in placement of new tellers.
3. Handles money.
4. Relieves in other positions in the bank when needed.

ORGANIZATION
1. Initiate changes in the basic organization structure and complement of the planning function in order to accomplish objectives as developed in concert with the Director, Personnel and Training.
2. Activate new work procedures and systems to accomplish planning and bank development objectives more efficiently.

FINANCES
Prepare the annual budget for Personnel and Training, administering allotted funds in accordance with the budget and approved fiscal procedures; and, recommend capital expenditures for planning and bank development.

RELATIONSHIPS
1. Responsible to the Director, Personnel and Training for the fulfillment of his or her functions, responsibilities, and authority and for their proper interpretation.
2. Will advise and assist department managers, officers, and staff in their respective functions associated with the areas for which he or she has direct responsibility.
3. Will have extensive contact with customers, the public and the community, and is to conduct relationships in a manner that will enhance the overall marketing effort of the bank.
4. Will be called upon from time to time to participate with community organizations and in community projects.

JOB DESCRIPTION: Teller Trainee
DEPARTMENT/DIVISION: Personnel and Training
REPORTS TO: Teller Training Officer
SUPERVISES: Has no supervisory responsibility.

JOB SUMMARY

Learns to accept cash items for deposit, maintain cash drawer, pay or cash checks. Must be trained to be familiar with all phases of teller operations. Requires ability to handle and count money, familiarity with bookkeeping transactions, ability to cheerfully deal with customers of the bank, cross-selling of other bank services. Exercises some independent judgment under close supervision.

DUTIES

1. Accepts cash item deposits.
2. Accepts savings deposits.
3. Accepts coupon payments.
4. Accepts commercial and installment payments.
5. Accepts credit card payments and applications.
6. Redeems series "E" savings bonds.
7. Cashes checks up to a certain limit.
8. Helps get out customer bank statements.
9. Prepares cash-in debit tickets for cash taken in.
10. Cross-sells other bank services.

ORGANIZATION

Has an inherent duty and responsibility to make recommendations to supervisor concerning possible methods to improve department.

FINANCES

Has the responsibility to make recommendations to supervisor concerning the budgetary needs of the department.

RELATIONSHIPS

1. Responsible to the Teller Training Officer for the fulfillment of functions, responsibilities, and authority and for their proper interpretation.
2. Will have extensive contact with customers and the public, and is to conduct relationships in a manner that will enhance the overall marketing effort of the bank.
3. Will be called upon from time to time to participate with community organizations and in community projects.

11

BRANCH BANK JOB DESCRIPTIONS

Branch banking in the United States is "a type of multiple office banking under which a bank as a single legal entity operates more than one banking office" (F.L. Garcia, *Encyclopedia of Banking and Finance*, eighth edition. Boston: Bankers Publishing Company, 1983). Since the branches of a bank are considered separate and distinct, a staff of able employees must be assembled for smooth branch operations.

There will be some duplication in jobs from branch to branch of the same bank. Managers, tellers, secretaries, and cashiers will be necessary at most branches. The job descriptions included here should give you a base to work from when putting together your branch staff.

JOB DESCRIPTION: Branch Manager
DEPARTMENT/DIVISION: Branch
REPORTS TO: Vice President and Branch Administrator
SUPERVISES: Assistant Branch Manager
              Head Teller
              Branch Secretary

JOB SUMMARY
Manages a branch and supervises branch tellers and secretaries. Takes loan applications and approves or rejects loan requests.

Branch Manager (continued)

DUTIES

1. Supervise branch personnel.
2. Take loan applications (consumer, commercial, and VISA).
3. Approve or reject loan requests.
4. Approve checks.
5. Achieves collection of loans and checks.
6. Branch security (supervision).
7. Open branch.
8. Close branch.
9. Supervise preparation of branch reports.
10. On call (24 hours) from police (for branch security).
11. Handle customer complaints/inquiries.
12. Supervise balancing/procedures.
13. Safe deposit entries.
14. Maintain and update bank lending policy.
15. Maintain and update bank operational policies.
16. Supervise branch activities for special promotions/projects.
17. Branch maintenance.
18. Recommend salary increases.
19. Hire new employees.
20. Recommend employee discharges/discipline.
21. Act on employee problems.
22. Responsible for customer relationships.
23. Responsible for employee training.
24. Supervise branch audits.
25. Sell cashiers checks, travelers checks (occasionally).
26. Open new accounts (occasionally).
27. Conduct staff meetings.
28. Assist secretaries' balancing.
29. Supervise work time for employees (early days, off time, attempt to avoid overtime).
30. Schedule vacations.
31. Attend branch and bank meetings.
32. Take branch work to main office.
33. Assist main office loan officers in customer relationships.
34. Assist other branch officers.
35. Assist bank security officer with fraud or possible fraud cases.
36. Handle drunks and other loud or difficult customers or non-customers.
37. Improve branch efficiency with new procedures and policies as required.

ORGANIZATION

1. Initiate changes in the basic organization structure and complement of the planning function in order to accomplish objectives as developed in concert with the Vice President and Branch Administrator.
2. Activate new work procedures and systems to accomplish planning and bank development objectives more efficiently.

FINANCES

Prepare the annual budget for branch, administering allotted funds in accordance with the budget and approved fiscal procedures; and, recommend capital expenditures for planning and bank development.

RELATIONSHIPS

1. Responsible to the Vice President and Branch Administrator for the fulfillment of his or her functions, responsibilities, and authority and for their proper interpretation.
2. Will advise and assist department managers, officers, and staff in their respective functions associated with the areas for which he or she has direct responsibility.
3. Will have extensive contact with customers, the public and the community, and is to conduct relationships in a manner that will enhance the overall marketing effort of the bank.
4. Will be called upon from time to time to participate with community organizations and in community projects.

JOB DESCRIPTION: Assistant Branch Manager
DEPARTMENT/DIVISION: Branch
REPORTS TO: Branch Manager
SUPERVISES: In the absence of Branch Manager, assumes supervision of the Branch.

JOB SUMMARY

Coordinate with manager in implementing and carrying out bank policy with respect to overall operations of branch. Includes all phases from responsibility for maintenance of building and grounds to handling of consumer and commercial loans.

DUTIES

1. Open bank.
2. Activate security clearance and alarm system.
3. Raise flag.
4. Check for absent personnel.
5. Attempt to obtain rover where possible.
6. Check lobby area for supplies.
7. Check PAT machine supplies.
8. Be available to approve checks and assist tellers in any way possible.
9. Take all types of loan applications and follow through to approval or rejection.
10. Check to see that customers in lobby area receive prompt attention.
11. Recognize customers who are waiting when bank is crowded and assure them that they are not overlooked.
12. Meet with customers who request financial counsel and offer all possible assistance.
13. Pick up mail at post office.
14. Meet with employees who have special problems.
15. During peak periods assist desk personnel in opening new accounts and meeting other customer needs.
16. Supervise preparation of all loan documentation and other documents normally prepared in branches.

Assistant Branch Manager (continued)

17. Make report to management of any teller shortages or overages according to bank policy.
18. Close bank.
19. Make security check of building and all teller stations.
20. Prepare lobby area for next day's opening.
21. Change dates and check supplies.
22. Attend Friday meetings and any others designated by management.
23. Call on new business prospects and, on occasion, take old customers out to lunch.

ORGANIZATION

1. Initiate changes in the basic organization structure and complement of the planning function in order to accomplish objectives as developed in concert with the Branch Manager.
2. Activate new work procedures and systems to accomplish planning and bank development objectives more efficiently.

FINANCES

Prepare the annual budget for branch, administering allotted funds in accordance with the budget and approved fiscal procedures; and, recommend capital expenditures for planning and bank development.

RELATIONSHIPS

1. Responsible to the Branch Manager for the fulfillment of his or her functions, responsibilities, and authority and for their proper interpretation.
2. Will advise and assist department managers, officers, and staff in their respective functions associated with the areas for which he or she has direct responsibility.
3. Will have extensive contact with customers, the public and the community, and is to conduct relationships in a manner that will enhance the overall marketing effort of the bank.
4. Will be called upon from time to time to participate with community organizations and in community projects.

JOB DESCRIPTION: Branch Secretary
DEPARTMENT/DIVISION: Branch
REPORTS TO: Branch Manager
SUPERVISES: Has no supervisory responsibility.

JOB SUMMARY

Acts as receptionist to customers. Opens accounts and sells certificates of deposit. Types necessary papers to complete installment and commercial loan transactions. May or may not be able to take shorthand. Answers telephone. May handle a variety of bank services. Performs most duties under moderate supervision and exercises a reasonable amount of judgment.

DUTIES

1. Answers telephone and greets customers.
2. Financial advisor on all deposit instruments.
3. Opens checking and savings accounts (business and personal) preparing all permanent records.

4. Orders and keeps records for personal and business check orders, deposits and other supplies for depositors.
5. Aids customers in reconciling their bank accounts.
6. PAT Machine card requests; new, replacements and deletions.
7. Deletes and adds names to existing accounts, changes addresses, etc. securing current permanent records and paper work to justify change.
8. Sends wire transfers and on occasion receives one for non-customer.
9. Prepares all direct deposits.
10. Orders, issues, and keeps records for Series EE Bond transactions. Orders or sends for redemption Series HH Bonds on request. Reconciles Branch Bond account statement quarterly.
11. Maintains all records for safe deposit boxes. Admits customer to vault area.
12. Issues cashier's checks and certifies checks.
13. Handles all collection items, recording each in daily records.
14. Receives all payments to Commercial Loan Department recording each in daily records.
15. Issues, renews and redeems all Certificates of Deposits.
16. Orders and issues travelers cheques, maintaining complete records for each transaction.
17. Prepares detailed monthly report of branch transactions.
18. Records all promotions, through Marketing Department or whatever, keeping records when necessary.
19. Is usually a Notary Public, therefore, all requests for this service would be directed to this person.
20. Prepares all paper work for Consumer Loan and Commercial Loan transactions (new and renewal loans). "Paper work" depends on type of loan. Some are relatively simple, while others are quite detailed and time consuming. This duty alone is a constant learning situation because of changing legislation.

ORGANIZATION

Has an inherent duty and responsibility to make recommendations to supervisor concerning possible methods to improve department.

FINANCES

Has the responsibility to make recommendations to supervisor concerning the budgetary needs of the department.

RELATIONSHIPS

1. Responsible to the Branch Manager for the fulfillment of functions, responsibilities, and authority and for their proper interpretation.
2. Will have extensive contact with customers and the public, and is to conduct relationships in a manner that will enhance the overall marketing effort of the bank.
3. Will be called upon from time to time to participate with community organizations and in community projects.

JOB DESCRIPTION: ATM Supervisor
DEPARTMENT/DIVISION: Branch
REPORTS TO: Branch Operations head.
SUPERVISES: ATM Staff

ATM Supervisor (continued)

JOB SUMMARY

General supervision of clerical personnel and overall C. P. MAC operation.

DUTIES

1. Problem identification and documentation in monitoring ATM up-time.
2. Communicates with branches.
3. Review and settlement of MAC accounts.
4. Assists in general control and operation of MAC accounts (C.P.).
5. Maintain hot card file.
6. Process fraud losses.
7. Training of department personnel.
8. Maintain and control after hours call list.
9. Review system reports and statistical information.
10. Prepare appropriate system and management reports.

ORGANIZATION

Has an inherent duty and responsibility to make recommendations to supervisor concerning possible methods to improve department.

FINANCES

Has the responsibility to make recommendations to supervisor concerning the budgetary needs of the department.

RELATIONSHIPS

Considerable telephone and written communication with customers, branch and bank personnel and MAC headquarters.

JOB DESCRIPTION: Head Teller
DEPARTMENT/DIVISION: Branch
REPORTS TO: Branch Manager
SUPERVISES: Tellers

JOB SUMMARY

Maintains records for Paying and Receiving area (i.e. monthly teller reports on cash received and paid out, deposits and checks, when teller alarms are checked). Maintains money supply in vault. Responsible for vault security and teller alarm equipment. Authorizes payment of checks. Collects on returned checks. Responsible for ordering, shipping and receiving vault money for main office and branches. Maintains money supply at each teller window. Relieves management of some administrative and supervisory duties (i.e. checking time cards for tellers). Position requires a general knowledge of bank operations, personnel policies and various departmental policies. Moderate amount of independent judgment required under minimum supervision.

DUTIES

1. Authorizes payment of checks.
2. Responsible for vault security.

3. Orders and receives money for main office and branches.
4. Ships money to Federal Reserve in case of oversupply or mutilation.
5. Takes and prepares merchants orders for money.
6. Collects checks returned to tellers.
7. Maintains money supply at each teller location.
8. Keeps records of all cash transactions.
9. Reviews and O.K.s tellers' time cards.

ORGANIZATION

1. Initiate changes in the basic organization structure and complement of the planning function in order to accomplish objectives as developed in concert with the Branch Manager.
2. Activate new work procedures and systems to accomplish planning and bank development objectives more efficiently.

FINANCES

Prepare the annual budget for branch, administering allotted funds in accordance with the budget and approved fiscal procedures; and, recommend capital expenditures for planning and bank development.

RELATIONSHIPS

1. Responsible to the Branch Manager for the fulfillment of his or her functions, responsibilities, and authority and for their proper interpretation.
2. Will advise and assist department managers, officers, and staff in their respective functions associated with the areas for which he or she has direct responsibility.
3. Will have extensive contact with customers, the public and the community, and is to conduct relationships in a manner that will enhance the overall marketing effort of the bank.
4. Will be called upon from time to time to participate with community organizations and in community projects.

JOB DESCRIPTION: Teller I
DEPARTMENT/DIVISION: Branch
REPORTS TO: Head Teller
SUPERVISES: Has no supervisory responsibility.

JOB SUMMARY

Accepts cash items from customers for deposit. Handles withdrawal and deposits from savings. Has limited authority to cash checks. Takes some installment and credit card payments. Maintains a running account on all transactions. Job involves considerable customer contact. Watches for checks on which stop payment orders have been issued. Job requires extensive on the job training for job proficiency. Exercises some judgment with moderate supervision.

DUTIES

1. Accepts cash item deposits.
2. Accepts savings deposits and makes withdrawals.
3. Accepts coupon payments and installment loan payments.
4. Balances cash each day.

Teller I (continued)

5. Redeems Series E savings bonds.
6. Helps get out customer bank statements.
7. Cashes checks.
8. Prepares cash-in debit tickets for cash taken in.

ORGANIZATION

Has an inherent duty and responsibility to make recommendations to supervisor concerning possible methods to improve department.

FINANCES

Has the responsibility to make recommendations to supervisor concerning the budgetary needs of the department.

RELATIONSHIPS

1. Responsible to the Head Teller for the fulfillment of functions, responsibilities, and authority and for their proper interpretation.
2. Will have extensive contact with customers and the public, and is to conduct relationships in a manner that will enhance the overall marketing effort of the bank.
3. Will be called upon from time to time to participate with community organizations and in community projects.

JOB DESCRIPTION: Teller II
DEPARTMENT/DIVISION: Branch
REPORTS TO: Head Teller
SUPERVISES: Has no supervisory responsibility.

JOB SUMMARY

Opens night depository chest; keeps records of all night deposits; returns bags to customers; receives deposits of cash items; verifies and maintains records of cash in and cash out. Pays or cashes items in limited amounts. Exercises some independent judgment under moderate supervision.

DUTIES

1. Opens night deposit chest.
2. Records night deposit bags.
3. Has customer sign book when receiving bags.
4. Accepts deposits of cash items.
5. Verifies cash.
6. May handle some savings deposits and withdrawals.
7. Balances cash drawer each day.

ORGANIZATION

Has an inherent duty and responsibility to make recommendations to supervisor concerning possible methods to improve department.

FINANCES

Has the responsibility to make recommendations to supervisor concerning the budgetary needs of the department.

RELATIONSHIPS

1. Responsible to the Head Teller for the fulfillment of functions, responsibilities, and authority and for their proper interpretation.
2. Will have extensive contact with customers and the public, and is to conduct relationships in a manner that will enhance the overall marketing effort of the bank.
3. Will be called upon from time to time to participate with community organizations and in community projects.

JOB DESCRIPTION: Teller III
DEPARTMENT/DIVISION: Branch
REPORTS TO: Head Teller
SUPERVISES: Has no supervisory responsibility.

JOB SUMMARY

Handles all phases of teller operations, including collections, savings, demand deposits and loan payments. Requires extensive knowledge of bank operations. Acts as a group leader for other tellers. Relieves management of some routine duties. Exercises independent judgment in most instances requiring minimum supervision.

DUTIES

1. Accepts demand deposits.
2. Accepts savings deposits.
3. Has authority to cash checks up to a certain limit.
4. Accepts loan payments, commercial and installment.
5. Accepts payments on collection items.
6. Prepares collection letters and tracers.
7. Writes expense checks.
8. Orders money for branch.
9. Countersigns charge tickets.
10. Balances cash drawer.
11. Helps get out customer statements.
12. Verifies cash.
13. Redeems savings bonds.

ORGANIZATION

Has an inherent duty and responsibility to make recommendations to supervisor concerning possible methods to improve departments.

FINANCES

Has the responsibility to make recommendations to supervisor concerning the budgetary needs of the department.

Teller III (continued)

RELATIONSHIPS

1. Responsible to the Head Teller for the fulfillment of functions, responsibilities, and authority and for their proper interpretation.
2. Will have extensive contact with customers and the public, and is to conduct relationships in a manner that will enhance the overall marketing effort of the bank.
3. Will be called upon from time to time to participate with community organizations and in community projects.

JOB DESCRIPTION: Relief Teller
DEPARTMENT/DIVISION: Branch
REPORTS TO: Vice President and Branch Administrator
SUPERVISES: Has no supervisory responsibility.

JOB SUMMARY

Performs usual paying and receiving teller functions plus may handle savings deposits and withdrawals, loan payments, savings bond redemption, collections, night deposit, etc. Relieves tellers who are absent in whatever capacity and location needed. Required extensive knowledge of all teller operations and flexibility in the performance of teller duties. Considerable customer contact required. Exercises independent judgment in some instances under limited supervision.

DUTIES

1. Accepts demand deposits.
2. Accepts savings deposits.
3. Has authority to cash checks up to a certain limit.
4. Accepts loan payments, commercial and installment.
5. Accepts payments on collection items.
6. Prepares collection letters and tracers.
7. Writes expense checks.
8. Orders money for branch.
9. Countersigns charge tickets.
10. Balances cash drawer.
11. Helps get out customer statements.
12. Verifies cash.
13. Redeems savings bonds.

ORGANIZATION

Has an inherent duty and responsibility to make recommendations to supervisor concerning possible methods to improve department.

FINANCES

Has the responsibility to make recommendations to supervisor concerning the budgetary needs of the department.

RELATIONSHIPS

1. Responsible to the Vice President and Branch Administrator for the fulfillment of functions, responsibilities, and authority and for their proper interpretation.
2. Will have extensive contact with customers and the public, and is to conduct relationships in a manner that will enhance the overall marketing effort of the bank.
3. Will be called upon from time to time to participate with community organizations and in community projects.

JOB DESCRIPTION: Secretary — Branch Administration
DEPARTMENT/DIVISION: Branch
REPORTS TO: Vice President and Branch Administrator
SUPERVISES: Has no supervisory responsibility.

JOB SUMMARY

Acts as a receptionist; answers telephone; types executive letters, reports and memos to branch personnel. May relieve supervisor of routine administrative duties. May be responsible for supervisor's routine bookkeeping duties. May be responsible for handling records on own initiative under limited supervision. Reasonable amount of judgment required.

DUTIES

1. Greets customers.
2. Keeps up with supervisor's appointment schedule.
3. Answers telephone.
4. Takes shorthand.
5. Types letters, reports and memos.
6. Maintains certain records for Executive Officers.
7. May do balance sheets or financial statements.

ORGANIZATION

Has an inherent duty and responsibility to make recommendations to supervisor concerning possible methods to improve department.

FINANCES

Has the responsibility to make recommendations to supervisor concerning the budgetary needs of the department.

RELATIONSHIPS

1. Responsible to the Vice President and Branch Administrator for the fulfillment of functions, responsibilities, and authority and for their proper interpretation.
2. Will have extensive contact with customers and the public, and is to conduct relationships in a manner that will enhance the overall marketing effort of the bank.
3. Will be called upon from time to time to participate with community organizations and in community projects.

JOB DESCRIPTION: Assistant Cashier and Savings and Collection Officer
DEPARTMENT/DIVISION: Branch
REPORTS TO: Vice President and Branch Manager
SUPERVISES: Savings and Collection Tellers

JOB SUMMARY

Responsible for savings and collection activities and supervision of savings and collection tellers.

DUTIES

1. Savings: Run window, separate branch work and handle rejects; verify savings maintenance, signature cards to new accounts; pull and file closed savings cards; film and file new savings accounts cards; balance savings; answer phone; help customers balance savings accounts; make error corrections; mail direct deposits, PAT Statements each month and interest statements each quarter.
2. Christmas Club accounts: open new accounts, file signature cards, take deposits, balance, close accounts, mail checks.
3. Federal Tax Deposits: Balance and film tax deposits for main office; film tax deposits for main office and branches; look up on film if necessary.
4. Travelers Checks: Order, sell, balance, make refunds.
5. Collection Department: Issue cashier checks and New York drafts; mortgage collections; handle incoming collection; supervise and advise.
6. Director, Profit Sharing and Pension Plan.

ORGANIZATION

1. Initiate changes in the basic organization structure and complement of the planning function in order to accomplish objectives as developed in concert with the Vice President and Branch Manager.
2. Activate new work procedures and systems to accomplish planning and bank development objectives more efficiently.

FINANCES

Prepare the annual budget for branch, administering allotted funds in accordance with the budget and approved fiscal procedures; and, recommend capital expenditures for planning and bank development.

RELATIONSHIPS

1. Responsible to the Vice President and Branch Manager for the fulfillment of his or her functions, responsibilities, and authority and for their proper interpretation.
2. Will advise and assist department managers, officers, and staff in their respective functions associated with the areas for which he or she has direct responsibility.
3. Will have extensive contact with customers, the public and the community, and is to conduct relationships in a manner that will enhance the overall marketing effort of the bank.
4. Will be called upon from time to time to participate with community organizations and in community projects.

JOB DESCRIPTION: Savings and Collection Teller
DEPARTMENT/DIVISION: Branch

REPORTS TO: Branch Manager — Main
SUPERVISES: Has no supervisory responsibility.

JOB SUMMARY

Maintains cash drawer. Receives savings deposits. Pays withdrawals from accounts. Makes changes in account records. Makes transfers from checking to savings and savings to checking. Deals directly with customers on any matter concerning their savings account. Issues travelers checks. Some typing is required. Takes Federal Withholding Tax payments from customers. Exercises independent judgment on savings matters with moderate supervision.

DUTIES

1. Receives deposits and withdrawals on savings accounts.
2. Sets up customers in automatic savings plans.
3. Handles deposits to Christmas Club accounts.
4. Photographs savings deposits and withdrawals at the end of the day.
5. Answers telephone inquiries regarding savings accounts.
6. Issues travelers checks.
7. Accepts Federal Withholding payments.

ORGANIZATION

Has an inherent duty and responsibility to make recommendations to supervisor concerning possible methods to improve department.

FINANCES

Has the responsibility to make recommendations to supervisor concerning the budgetary needs of the department.

RELATIONSHIPS

1. Responsible to the Branch Manager — Main for the fulfillment of functions, responsibilities, and authority and for their proper interpretation.
2. Will have extensive contact with customers and the public, and is to conduct relationships in a manner that will enhance the overall marketing effort of the bank.
3. Will be called upon from time to time to participate with community organizations and in community projects.

JOB DESCRIPTION: Safe Deposit Officer
DEPARTMENT/DIVISION: Branch — Main
REPORTS TO: Vice President and Branch Manager — Main
SUPERVISES: Safe Deposit Clerk

JOB SUMMARY

Coordinates clerical activities of the department. Relieves administrator of some routine management details. Sells safety deposit boxes, collects rent and keeps records of all transactions in the department. Handles correspondence for own as well as other departments. Maintains files and keeps some confidential records. Makes reports and keeps records for operations department. Handles items requiring special handling. Exercises independent judgment with minimum supervision.

Safe Deposit Officer (continued)

DUTIES

1. Sells safe deposit boxes.
2. Maintains safe deposit box entry files.
3. Keeps rent records and sends out due notices.
4. Maintains all records related to boxes.
5. Responsible for security and vault entry.
6. Requisitions supplies.
7. Handles duties not involved with safe deposit area such as:
   a. Stock dividends for bank.
   b. Figures income tax on Bank Building Company.
   c. Correspondence with Board of Directors.

ORGANIZATION

1. Initiate changes in the basic organization structure and complement of the planning function in order to accomplish objectives as developed in concert with the Vice President and Branch Manager — Main.
2. Activate new work procedures and systems to accomplish planning and bank development objectives more efficiently.

FINANCES

Prepare the annual budget for Branch — Main, administering funds in accordance with the budget and approved fiscal procedures; and, recommend capital expenditures for planning and bank development.

RELATIONSHIPS

1. Responsible to the Vice President and Branch Manager — Main for the fulfillment of his or her functions, responsibilities, and authority and for their proper interpretation.
2. Will advise and assist department managers, officers, and staff in their respective functions associated with the areas for which he or she has direct responsibility.
3. Will have extensive contact with customers, the public and the community, and is to conduct relationships in a manner that will enhance the overall marketing effort of the bank.
4. Will be called upon from time to time to participate with community organizations and in community projects.

JOB DESCRIPTION: Safe Deposit Clerk
DEPARTMENT/DIVISION: Branch — Main
REPORTS TO: Safe Deposit Officer
SUPERVISES: Has no supervisory responsibility.

JOB SUMMARY

Handles routine customer inquiries and problems. Sells safe deposit boxes and collects box rent. Admits customers to safe deposit vault. Sells savings bonds. Handles customer correspondence through the use of form letters for own as well as other departments. Keeps records of all transactions. Maintains cash box. Makes routine reports and keeps files up to date. Must be able to type routine notices. May handle items requiring special handling, exercising independent judgment under moderate supervision.

DUTIES

1. Types notices and reports.
2. Sells safe deposit boxes.
3. Admits customers to safe deposit vault and keeps record of entries.
4. Handles customer inquiries and problems.
5. Files letters, records, etc.
6. Handles minimum amount of money collected from sales and rentals of safe deposit boxes.
7. Keeps records of all transactions.
8. Responsible for key security.
9. Sells Series E and H savings bonds.
10. Requisitions supplies.

ORGANIZATION

Has an inherent duty and responsibility to make recommendations to supervisor concerning possible methods to improve department.

FINANCES

Has the responsibility to make recommendations to supervisor concerning the budgetary needs of the department.

RELATIONSHIPS

1. Responsible to the Safe Deposit Officer for the fulfillment of functions, responsibilities, and authority and for their proper interpretation.
2. Will have extensive contact with customers and the public, and is to conduct relationships in a manner that will enhance the overall marketing effort of the bank.
3. Will be called upon from time to time to participate with community organizations and in community projects.

12

OPERATIONS AND ADMINISTRATION DEPARTMENT

The jobs included in the operations department of a bank make up a team which keeps the bank running day in and day out. We have broken the operations and administration department job descriptions into six categories: bookkeeping, proof, operations, data processing, auditing, and purchasing.

All of the following job descriptions are integral to the policies, procedures, and objectives of a successful bank. The job descriptions here should serve well as guidelines to the type of individual and performance necessary for smooth bank operations.

JOB DESCRIPTION: Senior Vice President and Cashier
DEPARTMENT/DIVISION: Operations and Administration
REPORTS TO: Executive Vice President
SUPERVISES: Division Secretary
     Security Officer
     Assistant Vice President — Proof Department
     Vice President — Bookkeeping Department
     Vice President and Controller
     Vice President and Data Processing Officer
     Auditor (Indirect reporting relationship)

JOB SUMMARY

Coordinate and administer operations and data processing activities of the bank. Develop and recommend policies, procedures, and objectives in the area of operations and data processing. Provide advice and guidance to operations and data processing officers who implement departmental objectives and programs. Work with top management in developing plans and policies which may affect the bank as a whole.

DUTIES

1. Secretary of Board of Directors and Stockholders meetings — prepare agendas, keep all minutes and records of meetings, and see that all requirements of bank and stockholders are met for regulations.
2. Approve for payment much of bank's expense invoices.
3. Stay abreast of all regulations and rules of all supervisory and regulatory agencies pertaining to operations division functions. Analyze, plan and implement rule and regulation changes through appropriate operational departments.
4. Supervise and participate in the setting and developing of policies in the Operations Division.
5. Keep abreast of technological developments in electronic funds transfer, hardware, software, systems and procedures.
6. Evaluate, analyze, and/or approve the purchase of most of the bank's machinery and equipment.
7. Guide department heads in progressive and innovative efforts to evaluate systems and procedures for more efficient operation of their areas of responsibility.
8. Supervise and participate in the setting of all prices for operational services for the bank.
9. Guide the development of new services provided by the Operations Division.
10. Talk to salesmen regarding equipment, systems and procedures, services, etc.
11. Present, instruct, and train groups of employees throughout the bank on new bank-wide operational changes in services and procedures.
12. Stay abreast of and participate in decisions regarding accounting developments.
13. Stay abreast of and participate in decisions regarding tax developments.
14. Stay abreast of and participate in decisions regarding auditing developments.
15. Plan, coordinate and supervise remodeling and construction in operations area.
16. Do long-range planning for Operations Division and plan its interrelations with other areas of the bank.
17. Monitor income statement and balance sheet changes and progress. Approve published format of financial statements.
18. Work with supervisory examiners (Office of Comptroller of Currency) while they perform their examinations, etc.
19. Liaison officer for bank with outside auditing firm.
20. Plan, participate and make recommendations on long-range planning for whole bank.
21. Manage bank's total insurance program (except employee benefit insurance).
22. Advise and guide department heads in policy and regulation interpretation and implementation.
23. Member — Asset/Liability Management Committee.
24. Chairman — Pricing Committee.
25. Chairman — EDP Steering Committee.
26. Chairman — Pension and Profit Sharing Committee.
27. Member and Secretary — Charitable Trust Committee.

Senior Vice President and Cashier (continued)

28. Member and Secretary — Senior Management Committee.
29. Member — Capital Subcommittee.
30. Member — Facilities Subcommittee.

ORGANIZATION

1. Initiate changes in the basic organization structure and complement of the planning function in order to accomplish objectives as developed in concert with the Executive Vice President.
2. Activate new work procedures and systems to accomplish planning and bank development objectives more efficiently.

FINANCES

Prepare the annual budget for Operations and Administration, administering allotted funds in accordance with the budget and approved fiscal procedures; and, recommend capital expenditures for planning and bank development.

RELATIONSHIPS

1. Responsible to the Executive Vice President for the fulfillment of his or her functions, responsibilities, and authority and for their proper interpretation.
2. Will advise and assist department managers, officers, and staff in their respective functions associated with the areas for which he or she has direct responsibility.
3. Will have extensive contact with customers, the public and the community, and is to conduct relationships in a manner that will enhance the overall marketing effort of the bank.
4. Will be called upon from time to time to participate with community organizations and in community projects.

JOB DESCRIPTION: Executive Secretary
DEPARTMENT/DIVISION: Operations and Administration
REPORTS TO: Senior Vice President and Cashier
SUPERVISES: Has no supervisory responsibility.

JOB SUMMARY

Acts as receptionist, greets visitors and customers, answers telephone. Skilled in taking dictation, writing letters, etc. Handles confidential material. Makes routine decisions and handles routine matters so that supervisor will be free to handle more important matters.

DUTIES

1. Greet customers and visitors.
2. Answer telephone.
3. Open mail for supervisor and handle material that does not require his or her attention.
4. Handle filing of general correspondence and reports.
5. Check large number of accounts payable invoices for bank (repairs, utility bills, etc.) and route to various supervisors for their authority to pay.
6. Maintain schedule of bank's insurance coverage. Accumulate information for filing claims, etc. Make sure claims are paid and received by us.
7. Send out notices for Board Meeting each month.

8. Type Board of Directors Meeting minutes each month, agenda, and various information necessary for meeting. Type reports, memos, etc. as a result of this meeting. This information is confidential and most months requires extensive typing and preparation.
9. Prepare notices for Annual Shareholders Meeting each year.
10. Prepare minutes, agenda, and any related material for Annual Shareholders Meeting each year. Handle proxy material for this meeting.
11. Type various reports that have to be submitted to the Comptroller of the Currency as a result of Directors Meetings or Shareholders Meeting.
12. Type reports of crime that have to be submitted to the Regional Administrator of National Banks when we have a robbery, defalcation, etc. and maintain record of this information.
13. Type and distribute Interest Rate Schedule to department heads in Operations and Administration Division at least twice weekly and more often when necessary.
14. Maintain a schedule of meetings for Operations Division conference room.
15. Type minutes of Senior Management Committee Meeting each month.
16. Type minutes of bank's charitable Trust Committee Meetings.
17. Type minutes of division heads meetings each week.
18. Maintain file of signatures of our bank people who are authorized to sign on our accounts with various correspondent banks.
19. Make application for purchase of additional Federal Reserve Bank stock when necessary.
20. Take dictation and type general correspondence for supervisor.
21. Maintain file on Bylaws and Articles of Association and make sure changes are reported to Comptroller of the Currency as they are made at Directors Meetings or Annual Shareholders Meeting.
22. Prepare budget for our area.
23. Be alert for and report any potential new business or potential business opportunities.

ORGANIZATION

Has an inherent duty and responsibility to make recommendations to supervisor concerning possible methods to improve department.

FINANCES

Has the responsibility to make recommendations to supervisor concerning the budgetary needs of the department.

RELATIONSHIPS

1. Responsible to the Senior Vice President and Cashier, Operations and Administration Division, for the fulfillment of functions, responsibilities, and authority and for their proper interpretation.
2. Will have extensive contact with customers and the public, and is to conduct relationships in a manner that will enhance the overall marketing effort of the bank.
3. Will be called upon from time to time to participate with community organizations and in community projects.

JOB DESCRIPTION: Vice President and Controller
DEPARTMENT/DIVISION: Operations and Administration

Vice President and Controller (continued)

REPORTS TO: Senior Vice President and Cashier — Operations and Administration.
SUPERVISES: Secretary
             Accounting Clerk III
             Accounting Clerk IV

JOB SUMMARY

Manage the day-to-day activities and the evolvement of the bank's general accounting systems, internal management information and external reporting.

DUTIES

1. Transfer bank stock.
2. Prepare tax returns.
3. Check and sign expense checks.
4. Pricing Committee member.
5. Data Processing Steering Committee member.
6. CIF Committee member.
7. Prepare Net Interest Margin Report.
8. Open new general ledger accounts.
9. Handle accounting on other real estate.
10. Prepare projected income reports.
11. Prepare annual earnings plan.
12. Ad valorem taxes on personal property.
13. Annual Report financial statements and notes.
14. Cash dividends on stock.
15. Assist other departments with their internal accounting problems.
16. Design and implement new systems and reports for internal and external reporting.
17. Install and coordinate budgeting and cost accounting.

ORGANIZATION

1. Initiate changes in the basic organization structure and complement of the planning function in order to accomplish objectives as developed in concert with the Senior Vice President and Cashier — Operations and Administration.
2. Activate new work procedures and systems to accomplish planning and bank development objectives more efficiently.

FINANCES

Prepare the annual budget for Operations and Administration, administering allotted funds in accordance with the budget and approved fiscal procedures; and, recommend capital expenditures for planning and bank development.

RELATIONSHIPS

1. Responsible to the Senior Vice President and Cashier — Operations and Administration for the fulfillment of his or her functions, responsibilities, and authority and for their proper interpretation.
2. Will advise and assist department managers, officers, and staff in their respective functions associated with the areas for which he or she has direct responsibility.

3. Will have extensive contact with customers, the public and the community, and is to conduct relationships in a manner that will enhance the overall marketing effort of the bank.
4. Will be called upon from time to time to participate with community organizations and in community projects.

JOB DESCRIPTION: Secretary
DEPARTMENT/DIVISION: Operations and Administration
REPORTS TO: Vice President and Controller
SUPERVISES: Has no supervisory responsibility.

JOB SUMMARY

Performs specialized clerical work in keeping accounting records of moderate complexity and variety. Balances various accounts. Prepares various reports. Keeps records. Audits some accounting records. Requires some independent judgment with moderate supervision.

DUTIES

1. Balance correspondent banks.
2. Balance Federal Reserve statement daily.
3. Balance Treasury Tax and Loan monthly.
4. Certified and officers checks daily; check endorsement, put in numerical order by account and check number; call branches and verify amounts of cashier's checks; balance monthly.
5. Check figures on required reserve report weekly.
6. Check general ledger tickets daily.
7. File checks.
8. Learning to key punch.
9. Keys financial management transactions daily.
10. Reconciles DDA Control summary to general ledger daily.
11. Acts as control for Data Processing Service Bureau fees.
12. Compile figures for functional cost analysis.
13. Microfilm.
14. Get out dividend checks quarterly.

ORGANIZATION

Has an inherent duty and responsibility to make recommendations to supervisor concerning possible methods to improve department.

FINANCES

Has the responsibility to make recommendations to supervisor concerning the budgetary needs of the department.

RELATIONSHIPS

1. Responsible to the Vice President and Controller for the fulfillment of functions, responsibilities, and authority and for their proper interpretation.
2. Will have extensive contact with customers and the public, and is to conduct relationships in a manner that will enhance the overall marketing effort of the bank.
3. Will be called upon from time to time to participate with community organizations and in community projects.

JOB DESCRIPTION: Accounting Clerk IV
DEPARTMENT/DIVISION: Operations and Administration
REPORTS TO: Vice President and Controller
SUPERVISES: Has no supervisory responsibility.

JOB SUMMARY

Performs highly specialized clerical work for maintenance and recording of financial transactions and audits. Prepares operating and status reports for owners, management, and regulatory governmental agencies. Requires judgment and decisions based on experience and knowledge of generally accepted accounting principles. Works under minimum supervision.

DUTIES

1. Monthly management report.
2. FDIC Report of Conditions.
3. FDIC Report of Income.
4. Income and Expense Accruals.
5. Depreciation records on equipment and leaseholds.
6. Balance computer payroll account.
7. Balance Christmas Club account.
8. Use tax.
9. Comparison of Report of Conditions.
10. Answer phone.
11. Balance general ledger entry run.
12. Balance investment accounts.
13. Microfilm.
14. Get out dividend checks quarterly.

ORGANIZATION

Has an inherent duty and responsibility to make recommendations to supervisor concerning possible methods to improve department.

FINANCES

Has the responsibility to make recommendations to supervisor concerning the budgetary needs of the department.

RELATIONSHIPS

1. Responsible to the Vice President and Controller for the fulfillment of functions, responsibilities, and authority and for their proper interpretation.
2. Will have extensive contact with customers and the public, and is to conduct relationships in a manner that will enhance the overall marketing effort of the bank.
3. Will be called upon from time to time to participate with community organizations and in community projects.

JOB DESCRIPTION: Accounting Clerk III
DEPARTMENT/DIVISION: Operations and Administration
REPORTS TO: Vice President and Controller
SUPERVISES: Has no supervisory responsibility.

JOB SUMMARY

Typing and balancing accounts.

DUTIES

1. Type for the department and Security Officer.
2. Answer phone for Security Officer when he or she is out of the office.
3. Balance cash accounts on general ledger for main office and branches.
4. Post payment and charge offs on Reserve for bad debts and balance them.
5. Write expense checks.
6. Balance expense book.
7. Transfer accounts from expense book to general ledger accounts at the end of month.
8. Photograph cashier checks, teller tickets and general ledger tickets each day.
9. Make copies of condensed statement of general ledger and give to officers.
10. Send statement to correspondent banks.
11. Balance general ledger entry run.
12. Make two reports each week that go to Federal Reserve (Required Reserves and Loans and Investments).
13. Get dividend check out each quarter.
14. Mark off tickets from correspondent banks.
15. Learn to key punch.
16. Keys financial management transactions daily.

ORGANIZATION

Has an inherent duty and responsibility to make recommendations to supervisor concerning possible methods to improve department.

FINANCES

Has the responsibility to make recommendations to supervisor concerning the budgetary needs of the department.

RELATIONSHIPS

1. Responsible to the Vice President and Controller for the fulfillment of functions, responsibilities, and authority and for their proper interpretation.
2. Will have extensive contact with customers and the public, and is to conduct relationships in a manner that will enhance the overall marketing effort of the bank.
3. Will be called upon from time to time to participate with community organizations and in community projects.

JOB DESCRIPTION: Accounting Clerk II
DEPARTMENT/DIVISION: Operations and Administration
REPORTS TO: Vice President and Controller
SUPERVISES: Has no supervisory responsibility.

JOB SUMMARY

Typing and balancing accounts.

Accounting Clerk II (continued)

DUTIES

1. Type for the department and Security Officer.
2. Answer phone for Security Officer when needed.
3. Balance cash accounts on general ledger for main office and branches.
4. Post payment and charge offs on Reserve for bad debts and balance.
5. Write expense checks and key R.C. distribution.
6. Transfer accounts from expense book to general ledger accounts at the end of month.
7. Photograph cashier checks, teller tickets and general ledger tickets each day.
8. Make copies of condensed statement of general ledger and give to officers.
9. Send statement to correspondent banks.
10. Make three reports each week that go to Federal Reserve (Required Reserves and Loans and Investments).
11. Get dividend check out each quarter.
12. Mark off tickets from correspondent banks.
13. Keys and balances financial management transactions daily.
14. Be alert for and report any potential new business or potential business opportunities.

ORGANIZATION

Has an inherent duty and responsibility to make recommendations to supervisor concerning possible methods to improve department.

FINANCES

Has the responsibility to make recommendations to supervisor concerning the budgetary needs of the department.

RELATIONSHIPS

1. Responsible to the Vice President and Controller for the fulfillment of functions, responsibilities and authority and for their proper interpretation.
2. Will have extensive contact with customers and the public, and is to conduct relationships in a manner that will enhance the overall marketing effort of the bank.
3. Will be called upon from time to time to participate with community organizations and in community projects.

JOB DESCRIPTION: Vice President
DEPARTMENT/DIVISION: Operations
REPORTS TO: Senior Vice President — Operations and Administration
SUPERVISES: Supervisor of Customer Service, Wire Department, Mail, Telephone, Inter-
Bank Delivery
Supervisor of Repurchase Agreement, Accounts Record Support, Bookkeeping
Supervisor of Purchasing and Issuing (Forms, Supplies, Printing)
Supervisor of Return Check Department
Secretary II

JOB SUMMARY

Responsible for management of following departments: Bookkeeping, Customer Service, Mail, Wire Transfer Telephone System, Repurchase Agreement, Return Check, Accounts Record Support Department, Purchasing of Bank Supplies, Printing and Forms, Supply Inventory Program, Correspondent Banking Department, Daily Cash Management and Investment, and Inter-Bank Delivery System.

DUTIES

1. Read and answer mail.
2. Communicate with various individuals and groups on telephone.
3. Make decisions.
4. Motivate leaders.
5. Planning.
6. Customer relations and problem-solving.
7. Employee counseling and problem-solving.
8. Listen to ideas and suggestions from officers and employees.
9. Review reports and then take any necessary action.
10. Serve on management committees.
11. Calculate bank's reserve-cash position daily and make investments or borrow funds as appropriate.
12. Attend seminars and meetings.
13. Approve overdraft privileges.
14. Calculate and set rates on repurchase agreements in accordance with bank policy.
15. Advise and assist in police cases involving fraud or forgery on accounts.
16. Purchase automobile used by the department.
17. Make recommendations concerning salary changes and promotions for employees and officers.
18. Approve payment on bank purchases of supplies, printing, and forms.
19. Advise and assist other departments and branches in operation procedures.
20. Recommend and implement new bank services and operating procedures.
21. Coordinate telephone equipment changes and additions.

ORGANIZATION

1. Initiate changes in the basic organization structure and complement of the planning function in order to accomplish objectives as developed in concert with the Senior Vice President — Operations and Administration.
2. Activate new work procedures and systems to accomplish planning and bank development objectives more efficiently.

FINANCES

Prepare the annual budget for Operations, administering allotted funds in accordance with the budget and approved fiscal procedures; and, recommend capital expenditures for planning and bank development.

RELATIONSHIPS

1. Responsible to the Senior Vice President — Operations and Administration for the fulfillment of his or her functions, responsibilities, and authority and for their proper interpretation.

Vice President (continued)

2. Will advise and assist department managers, officers, and staff in their respective functions associated with the areas for which he or she has direct responsibility.
3. Will have extensive contact with customers, the public and the community, and is to conduct relationships in a manner that will enhance the overall marketing effort of the bank.
4. Will be called upon from time to time to participate with community organizations and in community projects.

Bookkeeping Division

JOB DESCRIPTION: Secretary — Bookkeeping
DEPARTMENT/DIVISION: Bookkeeping
REPORTS TO: Vice President — Bookkeeping
SUPERVISES: Has no supervisory responsibility.

JOB SUMMARY

Secretary to Vice President of Bookkeeping Department.

DUTIES

1. Daily Interbank Transfer.
2. Letters to customers concerning problem accounts.
3. Occasionally write overdraft letters due to overdraft agreement.
4. Prepare minutes for supervisor's meetings weekly.
5. Prepare memos for all branches when necessary.
6. Prepare department manuals.
7. Photocopy daily numerous documents for supervisor, branches and customers.
8. Responsible for separate files for collection procedures for Treasury Refund Requests for deceased customers.
9. Handle direct deposits for deceased customers by charging account monthly for amount of direct deposit; hold cashier's checks until Treasury requests funds.
10. Sell postage stamps to employees.
11. Make photocopies of monthly statements for customers by phone and photocopies for branch employees requests for customers.
12. Control direct deposit tapes to be run on specified dates.
13. Wire transfer requests daily.
14. Handle accounts in bankruptcy under Chapter 10 Division monthly as a collection service.
15. Handle customer complaints/inquiries.
16. Refund service charges.
17. Charge off accounts.
18. Act as receptionist.
19. Quote rates for potential investment customers.
20. Quote Foreign Currency Exchange rates.
21. Take deliveries for supplies.
22. Make DDA maintenance changes/requests.
23. Type letters to businesses to explain bank errors for customers.
24. Order supplies for daily use.

25. Count end of month statements.
26. Prepare Forgery Affidavits for security officer.
27. Occasionally handle tax levies and garnishments.

ORGANIZATION

Has an inherent duty and responsibility to make recommendations to supervisor concerning possible methods to improve department.

FINANCES

Has the responsibility to make recommendations to supervisor concerning the budgetary needs of the department.

RELATIONSHIPS

1. Responsible to the Vice President — Bookkeeping for the fulfillment of functions, responsibilities, and authority and for their proper interpretation.
2. Will have extensive contact with customers and the public, and is to conduct relationships in a manner that will enhance the overall marketing effort of the bank.
3. Will be called upon from time to time to participate with community organizations and in community projects.

JOB DESCRIPTION: Assistant Cashier
DEPARTMENT/DIVISION: Bookkeeping
REPORTS TO: Vice President — Bookkeeping
SUPERVISES: Front Bookkeeping
　　　　　　　Mail Room Clerk
　　　　　　　Switchboard Operator
　　　　　　　Wire Transfer Clerk

JOB SUMMARY

To insure that the wire transfer department, the switchboard operator, the mail room, and the customer service personnel are performing quality work while implementing bank policy and procedure. Do whatever is necessary, as long as it is within banking procedure, to give customers the very best service that is available.

DUTIES

1. Supervise the wire transfer department, the mail room, switchboard operator, and the customer service personnel.
2. Charge off overdrawn accounts.
3. Reconcile customer bank statements.
4. Refund service charges to customers' accounts whenever necessary.
5. Handle cash management program for various accounts.
6. Check for accuracy and sign all oil lease checks going to customers.
7. Make entries to the general ledger.
8. Sign all entries made to the general ledger or customer accounts concerning incoming or outgoing wire transfers.
9. Authorize all outgoing wire transfers that are over $2,500.00.

Assistant Cashier (continued)

10. Obtain and report various balance information over the phone to certain business customers.
11. Review the Demand Deposit Drawing on Today's Deposits Report each day for the purpose of exposing any customer that might be kiting.
12. Approve or deny overdraft privilege request from customers for their checking account.
13. Meet with other officers within bookkeeping department each day and settle the bank's cash position.
14. Purchase postage for the bank.
15. Fill out performance appraisal report on each employee as necessary.
16. Make recommendations as applicable for employee raises.
17. By phone correspondence, have excess monies transferred from various correspondent bank accounts to our account at the Federal Reserve Bank.
18. Review outgoing wire transfers for accuracy after they have been typed on the TWX machine, before they are actually sent by the wire transfer clerk.
19. Maintain a file containing all employee appraisals and other management data.
20. Look up copies of statements and checks on microfilm for customers.
21. Correct errors made on customers' checking accounts.
22. Answer incoming mail.
23. Perform the wire transfer clerk's job in her or his absence.
24. Delegate duties to employees as necessary.
25. Look for ways to increase productivity of employees.
26. Counsel with employees as necessary.
27. Interview job applicants.
28. Sign and mail letters to customers who are over their overdraft limit.

ORGANIZATION

1. Initiate changes in the basic organization structure and complement of the planning function in order to accomplish objectives as developed in concert with the Vice President — Bookkeeping.
2. Activate new work procedures and systems to accomplish planning and bank development objectives more efficiently.

FINANCES

Prepare the annual budget for Bookkeeping, administering allotted funds in accordance with the budget and approved fiscal procedures; and, recommend capital expenditures for planning and bank development.

RELATIONSHIPS

1. Responsible to the Vice President — Bookkeeping for the fulfillment of his or her functions, responsibilities, and authority and for their proper interpretation.
2. Will advise and assist department managers, officers, and staff in their respective functions associated with the areas for which he or she has direct responsibility.
3. Will have extensive contact with customers, the public and the community, and is to conduct relationships in a manner that will enhance the overall marketing effort of the bank.
4. Will be called upon from time to time to participate with community organizations and in community projects.

JOB DESCRIPTION: Clerk I — Front Bookkeeping
DEPARTMENT/DIVISION: Bookkeeping
REPORTS TO: Assistant Cashier
SUPERVISES: Has no supervisory responsibility.

JOB SUMMARY

Performs customer assistance function relative to their account relationships to the bank.

DUTIES

1. Helps customers over the phone as well as in person with any problem related to their checking accounts.
2. Take stop payment requests from customers and teller personnel.
3. Types and distributes various reports.
4. Maintains files.
5. Assists tellers as the need arises by giving them information on customers checking accounts.
6. Issue certified checks.
7. Place holds on checking accounts.
8. Process verifications of deposits.
9. General maintenance on checking accounts. Look up checks on microfiche.

ORGANIZATION

Has an inherent duty and responsibility to make recommendations to supervisor concerning possible methods to improve department.

FINANCES

Has the responsibility to make recommendations to supervisor concerning the budgetary needs of the department.

RELATIONSHIPS

1. Responsible to the Assistant Cashier for the fulfillment of functions, responsibilities, and authority and for their proper interpretation.
2. Will have extensive contact with customers and the public, and is to conduct relationships in a manner that will enhance the overall marketing effort of the bank.
3. Will be called upon from time to time to participate with community organizations and in community projects.

JOB DESCRIPTION: Front Bookkeeping
DEPARTMENT/DIVISION: Bookkeeping
REPORTS TO: Assistant Cashier
SUPERVISES: Has no supervisory responsibility.

JOB SUMMARY

Handles routine customer inquiries and problems regarding their checking accounts. Discusses accounts and discrepancies with customers both over the phone and in person. Originates stop payment orders at the customer's request. Considerable tact and public relations ability is re-

Front Bookkeeping (continued)

quired. Types routine notices and reports. Maintains files. Verifies customer account to government agencies. Requires ability to work well with others. Some training is required for job proficiency. Works under close supervision.

DUTIES

1. Answers customer and other telephone inquiries regarding demand deposit accounts.
2. Answers telephone inquiries from branches.
3. Takes check stop payment orders.
4. Prepares big check list for distribution.
5. Files new accounts.
6. Types closed account list for distribution.
7. Originates special action requests to data processing.
8. Helps customers reconcile bank statements.

ORGANIZATION

Has an inherent duty and responsibility to make recommendations to supervisor concerning possible methods to improve department.

FINANCES

Has the responsibility to make recommendations to supervisor concerning the budgetary needs of the department.

RELATIONSHIPS

1. Responsible to the Assistant Cashier for the fulfillment of functions, responsibilities, and authority and for their proper interpretation.
2. Will have extensive contact with customers and the public, and is to conduct relationships in a manner that will enhance the overall marketing effort of the bank.
3. Will be called upon from time to time to participate with community organizations and in community projects.

JOB DESCRIPTION: Mail Clerk
DEPARTMENT/DIVISION: Bookkeeping
REPORTS TO: Assistant Cashier
SUPERVISES: Has no supervisory responsibility.

JOB SUMMARY

Handles all incoming and outgoing mail. Makes pick ups and deliveries of mail between banks, branches, and post office through the use of bank vehicle. Operates postage meter machine. Makes inner-bank mail pick ups and deliveries. Does incidental posting of postage used in ledger. Performs other routine tasks related to bank mailing. Works under close supervision. A minimum of training is required for job proficiency.

DUTIES

1. Delivers mail to post office.
2. Picks up incoming mail at post office.

3. Sorts, stamps and seals all outgoing mail.
4. Folds bank statements.
5. Picks up mail at branches.
6. Tags and determines postage on registered and certified mail.
7. Delivers returned checks to local banks and businesses.
8. Runs errands.

ORGANIZATION

Has an inherent duty and responsibility to make recommendations to supervisor concerning possible methods to improve department.

FINANCES

Has the responsibility to make recommendations to supervisor concerning the budgetary needs of the department.

RELATIONSHIPS

1. Responsible to the Assistant Cashier for the fulfillment of functions, responsibilities, and authority and for their proper interpretation.
2. Will have extensive contact with customers and the public, and is to conduct relationships in a manner that will enhance the overall marketing effort of the bank.
3. Will be called upon from time to time to participate with community organizations and in community projects.

JOB DESCRIPTION: Mail Clerk
DEPARTMENT/DIVISION: Bookkeeping
REPORTS TO: Assistant Cashier
SUPERVISES: Has no supervisory responsibility.

JOB SUMMARY

Pick up, separate, and deliver mail for the bank.

DUTIES

1. Processes all incoming and outgoing mail.
2. By the use of a bank vehicle makes pick ups and deliveries between the main office, branches, Post Office and various banks in the city.
3. Operates postage machine and folding machine.
4. Delivers and picks up mail at various locations within the bank.
5. Runs errands as necessary for bank officers.

ORGANIZATION

Has an inherent duty and responsibility to make recommendations to supervisor concerning possible methods to improve department.

FINANCES

Has the responsibility to make recommendations to supervisor concerning the budgetary needs of the department.

Mail Clerk (continued)

RELATIONSHIPS

1. Responsible to the Assistant Cashier for the fulfillment of functions, responsibilities, and authority and for their proper interpretation.
2. Will have extensive contact with customers and the public, and is to conduct relationships in a manner that will enhance the overall marketing effort of the bank.
3. Will be called upon from time to time to participate with community organizations and in community projects.

JOB DESCRIPTION: Clerk II — Mail Room
DEPARTMENT/DIVISION: Bookkeeping
REPORTS TO: Assistant Cashier
SUPERVISES: Has no supervisory responsibility.

JOB SUMMARY

Work is of moderately complex clerical type. Makes deliveries and pick up of various banking items for the entire bank system. Operates bank vehicle as needed. Ability to handle office machines such as postage machine, folding machine, electronic and manual scales. Work is performed under relatively moderate supervision.

DUTIES

1. Pick up and deliver teller work.
2. Pick up and deliver DDA bank statements.
3. Deliver mail to all departments.
4. Deliver return items to branches.
5. Deliver statements, night deposit bags and data processing work to merchants.
6. Pick up mail at post office.
7. Maintenance of bank vehicle.

ORGANIZATION

Has an inherent duty and responsibility to make recommendations to supervisor concerning possible methods to improve department.

FINANCES

Has the responsibility to make recommendations to supervisor concerning the budgetary needs of the department.

RELATIONSHIPS

1. Responsible to the Assistant Cashier for the fulfillment of functions, responsibilities, and authority and for their proper interpretation.
2. Will have extensive contact with customers and the public, and is to conduct relationships in a manner that will enhance the overall marketing effort of the bank.
3. Will be called upon from time to time to participate with community organizations and in community projects.

JOB DESCRIPTION: Runner
DEPARTMENT/DIVISION: Bookkeeping
REPORTS TO: Assistant Cashier
SUPERVISES: Has no supervisory responsibility.

JOB SUMMARY

Makes pick up and deliveries of various banking items for several bank departments. Operates bank vehicle between main office and branches. Assists in stock room work. Performs routine tasks under close supervision. A minimum of training is required for job proficiency.

DUTIES

1. Picks up work at branches.
2. Delivers work to branches.
3. Keeps stock in supply room in order.
4. Delivers customer bank statements to branches.
5. Makes other deliveries and pickups between branches and main office.

ORGANIZATION

Has an inherent duty and responsibility to make recommendations to supervisor concerning possible methods to improve department.

FINANCES

Has the responsibility to make recommendations to supervisor concerning the budgetary needs of the department.

RELATIONSHIPS

1. Responsible to the Assistant Cashier for the fulfillment of functions, responsibilities, and authority and for their proper interpretation.
2. Will have extensive contact with customers and the public, and is to conduct relationships in a manner that will enhance the overall marketing effort of the bank.
3. Will be called upon from time to time to participate with community organizations and in community projects.

JOB DESCRIPTION: Secretary I
DEPARTMENT/DIVISION: Bookkeeping
REPORTS TO: Assistant Cashier
SUPERVISES: Has no supervisory responsibility.

JOB SUMMARY

Performs such secretarial duties as typing, receptionist work and answering the telephone. Handles all typing and correspondence for management. Puts customers who have signed overdraft agreements on overdraft cycles and performs other duties related to checking accounts. Contacts customers by mail regarding their accounts and checks they have written. Does some filing. Wires money for depositors. Uses own judgment in some instances. Requires moderate supervision. Job requires extensive on-the-job training for job proficiency.

Secretary I (continued)

DUTIES

1. Greets customers.
2. Answers telephone.
3. Balances dormant accounts.
4. Makes corresponding bank transfers.
5. Charges depositors accounts for garnishment and tax levys.
6. Opens and closes accounts by mail.
7. Corrects bank statements.
8. Wires money for depositors.
9. Credits accounts for oil lease payments.
10. Repurchase agreements.

ORGANIZATION

Has an inherent duty and responsibility to make recommendations to supervisor concerning possible methods to improve department.

FINANCES

Has the responsibility to make recommendations to supervisor concerning the budgetary needs of the department.

RELATIONSHIPS

1. Responsible to the Assistant Cashier for the fulfillment of functions, responsibilities, and authority and for their proper interpretation.
2. Will have extensive contact with customers and the public, and is to conduct relationships in a manner that will enhance the overall marketing effort of the bank.
3. Will be called upon from time to time to participate with community organizations and in community projects.

JOB DESCRIPTION: Switchboard Operator
DEPARTMENT/DIVISION: Bookkeeping
REPORTS TO: Assistant Cashier
SUPERVISES: Has no supervisory responsibility.

JOB SUMMARY

Distribute incoming phone calls to the proper person or department. Distribute the Watts line to employees of the bank who are authorized to use it. Set up conference calls for bank officers. Verifies and files teller tapes. Talks with creative displays personnel and records deposit information to be used in their cash management program.

DUTIES

1. Answer switchboard.
2. Help customers find department that they need.
3. Take creative deposits over phone.
4. Write out checks for creative displays.

5. Distribute Watts line.
6. Proof date and machine number of tellers machine tapes.
7. Write tellers up if there is an error.
8. File tellers tapes.
9. Look up phone numbers for employees.

ORGANIZATION

Has an inherent duty and responsibility to make recommendations to supervisor concerning possible methods to improve department.

FINANCES

Has the responsibility to make recommendations to supervisor concerning the budgetary needs of the department.

RELATIONSHIPS

1. Responsible to the Assistant Cashier for the fulfillment of functions, responsibilities, and authority and for their proper interpretation.
2. Will have extensive contact with customers and the public, and is to conduct relationships in a manner that will enhance the overall marketing effort of the bank.
3. Will be called upon from time to time to participate with community organizations and in community projects.

JOB DESCRIPTION: PBX Switchboard Operator
DEPARTMENT/DIVISION: Bookkeeping
REPORTS TO: Assistant Cashier
SUPERVISES: Has no supervisory responsibility.

JOB SUMMARY

Operates a PBX switchboard; may do incidental clerical work. Requires some experience or training in switchboard operation.

DUTIES

1. Operates PBX switchboard.
2. Keeps log of incoming and outgoing calls.

ORGANIZATION

Has an inherent duty and responsibility to make recommendations to supervisor concerning possible methods to improve department.

FINANCES

Has the responsibility to make recommendations to supervisor concerning the budgetary needs of the department.

RELATIONSHIPS

1. Responsible to the Assistant Cashier for the fulfillment of functions, responsibilities, and authority and for their proper interpretations.

PBX Switchboard Operator (continued)

2. Will have extensive contact with customers and the public, and is to conduct relationships in a manner that will enhance the overall marketing effort of the bank.
3. Will be called upon from time to time to participate with community organizations and in community projects.

JOB DESCRIPTION: Wire Transfer Clerk — I
DEPARTMENT/DIVISION: Bookkeeping
REPORTS TO: Assistant Cashier
SUPERVISES: Has no supervisory responsibility.

JOB SUMMARY

Wire funds, do maintenance on NOW accounts, acquire information on tax levy, and garnishments. Answer subpoenas with information requested.

DUTIES

1. Responsible for maintenance of wire transfers, oil leases, first one accounts and overdraft cards.
2. By using the TWX terminal, sends wire transfers and securities electronically to various banks.
3. Orders supplies for the mail room, wire transfer department and supervisor.
4. Does maintenance on garnishments, tax levys and subpoenas.
5. Types correspondence for supervisor.

ORGANIZATION

Has an inherent duty and responsibility to make recommendations to supervisor concerning possible methods to improve department.

FINANCES

Has the responsibility to make recommendations to supervisor concerning the budgetary needs of the department.

RELATIONSHIPS

1. Responsible to the Assistant Cashier for the fulfillment of functions, responsibilities, and authority and for their proper interpretation.
2. Will have extensive contact with customers and the public, and is to conduct relationships in a manner that will enhance the overall marketing effort of the bank.
3. Will be called upon from time to time to participate with community organizations and in community projects.

JOB DESCRIPTION: Wire Transfer Clerk — II
DEPARTMENT/DIVISION: Bookkeeping
REPORTS TO: Assistant Cashier
SUPERVISES: Has no supervisory responsibility.

JOB SUMMARY

Work is of moderately complex clerical type. Reasonable amount of judgment required. Ability to handle office machines such as typewriter, calculator and TWX machine. Job requires extensive on-the-job training for job proficiency. Work is performed under close supervision.

DUTIES

1. Types letters and reports required by department.
2. Handles some confidential records for department.
3. Operates office machines: typewriter, calculator and TWX machine.
4. Takes wire transfer instructions for customers.
5. Makes entries to the general ledger.
6. Maintains files for wire transfer written authorizations.

ORGANIZATION

Has an inherent duty and responsibility to make recommendations to supervisor concerning possible methods to improve department.

FINANCES

Has the responsibility to make recommendations to supervisor concerning the budgetary needs of the department.

RELATIONSHIPS

1. Responsible to the Assistant Cashier for the fulfillment of functions, responsibilities, and authority and for their proper interpretation.
2. Will have extensive contact with customers and the public, and is to conduct relationships in a manner that will enhance the overall marketing effort of the bank.
3. Will be called upon from time to time to participate with community organizations and in community projects.

JOB DESCRIPTION: Assistant Vice President
DEPARTMENT/DIVISION: Bookkeeping
REPORTS TO: Vice President — Bookkeeping
SUPERVISES: Secretary
               Administrative Assistant — Check File
               Relief Switchboard — Addressograph

JOB SUMMARY

Supervising bookkeeping operations and addressograph. Figuring cash difference; buy-sell federal funds. Handle repurchase agreements.

DUTIES

1. Balance checking accounts.
2. Handle repurchase agreements.
3. Handle problems with customer accounts.
4. Close checking accounts.

Assistant Vice President (continued)

5. Sell federal funds.
6. Buy federal funds.
7. Figure statement cycles.
8. Supervise operations of Bookkeeping Department.
9. Supervise operation of addressograph.
10. Settle cash management position.
11. Supervise in return section with problems.
12. Reproduce copies of checks and statements.
13. Handle court orders on checking accounts.
14. Handle estate accounts.
15. Balance unidentified accounts.
16. Handle dormant accounts.
17. In charge of stuffers that go out in statements.
18. See that signature cards and authorizations are correct.

ORGANIZATION

1. Initiate changes in the basic organization structure and complement of the planning function in order to accomplish objectives as developed in concert with the Vice President — Bookkeeping.
2. Activate new work procedures and systems to accomplish planning and bank development objectives more efficiently.

FINANCES

Prepare the annual budget for Bookkeeping, administering allotted funds in accordance with the budget and approved fiscal procedures; and, recommend capital expenditures for planning and bank development.

RELATIONSHIPS

1. Responsible to the Vice President — Bookkeeping for the fulfillment of his or her functions, responsibilities, and authority and for their proper interpretation.
2. Will advise and assist department managers, officers, and staff in their respective functions associated with the areas for which he or she has direct responsibility.
3. Will have extensive contact with customers, the public and the community, and is to conduct relationships in a manner that will enhance the overall marketing effort of the bank.
4. Will be called upon from time to time to participate with community organizations and in community projects.

JOB DESCRIPTION: Secretary
DEPARTMENT/DIVISION: Bookkeeping
REPORTS TO: Assistant Vice President
SUPERVISES: Has no supervisory responsibility.

JOB SUMMARY

Secretary to Assistant Vice President. Invest and mature repurchase agreements and close checking and savings accounts.

DUTIES

1. Act as receptionist.
2. Take wire transfers.
3. Make interbank corrections (encoding errors).
4. Look up statements and checks.
5. Make DDA maintenance changes.
6. Refund service charges to customers.
7. Quote foreign currency exchange rate.
8. Make interbank transfers.
9. Take deliveries for supplies.
10. Order supplies.
11. Sell postage stamps.
12. Close checking and savings accounts (send closing letters to these customers).
13. Type letters to businesses to explain bank errors for customers.
14. Type statement schedule.
15. Type cycle schedule.
16. Charge customer's account for looking up checks and copies of checks.
17. Charge unidentified deposits for service charge once a month.
18. Type forgery affidavits.
19. Correct statements at the end of the month (business).
20. Transfers made to other banks due to deposit errors.
21. Repurchase Agreements — (Investing)
    a. Invest and type Repurchase Agreement for customers.
    b. Choose government security to use for repurchase agreement. Determine the rate of interest for repurchase agreement.
    c. Type letter to customer stating the terms of repurchase agreement.
22. Credit general ledger.
23. Make up computer sheet for repurchase agreement.
24. Repurchase Agreement (Maturing)
    a. Credit customer's account or issue cashier's check.
    b. Charge General Ledger.
25. Repurchase Agreement Report
    a. Balance the report.
    b. Make tickets for interest accrued.
26. Every morning balance securities.
27. On the last day of each month type up a list showing the securities used for each repurchase agreement.

ORGANIZATION

Has an inherent duty and responsibility to make recommendations to supervisor concerning possible methods to improve department.

FINANCES

Has the responsibility to make recommendations to supervisor concerning the budgetary needs of the department.

RELATIONSHIPS

1. Responsible to the Assistant Vice President for the fulfillment of functions, responsibilities, and authority and for their proper interpretation.

Secretary (continued)

2. Will have extensive contact with customers and the public, and is to conduct relationships in a manner that will enhance the overall marketing effort of the bank.
3. Will be called upon from time to time to participate with community organizations and in community projects.

JOB DESCRIPTION: Secretary II
DEPARTMENT/DIVISION: Bookkeeping
REPORTS TO: Assistant Vice President
SUPERVISES: Has no supervisory responsibility.

JOB SUMMARY

Performs such secretarial duties as typing, receptionist work and answering the telephone. Handles all typing and correspondence for management. Puts customers who have signed overdraft agreements on overdraft cycles and performs other duties related to checking accounts. Contacts customers by mail regarding their accounts and checks they have written. Does some filing. Wires money for depositors. Uses own judgment in some instances. Requires moderate supervision. Job requires extensive on-the-job training for job proficiency.

DUTIES

1. Greets customers.
2. Answers telephone.
3. Balances dormant accounts.
4. Makes corresponding bank transfers.
5. Charges depositors accounts for garnishment and tax levys.
6. Opens and closes accounts by mail.
7. Corrects bank statements.
8. Wires money for depositors.
9. Credits accounts for oil lease payments.

ORGANIZATION

Has an inherent duty and responsibility to make recommendations to supervisor concerning possible methods to improve department.

FINANCES

Has the responsibility to make recommendations to supervisor concerning the budgetary needs of the department.

RELATIONSHIPS

1. Responsible to the Assistant Vice President for the fulfillment of functions, responsibilities, and authority and for their proper interpretation.
2. Will have extensive contact with customers and the public, and is to conduct relationships in a manner that will enhance the overall marketing effort of the bank.
3. Will be called upon from time to time to participate with community organizations and in community projects.

JOB DESCRIPTION: Administrative Assistant — Check File
DEPARTMENT/DIVISION: Bookkeeping
REPORTS TO: Assistant Vice President
SUPERVISES: Has no supervisory responsibility.

JOB SUMMARY

Moderately advanced clerical work requiring some prior training or experience, either in a similar job or as Clerk I. Work involves light typing, filing, office machine operation, etc. Requires moderate amount of judgment, and is performed under moderate supervision.

DUTIES

1. Takes stop payment orders and sees they are taken care of.
2. Reopens dormant accounts.
3. Contacts customers regarding error on checks.
4. Routes form letters to customers.
5. Filing.

ORGANIZATION

Has an inherent duty and responsibility to make recommendations to supervisor concerning possible methods to improve department.

FINANCES

Has the responsibility to make recommendations to supervisor concerning the budgetary needs of the department.

RELATIONSHIPS

1. Responsible to the Assistant Vice President for the fulfillment of functions, responsibilities, and authority and for their proper interpretation.
2. Will have extensive contact with customers and the public, and is to conduct relationships in a manner that will enhance the overall marketing effort of the bank.
3. Will be called upon from time to time to participate with community organizations and in community projects.

JOB DESCRIPTION: Administrative Assistant — Check File
DEPARTMENT/DIVISION: Bookkeeping
REPORTS TO: Assistant Vice President
SUPERVISES: File Clerks

JOB SUMMARY

Supervise file room personnel; handle and balance all unpaid debits and credits. Perform various other supervisory duties.

DUTIES

1. Supervise file clerks.
2. Balance insufficient checks.
3. Balance deposits (no accounts).

Administrative Assistant — Check File (continued)

4. Balance no account checks.
5. Balance closed account checks.
6. Balance closed account deposits.
7. Reopen closed accounts.
8. Correct no account deposits.
9. Refund stop payment and unsigned checks.

ORGANIZATION

1. Initiate changes in the basic organization structure and complement of the planning function in order to accomplish objectives as developed in concert with the Assistant Vice President.
2. Activate new work procedures and systems to accomplish planning and bank development objectives more efficiently.

FINANCES

Prepare the annual budget for Bookkeeping, administering allotted funds in accordance with the budget and approved fiscal procedures; and, recommend capital expenditures for planning and bank development.

RELATIONSHIPS

1. Responsible to the Assistant Vice President for the fulfillment of his or her functions, responsibilities, and authority and for their proper interpretation.
2. Will advise and assist department managers, officers, and staff in their respective functions associated with the areas for which he or she has direct responsibility.
3. Will have extensive contact with customers, the public and the community, and is to conduct relationships in a manner that will enhance the overall marketing effort of the bank.
4. Will be called upon from time to time to participate with community organizations and in community projects.

JOB DESCRIPTION: Clerk II
DEPARTMENT/DIVISION: Bookkeeping
REPORTS TO: Administrative Assistant for Return Items Section
SUPERVISES: Has no supervisory responsibility.

JOB SUMMARY

Involves customer contact regarding returned checks, both by mail and by telephone. Balances checks with adding machine tapes and computer printout. Types customer notices. Handles relatively complex transactions. Exercises independent judgment in some instances and with moderate supervision. Job requires extensive on-the-job training for job proficiency.

DUTIES

1. Handles returned checks.
2. Contacts accounts overdrawn.
3. Prepares charge backs to last endorser of returned checks.
4. Sends notice of overdraft to customers.
5. Prepares daily and monthly reports on return items.

ORGANIZATION

Has an inherent duty and responsibility to make recommendations to supervisor concerning possible methods to improve department.

FINANCES

Has the responsibility to make recommendations to supervisor concerning the budgetary needs of the department.

RELATIONSHIPS

1. Responsible to the Administrative Assistant for Return Items Section for the fulfillment of functions, responsibilities, and authority and for their proper interpretation.
2. Will have extensive contact with customers and the public, and is to conduct relationships in a manner that will enhance the overall marketing effort of the bank.
3. Will be called upon from time to time to participate with community organizations and in community projects.

JOB DESCRIPTION: File Clerk
DEPARTMENT/DIVISION: Bookkeeping
REPORTS TO: Administrative Assistant — Check Files
SUPERVISES: Has no supervisory responsibility.

JOB SUMMARY

Does routine check and deposit slip filing by account number. A minimum amount of customer contact by phone is required. Must be alert to improper signatures and special instruction cards on checks. Job requires a minimum of judgment and little or no previous experience. Work is performed under close supervision. Must be able to work well with others. A minimum of training is required for job proficiency.

DUTIES

1. File checks and deposit tickets.
2. Photograph everything filed.
3. Watch for stop payment orders.
4. Check signatures for validity.
5. Pull checks and deposits for customer statements.

ORGANIZATION

Has an inherent duty and responsibility to make recommendations to supervisor concerning possible methods to improve department.

FINANCES

Has the responsibility to make recommendations to supervisor concerning the budgetary needs of the department.

RELATIONSHIPS

1. Responsible to the Administrative Assistant — Check Files for the fulfillment of functions, responsibilities, and authority and for their proper interpretation.

File Clerk (continued)

2. Will have extensive contact with customers and the public, and is to conduct relationships in a manner that will enhance the overall marketing effort of the bank.
3. Will be called upon from time to time to participate with community organizations and in community projects.

JOB DESCRIPTION: File Clerk
DEPARTMENT/DIVISION: Bookkeeping
REPORTS TO: Administrative Assistant — Check File
SUPERVISES: Has no supervisory responsibility.

JOB SUMMARY

The general function of this job is filing checks, sending out monthly statements and assisting customers by phone.

DUTIES

1. Assist customers on telephone.
2. Refer customers to other departments for further assistance.
3. File checks.
4. File rejects.
5. Make copies of checks and deposits for customers.
6. Send copies of checks, deposits, drafts, etc. to different branches.
7. Look up copies of checks on film.
8. Look up copies of statements on film.
9. Make sure proper signature and account number is on all checks as each check is filed.
10. Pull out insufficient checks.
11. Sort rejects.
12. Photograph rejects.
13. Request fullsheets.
14. Count fullsheets.
15. File back fullsheets.
16. Pull out checks on which a stop payment has been made.
17. Change out signature cards (from temporary to permanent).
18. File re-open account cards.
19. File new account cards.
20. Pull regular cycle statements.
21. Pull end of month statements.
22. Request and mail early or special statements at customer's request.
23. Check list daily for special requested statements.

ORGANIZATION

Has an inherent duty and responsibility to make recommendations to supervisor concerning possible methods to improve department.

FINANCES

Has the responsibility to make recommendations to supervisor concerning the budgetary needs of the department.

RELATIONSHIPS

1. Responsible to the Administrative Assistant — Check File for the fulfillment of functions, responsibilities, and authority and for their proper interpretation.
2. Will have extensive contact with customers and the public, and is to conduct relationships in a manner that will enhance the overall marketing effort of the bank.
3. Will be called upon from time to time to participate with community organizations and in community projects.

JOB DESCRIPTION: Relief Switchboard — Addressograph
DEPARTMENT/DIVISION: Bookkeeping
REPORTS TO: Assistant Vice President
SUPERVISES: Has no supervisory responsibility.

JOB SUMMARY

General bookkeeping and secretarial/clerical duties.

DUTIES

1. Change addresses on accounts.
2. File authorizations.
3. Answer telephone.
4. Relieve on switchboard.
5. Type changes of address.

ORGANIZATION

Has an inherent duty and responsibility to make recommendations to supervisor concerning possible methods to improve department.

FINANCES

Has the responsibility to make recommendations to supervisor concerning the budgetary needs of the department.

RELATIONSHIPS

1. Responsible to the Assistant Vice President for the fulfillment of functions, responsibilities, and authority and for their proper interpretation.
2. Will have extensive contact with customers and the public, and is to conduct relationships in a manner that will enhance the overall marketing effort of the bank.
3. Will be called upon from time to time to participate with community organizations and in community projects.

JOB DESCRIPTION: Relief Switchboard — Addressograph Operator
DEPARTMENT/DIVISION: Bookkeeping
REPORTS TO: Assistant Vice President
SUPERVISES: Has no supervisory responsibility.

Relief Switchboard — Addressograph Operator (continued)

JOB SUMMARY

Operates addressograph equipment including the plate maker and check printer. Maintains account files. Operates NCR encoder. Keeps records of all work done. Performs routine duties under close supervision. Requires ability to work well with others. A minimum of training is required for job proficiency.

DUTIES

1. Makes address plates.
2. Receives and fills orders for checks.
3. Changes addresses on all accounts.
4. Keeps stockholders list up to date.
5. Encodes account numbers on all pre-made deposit slips.
6. Relieves on telephone switchboard.

ORGANIZATION

Has an inherent duty and responsibility to make recommendations to supervisor concerning possible methods to improve department.

FINANCES

Has the responsibility to make recommendations to supervisor concerning the budgetary needs of the department.

RELATIONSHIPS

1. Responsible to the Assistant Vice President for the fulfillment of functions, responsibilities, and authority and for their proper interpretation.
2. Will have extensive contact with customers and the public, and is to conduct relationships in a manner that will enhance the overall marketing effort of the bank.
3. Will be called upon from time to time to participate with community organizations and in community projects.

JOB DESCRIPTION: Administrative Assistant — Bookkeeping
DEPARTMENT/DIVISION: Bookkeeping
REPORTS TO: Vice President — Bookkeeping
SUPERVISES: Clerk II

JOB SUMMARY

To handle all returns and any check that we have a problem with.

DUTIES

1. Get cash items from vault; balance and identify all numbers on tape; photograph and identify as cash items with previous date; add and balance.
2. Debit Federal Reserve for direct deposit then send items to different departments.
3. Get work from all three desks; add all insufficient checks balance and distribute to designated places.

4. Call all employees when overdrawn and count their statements.
5. Balance all work handled for the day.
6. Forgeries, foreign currency tickets, jury certificates, PAT rejects and missing checks are held in cash items until cleared.
7. Type back checks to our customers' accounts.

ORGANIZATION

1. Initiate changes in the basic organization structure and complement of the planning function in order to accomplish objectives developed in concert with the Vice President — Bookkeeping.
2. Activate new work procedures and systems to accomplish planning and bank development objectives more efficiently.

FINANCES

Prepare the annual budget for Bookkeeping, administering allotted funds in accordance with the budget and approved fiscal procedures; and, recommend capital expenditures for planning and bank development.

RELATIONSHIPS

1. Responsible to the Vice President — Bookkeeping for the fulfillment of his or her functions, responsibilities, and authority and for their proper interpretation.
2. Will advise and assist department managers, officers, and staff in their respective functions associated with the areas for which he or she has direct responsibility.
3. Will have extensive contact with customers, the public and the community, and is to conduct relationships in a manner that will enhance the overall marketing effort of the bank.
4. Will be called upon from time to time to participate with community organizations and in community projects.

JOB DESCRIPTION: Clerk II
DEPARTMENT/DIVISION: Bookkeeping
REPORTS TO: Administrative Assistant — Bookkeeping
SUPERVISES: Has no supervisory responsibility.

JOB SUMMARY

Purpose of job is to charge bank checks that have been refused for payment for any reason. Responsibility for detecting suspicious practices in checking account customers.

DUTIES

1. Film and charge back the checks from the Fed payable to our customers that are drawn on other banks.
2. Tear and separate the insufficient charges for our own customers, making sure everyone is charged accurately as we have several methods for charging customers.
3. Separate the checks on our customers into the groups that are payable through our correspondent banks and the checks that are payable through the Fed to any other banks.
4. Take phone calls from customers and help them in any way possible.

Clerk II (continued)

5. Look for suspicious activities in our checking account customers, forgery, fraud, etc., and let the security officer know and help him or her in any way possible.
6. Work both the supervisor desk and the other clerks' desks, which means having to keep informed on all jobs in our department.
7. Charge back the insufficient checks payable to our customers drawn on our correspondent banks.
8. Encode account numbers on the work we are going to send through proof.
9. File the insufficient charges that cannot be paid because of low balances.
10. Count the business statements at the end of the month.
11. Count and verify employee statements once a month.
12. Do research for the supervisor on accounts where there is a problem of some kind.
13. Order and store supplies for our department.
14. Film and send the checks drawn on us payable through the Federal Reserve Bank to the Federal Reserve by the courier.

ORGANIZATION
Has an inherent duty and responsibility to make recommendations to supervisor concerning possible methods to improve department.

FINANCES
Has the responsibility to make recommendations to supervisor concerning the budgetary needs of the department.

RELATIONSHIPS
1. Responsible to the Administrative Assistant — Bookkeeping for the fulfillment of functions, responsibilities, and authority and for their proper interpretation.
2. Will have extensive contact with customers and the public, and is to conduct relationships in a manner that will enhance the overall marketing effort of the bank.
3. Will be called upon from time to time to participate with community organizations and in community projects.

Proof Division

JOB DESCRIPTION: Assistant Vice President — Proof Department
DEPARTMENT/DIVISION: Proof
REPORTS TO: Senior Vice President and Cashier — Operations and Administration
SUPERVISES: Administrative Assistant and Assistant Department Manager

JOB SUMMARY
Direct supervision of employees in Proof Department. To be responsible for all functions performed within the department. To evaluate and review the employees in the department.

DUTIES
1. To see that all work is proofed and encoded for processing.
2. To see that all food stamps are counted, endorsed and ready for shipment.

3. To see that the general ledger is balanced and ready to be processed.
4. To see that all film is processed and delivered to departments.
5. To see that all direct coupons, drafts, etc. are handled.
6. To see that transit and clearing items are handled properly.
7. To see that all rejects are handled properly.
8. To see that teller's cash is in balance daily.
9. To make adjustments when needed.
10. To handle problems with customers and other departments in the bank.
11. To see that PAT (anytime teller machine) balances daily.
12. To see that adjustment with corresponding banks is handled.
13. To see that reports are done when needed.
14. To check equipment expense and charges to the department, to see if they are correct.
15. To see that the department completes its daily operations on time.
16. To see that business service charges are handled and charged correctly.
17. To be responsible for all functions performed in the department, and to see that the department is providing prompt services to customers and bank at the most economical cost.
18. To perform special projects upon request from immediate supervisor and top management.
19. To be able to handle unexpected situations that occur in the department.

ORGANIZATION

1. Initiate changes in the basic organization structure and complement of the planning function in order to accomplish objectives as developed in concert with the Senior Vice President and Cashier — Operations and Administration.
2. Activate new work procedures and systems to accomplish planning and bank development objectives more efficiently.

FINANCES

Prepare the annual budget for Proof, administering allotted funds in accordance with the budget and approved fiscal procedures; and, recommend capital expenditures for planning and bank development.

RELATIONSHIPS

1. Responsible to the Senior Vice President and Cashier — Operations and Administration for the fulfillment of his or her functions, responsibilities, and authority and for their proper interpretation.
2. Will advise and assist department managers, officers, and staff in their respective functions associated with the areas for which he or she has direct responsibility.
3. Will have extensive contact with customers, the public and the community, and is to conduct relationships in a manner that will enhance the overall marketing effort of the bank.
4. Will be called upon from time to time to participate with community organizations and in community projects.

JOB DESCRIPTION: Administrative Assistant and Assistant Department Manager
DEPARTMENT/DIVISION: Proof
REPORTS TO: Assistant Vice President — Proof Department

Administrative Assistant and Assistant Department Manager (continued)

SUPERVISES: Part-Time Proof Operator
Proof Operator
Clerk III
Balancing Supervisor

JOB SUMMARY

General supervision of Proof Department. This job requires a knowledge of every function of the department. One of the most important duties of this job is to be capable of making supervisory decisions and act as supervisor when the need arises.

DUTIES

1. Balance and encode general ledger daily work.
2. Balance tellers cash and make corrections on cash.
3. Balance sundry book and make entries for all incoming sundry items. Follow up on delinquent items.
4. Take phone call questions and complaints from customers concerning errors we correct on their deposits.
5. Research items on film for tellers, customers or other departments to clarify or verify item in question.
6. Prepare and balance tickets for the deferred account.
7. Help count and endorse food coupons. Balance and prepare food coupons for shipment.
8. Run proof machine.
9. Help proof operators with questions, errors, etc.
10. Do all of the typing, take messages, phone calls, etc. for proof manager.
11. In charge of proof and transit when proof manager is off or away from the department. Do the proof manager's job when he or she is off from work.
12. Prepare clearing checks to go to the computer.
13. Balance clearing runs.
14. Punch rejects.
15. Balance PAT work.
16. Correct Federal Reserve Bank errors.
17. Develop film.
18. Open and work up mail to proof department.
19. Balance runs.
20. Go through garbage for lost items.
21. Photograph checks.

ORGANIZATION

1. Initiate changes in the basic organization structure and complement of the planning function in order to accomplish objectives as developed in concert with the Assistant Vice President — Proof Department.
2. Activate new work procedures and systems to accomplish planning and bank development objectives more efficiently.

FINANCES

Prepare the annual budget for Proof, administering allotted funds in accordance with the budget and approved fiscal procedures; and, recommend capital expenditures for planning and bank development.

RELATIONSHIPS

1. Responsible to the Assistant Vice President — Proof Department for the fulfillment of his or her functions, responsibilities, and authority and for their proper interpretation.
2. Will advise and assist department managers, officers, and staff in their respective functions associated with the areas for which he or she has direct responsibility.
3. Will have extensive contact with customers, the public and the community, and is to conduct relationships in a manner that will enhance the overall marketing effort of the bank.
4. Will be called upon from time to time to participate with community organizations and in community projects.

JOB DESCRIPTION: Part-Time Proof Operator
DEPARTMENT/DIVISION: Proof
REPORTS TO: Administrative Assistant and Assistant Department Manager
SUPERVISES: Has no supervisory responsibility.

JOB SUMMARY

Operates slow speed proof machine and food stamp counter. Balances all incoming deposits and debit items. Sorts work in batches to be read by computer. Requires little independent judgment and work is performed under close supervision.

DUTIES

1. Operate slow speed proof machine.
2. Balance incoming deposits and debit items.
3. Sort work into batches.
4. Prepare transit work.
5. Photograph proof work.

ORGANIZATION

Has an inherent duty and responsibility to make recommendations to supervisor concerning possible methods to improve department.

FINANCES

Has the responsibility to make recommendations to supervisor concerning the budgetary needs of the department.

RELATIONSHIPS

1. Responsible to the Administrative Assistant and Assistant Department Manager for the fulfillment of functions, responsibilities, and authority and for their proper interpretation.
2. Will have extensive contact with customers and the public, and is to conduct relationships in a manner that will enhance the overall marketing effort of the bank.

Part-Time Proof Operator (continued)

3. Will be called upon from time to time to participate with community organizations and in community projects.

JOB DESCRIPTION: Operations Clerk III
DEPARTMENT/DIVISION: Proof
REPORTS TO: Administrative Assistant and Assistant Department Manager
SUPERVISES: Has no supervisory responsibility.

JOB SUMMARY

Work is somewhat complex and requires knowledge of policies, procedures and practices. Work may involve relieving Balancing Supervisor. Assist in balancing all work. Work requires some specialized knowledge such as operation of slow speed proof machine. Work requires use of office machines such as proof machine, typewriter, and calculator. Must be fully competent to work alone. Requires ability to take over management responsibilities.

DUTIES

1. Relieve supervisor of Balancing Department.
2. Operate proof machine.
3. Balance general ledger.
4. Develop proof film.
5. Transmit coupons, drafts, checks and other items to Federal Reserve.
6. Balance cash tickets.
7. Balance reject list.
8. Prepare transit items and clearing items for shipment.
9. Count food coupons.

ORGANIZATION

Has an inherent duty and responsibility to make recommendations to supervisor concerning possible methods to improve department.

FINANCES

Has the responsibility to make recommendations to supervisor concerning the budgetary needs of the department.

RELATIONSHIPS

1. Responsible to the Administrative Assistant and Assistant Department Manager for the fulfillment of functions, responsibilities, and authority and for their proper interpretation.
2. Will have extensive contact with customers and the public, and is to conduct relationships in a manner that will enhance the overall marketing effort of the bank.
3. Will be called upon from time to time to participate with community organizations and in community projects.

JOB DESCRIPTION: Proof Operator
DEPARTMENT/DIVISION: Proof
REPORTS TO: Administrative Assistant and Assistant Department Manager
SUPERVISES: Has no supervisory responsibility.

JOB SUMMARY

Operates proof machine and food stamp counter. Balances all incoming deposits and debit items. Sorts work in batches to be read by computer. Requires little independent judgment and work is performed under close supervision.

DUTIES

1. Operate proof machine.
2. Count food coupons.
3. Cancel food coupons.

ORGANIZATION

Has an inherent duty and responsibility to make recommendations to supervisor concerning possible methods to improve department.

FINANCES

Has the responsibility to make recommendations to supervisor concerning the budgetary needs of the department.

RELATIONSHIPS

1. Responsible to the Administrative Assistant and Assistant Department Manager for the fulfillment of functions, responsibilities and authority and for their proper interpretation.
2. Will have extensive contact with customers and the public, and is to conduct relationships in a manner that will enhance the overall marketing effort of the bank.
3. Will be called upon from time to time to participate with community organizations and in community projects.

JOB DESCRIPTION: Balancing Supervisor
DEPARTMENT/DIVISION: Proof
REPORTS TO: Administrative Assistant and Assistant Department Manager
SUPERVISES: Part Time Clerk I
                 Balancing Clerk V

JOB SUMMARY

Work is moderately complex and requires knowledge of policies, procedures, and practices of the bank. Work requires some specialized knowledge such as operation of slow speed proof machine. Balances over-the-counter entry run. Prepares transit items for shipment. Assists in balancing PAT work. Performs various other jobs as needed. Must be fully competent to work alone. Must be able to train others. Requires ability to take over management responsibilities.

Balancing Supervisor (continued)

DUTIES

1. Supervise all work in Balancing Department.
2. Balance all work for Data Processing.
3. Photograph all work.
4. Operate slow speed proof machine.
5. Prepare transit items for shipment.
6. Assists in balancing PAT work.

ORGANIZATION

1. Initiate changes in the basic organization structure and complement of the planning function in order to accomplish objectives as developed in concert with the Administrative Assistant and Assistant Department Manager.
2. Activate new work procedures and systems to accomplish planning and bank development objectives more efficiently.

FINANCES

Prepare the annual budget for Proof, administering allotted funds in accordance with the budget and approved fiscal procedures; and, recommend capital expenditures for planning and bank development.

RELATIONSHIPS

1. Responsible to the Administrative Assistant and Assistant Department Manager for the fulfillment of his or her functions, responsibilities, and authority and for their proper interpretation.
2. Will advise and assist department managers, officers, and staff in their respective functions associated with the areas for which he or she has direct responsibility.
3. Will have extensive contact with customers, the public and the community, and is to conduct relationships in a manner that will enhance the overall marketing effort of the bank.
4. Will be called upon from time to time to participate with community organizations and in community projects.

JOB DESCRIPTION: Balancing Clerk V
DEPARTMENT/DIVISION: Proof
REPORTS TO: Administrative Assistant and Assistant Department Manager
SUPERVISES: Has no supervisory responsibility.

JOB SUMMARY

See that all transit operations are completed as accurate and fast as possible on the night shift. This job requires knowledge of all transit operations and decision making and supervision of night employees on a limited basis.

DUTIES

1. Balance primary and secondary runs.
2. Operate multipocket proof machine.
3. Balance credit card, cash items, and food coupons.

4. Prepare outgoing cash letters.
5. Operate CRT terminal and microfilmer.
6. Assist balancing clerks with any problems they incur with their duties.

ORGANIZATION

Has an inherent duty and responsibility to make recommendations to supervisor concerning possible methods to improve department.

FINANCES

Has the responsibility to make recommendations to supervisor concerning the budgetary needs of the department.

RELATIONSHIPS

1. Responsible to the Administrative Assistant and Assistant Department Manager for the fulfillment of functions, responsibilities and authority and for their proper interpretation.
2. Will have extensive contact with customers and the public, and is to conduct relationships in a manner that will enhance the overall marketing effort of the bank.
3. Will be called upon from time to time to participate with community organizations and in community projects.

JOB DESCRIPTION: Balancing Clerk Part-time
DEPARTMENT/DIVISION: Proof
REPORTS TO: Balancing Clerk V
SUPERVISES: Has no supervisory responsibility.

JOB SUMMARY

Balances entry runs, operates microfilmer, and CRT terminal machine.

DUTIES

1. Microfilm all work run on proof machines.
2. Balance entry runs.
3. Prepare checks for shipment.
4. Balance credit card, cash items, food stamps.
5. Transport check to Federal Reserve when necessary.
6. Make branch runs when necessary.
7. Be alert for and report any potential new business or potential business opportunities.

ORGANIZATION

Has an inherent duty and responsibility to make recommendations to supervisor concerning possible methods to improve department.

FINANCES

Has the responsibility to make recommendations to supervisor concerning the budgetary needs of the department.

Balancing Clerk Part-time (continued)

RELATIONSHIPS

1. Responsible to the balancing supervisor Clerk V for the fulfillment of functions, responsibilities, and authority for their proper interpretation.
2. Will have some contact with customers and the public and is to conduct relationships in a manner that will enhance the overall marketing effort of the bank.

Operations Division

JOB DESCRIPTION: Security Officer
DEPARTMENT/DIVISION: Operations and Administration
REPORTS TO: Senior Vice President and Cashier — Operations and Administration
SUPERVISES: Has no supervisory responsibility.

JOB SUMMARY

Purpose is the protection of people, assets, and property through the development and administration of a protection program. To train and indoctrinate bank employees concerning protection measures. Functions include fire protection of banking offices, the investigation of employee crimes, liaison with the law enforcement agencies, and dealing with the investigation of all external crimes against the bank.

DUTIES

1. Regular survey of each banking office.
2. Recommend appropriate protection measures.
3. Administer the bank protection program.
4. Conduct periodic retraining of bank employees concerning their responsibilities under the security program.
5. Conduct liaison with the local, federal and criminal justice agencies.
6. Advise and assist all departments in protection measures.
7. Obtain information from the bank records to prevent check kiting and terminate check kiting in progress.
8. Prepare copies of all items necessary for processing a criminal case (checks, deposit slips, signature cards, forged signature affidavits, etc.).
9. Write, publish, and distribute memos concerning various activities that have occurred resulting in loss to the bank and recommend measures to prevent further losses.
10. Escort trouble makers and undesirable customers from the bank.
11. Assist the law enforcement agencies in apprehension of various bank crime perpetrators.
12. Investigate credit card frauds as necessary.
13. Conduct interviews and investigate internal crimes to the bank such as mail theft, embezzlements, property destruction, and theft.
14. Investigate PAT frauds and claims of fraud.
15. Develop and maintain a fire protection program.
16. Sign all warrants of arrest for persons apprehended who have committed criminal acts against the bank.
17. Appear at all Grand Jury Hearings and court trials involving the bank.

18. Maintain records of all criminal activities against the bank.
19. Carry out all the requirements for security protection as outlined in Title 12 — Bank and Banking, Chapter 1 — Bureau of the Comptroller of Currency, Part 21.
20. Remain calm when everyone else is shaken.

ORGANIZATION

Has an inherent duty and responsibility to make recommendations to supervisor concerning possible methods to improve department.

FINANCES

Has the responsibility to make recommendations to supervisor concerning the budgetary needs of the department.

RELATIONSHIPS

1. Responsible to the Senior Vice President and Cashier — Operations and Administration for the fulfillment of functions, responsibilities and authority and for their proper interpretation.
2. Will have extensive contact with customers and the public, and is to conduct relationships in a manner that will enhance the overall marketing effort of the bank.
3. Will be called upon from time to time to participate with community organizations and in community projects.

JOB DESCRIPTION: Assistant Cashier
DEPARTMENT/DIVISION: Operations
REPORTS TO: Vice President
SUPERVISES: Front Bookkeeping
               Mailroom/Runners/Van Run
               Switchboard
               Wire Transfer

JOB SUMMARY

Purchasing agent for the bank. Foreign Currency sales and related items. Customer service. Involved in settlement of daily cash position of the bank.

DUTIES

Purchasing:
1. Complete "On Order Forms" for each item ordered.
2. Complete "Stock Acquisition Forms" for each item received.
3. Complete all computer maintenance forms for the Supplies Inventory System.
4. See that all shipments are received and verified.
5. See that all supplies are dispersed properly.
6. See that all supplies are placed on the shelves.
7. Balance the "Inventory Control Report" twice weekly.
8. Take physical inventory.
9. Verify all invoices and statements for payment.
10. Issue monthly reports of requisition to each cost center and to the Controller Department.
11. Ok maintenance agreements on a good portion of the bank equipment.

Assistant Cashier (continued)

Foreign Currency Sales:
12. Buy and sell foreign currencies, bank drafts and foreign travellers checks.
13. Answer questions by phone and in person concerning currency rates of exchange, etc.

Customer Service:
14. Assist customers in solving problems concerning their checking account.
15. Help balance check books.
16. Reproduce microfilm records for different reasons.
17. Help customers understand checking account procedures.
18. Storage of microfilm and cataloging.
19. Involved in settlement of daily cash position of the bank.
20. Write letters for customers who have had checks returned as a result of a bank error.
21. Verify savings bonds report before sending to the Federal Reserve.

ORGANIZATION

1. Initiate changes in the basic organization structure and complement of the planning function in order to accomplish objectives as developed in concert with the Vice President.
2. Activate new work procedures and systems to accomplish planning and bank development objectives more efficiently.

FINANCES

Prepare the annual budget for the Operations Department, administering allotted funds in accordance with the budget and approved fiscal procedures; and, recommend capital expenditures for planning and bank development.

RELATIONSHIPS

1. Responsible to the Vice President for the fulfillment of his or her functions, responsibilities, and authority and for their proper interpretation.
2. Will advise and assist department managers, officers, and staff in their respective functions associated with the areas for which he or she has direct responsibility.
3. Will have extensive contact with customers, the public and the community, and is to conduct relationships in a manner that will enhance the overall marketing effort of the bank.
4. Will be called upon from time to time to participate with community organizations and in community projects.

Data Processing Division

JOB DESCRIPTION: Data Processing Manager
DEPARTMENT/DIVISION: Data Processing
REPORTS TO: Senior Vice President — Operations and Administration
SUPERVISES: Secretary and Receptionist
              Data Processing Officer
              Assistant Data Processing Officer
              CIF Coordinator

JOB SUMMARY

Plan, administer and control all data processing activities of the bank.

DUTIES

1. Select and supervise data processing personnel.
2. Recommend personnel for promotions.
3. Recommend salary increases.
4. Provide professional services for feasibility studies.
5. Select new computer hardware.
6. Select new computer software.
7. Do systems programming.
8. Do some applications programming.
9. Interpret and apply company policies and objectives across all data processing activities.
10. Secretary to the EDP Steering Committee.
11. Member of Pricing Committee.
12. Member of CIF Committee.
13. Call on bank customers (D.P. Services).
14. Trouble-shoot user problems.
15. Negotiate contracts with hardware and software vendors.

ORGANIZATION

1. Initiate changes in the basic organization structure and complement of the planning function in order to accomplish objectives as developed in concert with the Senior Vice President — Operations and Administration.

FINANCES

Prepare the annual budget for Data Processing, administering allotted funds in accordance with the budget and approved fiscal procedures; and, recommend capital expenditures for planning and bank development.

RELATIONSHIPS

1. Responsible to the Senior Vice President — Operations and Administration for the fulfillment of his or her functions, responsibilities, and authority and for their proper interpretation.
2. Will advise and assist department managers, officers, and staff in their respective functions associated with the areas for which he or she has direct responsibility.
3. Will have extensive contact with customers, the public and the community, and is to conduct relationships in a manner that will enhance the overall marketing effort of the bank.
4. Will be called upon from time to time to participate with community organizations and in community projects.

JOB DESCRIPTION: Secretary and Receptionist
DEPARTMENT/DIVISION: Data Processing
REPORTS TO: Vice President and Data Processing Officer
SUPERVISES: Has no supervisory responsibility.

Secretary and Receptionist (continued)

JOB SUMMARY

Acts as receptionist. Types letters. Answers telephone. Handles service bureau billing. May be responsible for handling records on own initiative under limited supervision. Reasonable amount of judgment required.

DUTIES

1. Greet customers.
2. Answer telephone.
3. Take shorthand.
4. Type letters and reports required by department.
5. Handle some confidential records for department.
6. Bill customers.

ORGANIZATION

Has an inherent duty and responsibility to make recommendations to supervisor concerning possible methods to improve department.

FINANCES

Has the responsibility to make recommendations to supervisor concerning the budgetary needs of the department.

RELATIONSHIPS

1. Responsible to the Vice President and Data Processing Officer for the fulfillment of functions, responsibilities, and authority and for their proper interpretation.
2. Will have extensive contact with customers and the public, and is to conduct relationships in a manner that will enhance the overall marketing effort of the bank.
3. Will be called upon from time to time to participate with community organizations and in community projects.

JOB DESCRIPTION: Data Processing Manager
DEPARTMENT/DIVISION: Data Processing
REPORTS TO: Vice President and Data Processing Officer
SUPERVISES: Programmer I
                        Programmer II

JOB SUMMARY

Plan, coordinate, and supervise the implementation and subsequent maintenance of all of the systems and applications software used by bank.

DUTIES

1. Plan and organize all software development and installation.
2. Research problems encountered by user departments.
3. Assign program changes to programmers.
4. Assist programmers when technical questions arise.

5. Review programmer's work.
6. Develop program specifications for new programs.
7. Develop and oversee programming standards.
8. Develop, code, test and document programs in COBOL language.
9. Develop, code, test and document programs in Command level language.
10. Install and maintain program source library software (vollie).
11. Install and maintain IBM system software.
12. Install and maintain Data Entry (Key/Master) software.
13. Install and maintain Audit software (CULPRIT/EDP AUDITOR).
14. Install and maintain central information file (CIF) software.
15. Maintain tables required for IBM CICS software.
16. Create VSAM data bases.
17. Assist DP Manager in selecting new employees.
18. Recommend salary increases for programming staff.

ORGANIZATION

1. Initiate changes in the basic organization structure and complement of the planning function in order to accomplish objectives as developed in concert with the Vice President and Data Processing Officer.
2. Activate new work procedures and systems to accomplish planning and bank development objectives more efficiently.

FINANCES

Prepare the annual budget for Data Processing, administering allotted funds in accordance with the budget and approved fiscal procedures; and, recommend capital expenditures for planning and bank development.

RELATIONSHIPS

1. Responsible to the Vice President and Data Processing Officer for the fulfillment of his or her functions, responsibilities, and authority and for their proper interpretation.
2. Will advise and assist department managers, officers, and staff in their respective functions associated with the areas for which he or she has direct responsibility.
3. Will have extensive contact with customers, the public and the community, and is to conduct relationships in a manner that will enhance the overall marketing effort of the bank.
4. Will be called upon from time to time to participate with community organizations and in community projects.

JOB DESCRIPTION: Assistant Data Processing Officer
DEPARTMENT/DIVISION: Data Processing
REPORTS TO: Vice President and Data Processing Officer
SUPERVISES: Data Entry Clerk
            Operations — First Shift
            Operations — Second Shift

JOB SUMMARY

Supervises operations personnel, maintaining all machines, service bureau contact.

Assistant Data Processing Officer (continued)

DUTIES

1. Operate computer.
2. Contact service bureau customers.
3. Install new equipment.
4. Purchase supplies.
5. Keep tape inventory.
6. Maintain employee relations.
7. Supervise data entry.
8. Supervise computer operations.
9. Communicate directly to customers on data processing matters.
10. Maintain minor equipment problems.
11. Assist night operations by phone.
12. Coordinate data entry with computer operations.

ORGANIZATION

1. Initiate changes in the basic organization structure and complement of the planning function in order to accomplish objectives as developed in concert with the Vice President and Data Processing Officer.
2. Activate new work procedures and systems to accomplish planning and bank development objectives more efficiently.

FINANCES

Prepare the annual budget for Data Processing, administer allotted funds in accordance with the budget and approved fiscal procedures; and, recommend capital expenditures for planning and bank development.

RELATIONSHIPS

1. Responsible to the Vice President and Data Processing Officer for the fulfillment of his or her functions, responsibilities, and authority and for their proper interpretation.
2. Will advise and assist department managers, officers, and staff in their respective functions associated with the areas for which he or she has direct responsibility.
3. Will have extensive contact with customers, the public and the community, and is to conduct relationships in a manner that will enhance the overall marketing effort of the bank.
4. Will be called upon from time to time to participate with community organizations and in community projects.

JOB DESCRIPTION: Systems Analyst
DEPARTMENT/DIVISION: Data Processing
REPORTS TO: Senior Systems Analyst.
SUPERVISES: Has no direct supervisory responsibility.

JOB SUMMARY

Prepares new EDP programs and refines current programs.

DUTIES

1. Confer with bank customers and officers to discuss ideas, objectives, and/or solutions to a proposed EDP program.
2. Design and document entire system for programming.
3. Examine and learn each stage of procedure.
4. Consider the volume, arithmetic formulas, forms and work flow of the data.
5. Review trade journals for pertinent information.
6. Visit, observe, and confer with personnel at other automated business institutions.
7. Develop flow charts.
8. Coordinate the purchase and design of input-output forms, keypunch instructions and familiarization of new duties with client departments.
9. Submit same to EDP officers for a review.
10. Act as the liaison between operating department and EDP management.
11. Assist or perform duties of Senior Systems Analyst as required.
12. Perform duties of Programmer/Analyst as necessary.

ORGANIZATION

Has an inherent duty and responsibility to make recommendations to supervisor concerning possible methods to improve department.

FINANCES

Has the responsibility to make recommendations to supervisor concerning the budgetary needs of the department.

RELATIONSHIPS

Personal contact with bank customers in our computer services program. Some telephone contact with other banks and business concerns.

JOB DESCRIPTION: CIF Coordinator
DEPARTMENT/DIVISION: Data Processing
REPORTS TO: Vice President and Data Processing Officer
SUPERVISES: Has no supervisory responsibility.

JOB SUMMARY

Relieves management of some routine management details. Acts as group leader over other employees while training bank personnel. Schedules and monitors CIF usage using Log reports. Has thorough knowledge of the operation of all equipment in the department. Initiate change requests as needed. Supervises CIF program. Knowledge of bank operations and thorough understanding of bank services are necessary. Exercises a reasonable amount of independent judgment under minimum supervision.

DUTIES

1. Train bank personnel.
2. Monitor CIF usage using Log reports.
3. Initiate change requests.

CIF Coordinator (continued)

4. Notify users of CIF scheduled down time.
5. Update/create CIF documentation.
6. Set up all CICS/CIF security.

ORGANIZATION

Has an inherent duty and responsibility to make recommendations to supervisor concerning possible methods to improve department.

FINANCES

Has the responsibility to make recommendations to supervisor concerning the budgetary needs of the department.

RELATIONSHIPS

1. Responsible to the Vice President and Data Processing Officer for the fulfillment of functions, responsibilities, and authority and for their proper interpretation.
2. Will have extensive contact with customers and the public, and is to conduct relationships in a manner that will enhance the overall marketing effort of the bank.
3. Will be called upon from time to time to participate with community organizations and in community projects.

JOB DESCRIPTION: Programmer I
DEPARTMENT/DIVISION: Data Processing
REPORTS TO: Data Processing Officer
SUPERVISES: Has no supervisory responsibility.

JOB SUMMARY

Writes and maintains application programs under direct supervision of the programming manager. Prepares JCL and systems documentation. Does no systems design work. Works with other departments. Usually works on one item at a time under direct supervision. Is learning to program. Considerable on-the-job training required.

DUTIES

1. Write and maintain applications.
2. Prepare JCL and systems documentation.
3. Work with other departments.
4. Learn to program.

ORGANIZATION

Has an inherent duty and responsibility to make recommendations to supervisor concerning possible methods to improve department.

FINANCES

Has the responsibility to make recommendations to supervisor concerning the budgetary needs of the department.

RELATIONSHIPS

1. Responsible to the Data Processing Officer for the fulfillment of functions, responsibilitites, and authority and for their proper interpretation.
2. Will have extensive contact with customers and the public, and is to conduct relationships in a manner that will enhance the overall marketing effort of the bank.
3. Will be called upon from time to time to participate with community organizations and in community projects.

JOB DESCRIPTION: Programmer II
DEPARTMENT/DIVISION: Data Processing
REPORTS TO: Data Processing Officer
SUPERVISES: Has no supervisory responsibility.

JOB SUMMARY

Writes and maintains application programs with some supervision from programming manager. Prepares JCL and systems documentation. Gives some assistance to junior programmers. Does some systems design work. Requires only some general direction and instruction. Usually works on only one or a few types of applications. Works with other departments.

DUTIES

1. Write and maintain application programs.
2. Prepare JCL and systems documentation.
3. Assist junior programmers.
4. Do some systems design work.
5. Work with other departments.

ORGANIZATION

Has an inherent duty and responsibility to make recommendations to supervisor concerning possible methods to improve department.

FINANCES

Has the responsibility to make recommendations to supervisor concerning the budgetary needs of the department.

RELATIONSHIPS

1. Responsible to the Data Processing Officer for the fulfillment of functions, responsibilities, and authority and for their proper interpretation.
2. Will have extensive contact with customers and the public, and is to conduct relationships in a manner that will enhance the overall marketing effort of the bank.
3. Will be called upon from time to time to participate with community organizations and in community projects.

JOB DESCRIPTION: Keypunch Operator
DEPARTMENT/DIVISION: Data Processing
REPORTS TO: Assistant Data Processing Officer
SUPERVISES: Has no supervisory responsibility.

Keypunch Operator (continued)

JOB SUMMARY
Keypunch and verify all bank work and service bureau work processed by this department.

DUTIES
1. Balance reconciliation.
2. Keypunch DDA, savings, payrolls, accounts, receivables, general ledger, ATM, and safe deposit work and trust work.
3. Balance accounts receivables and payrolls.
4. Set up applications on data screen.
5. Use of Univac Keypunch.
6. Verifying keypunch work.
7. Take amortization on the phone.
8. Keypunch CIF work.

ORGANIZATION
Has an inherent duty and responsibility to make recommendations to supervisor concerning possible methods to improve department.

FINANCES
Has the responsibility to make recommendations to supervisor concerning the budgetary needs of the department.

RELATIONSHIPS
1. Responsible to the Assistant Data Processing Officer for the fulfillment of functions, responsibilities, and authority and for their proper interpretation.
2. Will have extensive contact with customers and the public, and is to conduct relationships in a manner that will enhance the overall marketing effort of the bank.
3. Will be called upon from time to time to participate with community organizations and in community projects.

JOB DESCRIPTION: Data Entry Operator
DEPARTMENT/DIVISION: Data Processing
REPORTS TO: Assistant Data Processing Officer
SUPERVISES: Has no supervisory responsibility.

JOB SUMMARY
Operates Univac and IBM keypunch machines; transcribes information from various documents into punch cards for computer input. Assists with balancing and control work. Exercises minimum independent judgment under maximum supervision.

DUTIES
1. Operate Univac 1710 VIP keypunch machine.
2. Correct errors to punch card input.
3. Assist in balancing entry runs.
4. Assist in balancing and processing service bureau work for computer service users.

ORGANIZATION

Has an inherent duty and responsibility to make recommendations to supervisor concerning possible methods to improve department.

FINANCES

Has the responsibility to make recommendations to supervisor concerning the budgetary needs of the department.

RELATIONSHIPS

1. Responsible to the Assistant Data Processing Officer for functions, responsibilities, and authority and for their proper interpretation.
2. Will have extensive contact with customers and the public, and is to conduct relationships in a manner that will enhance the overall marketing effort of the bank.
3. Will be called upon from time to time to participate with community organizations and in community projects.

JOB DESCRIPTION: Operator III
DEPARTMENT/DIVISION: Data Processing
REPORTS TO: Assistant Data Processing Officer
SUPERVISES: Has no supervisory responsibility.

JOB SUMMARY

Post all daily transactions for all departments, print it, film it, trim it, burst it and back up important disk files to tape.

DUTIES

1. Print tape labels, label tapes, store tapes, input tapes, output tapes, scratch tapes, set up VISA machine with scratch tapes.
2. Print stock paper, 2 part stock, U part stock, payroll checks, payroll deposit slips, payroll register, payroll deductions slips, trust checks, trust statements, trust reviews and summaries, trust envelopes, COD checks, I/C collection cards, I/C late notices, I/C labels, NSF notices, DDA statements.
3. Run all the daily work, end of month, end of quarter, and end of year work for Trust, COD, Commercial Loans, Savings, Installment Loans, and DDA. Also run payroll for many different companies that bank with us.
4. Film important parts of printouts for each department.
5. Trim and burst special forms to be mailed out to the customers for almost each department.
6. Answer all console messages, credit card machine messages, ATM machine messages, and the telephone.
7. Assure that tapes and disk packs are secure in vault and that the computer room is secured before leaving.

ORGANIZATION

Has an inherent duty and responsibility to make recommendations to supervisor concerning possible methods to improve department.

Operator III (continued)

FINANCES

Has the responsibility to make recommendations to supervisor concerning the budgetary needs of the department.

RELATIONSHIPS

1. Responsible to the Assistant Data Processing Officer for the fulfillment of functions, responsibilities, and authority and for their proper interpretation.
2. Will have extensive contact with customers and the public, and is to conduct relationships in a manner that will enhance the overall marketing effort of the bank.
3. Will be called upon from time to time to participate with community organizations and in community projects.

JOB DESCRIPTION: Computer Operations Supervisor
DEPARTMENT/DIVISION: Data Processing
REPORTS TO: Operations Officer
SUPERVISES: Has no direct supervisory responsibility.

JOB SUMMARY

Responsible for all data processing equipment and three shift operation. Maintains the flow of work through the equipment, according to schedule. Recognizes production problems; corrects or recommends correction to other data processing supervisory personnel. Assures the equipment is in good operating order and oversees maintenance of same. Enforces standards and procedures for equipment operation and data security. Directs training program for computer operation personnel. Communicates with shift supervisors to assure continuation and completion of work.

DUTIES

1. Supervise all personnel of three shift operation.
2. Install and enforce standards and procedures for equipment operation, data and installment security, and troubleshooting.
3. Collect pertinent information and report on performance of equipment and resources.
4. Review work schedules and advise management of their impact on equipment and resources.
5. Communicate with shift supervisors and other data processing personnel to insure continuation and completion of work in progress.
6. Produce all data processing jobs according to schedules and standards.
7. Staff equipment operation function.
8. Maintain equipment and related facilities in good working order.

ORGANIZATION

Has an inherent duty and responsibility to make recommendations to supervisor concerning possible methods to improve department.

FINANCES

Has the responsibility to make recommendations to supervisor concerning the budgetary needs of the department.

RELATIONSHIPS

1. Contact with supervisory and managerial personnel within data processing and bank operation.
2. Contact with production control, technical support, area programming managers.
3. Contact with vendors maintenance staff.

JOB DESCRIPTION: Computer Operator
DEPARTMENT/DIVISION: Data Processing
REPORTS TO: Assistant Data Processing Officer
SUPERVISES: Has no supervisory responsibility.

JOB SUMMARY

Operates all computer equipment and runs all work for the day and sets up work for night shift.

DUTIES

1. Set up disk packs.
2. Clean sorter.
3. Run and print all day work (Dealer Floor Plan, Student Loans, Clearing, ACH, ATM, BAC, General Ledger, etc.).
4. Clean tape drives.
5. Send out tapes (mail).
6. Scratch tapes.
7. Get supplies (forms, printer ribbons, etc.).
8. Clean printer.
9. Make sure that all work gets out for the night before.
10. Check console log.

ORGANIZATION

Has an inherent duty and responsibility to make recommendations to supervisor concerning possible methods to improve department.

FINANCES

Has the responsibility to make recommendations to supervisor concerning the budgetary needs of the department.

RELATIONSHIPS

1. Responsible to the Assistant Data Processing Officer for the fulfillment of functions, responsibilities, and authority and for their proper interpretation.

Computer Operator (continued)

2. Will have extensive contact with customers and the public, and is to conduct relationships in a manner that will enhance the overall marketing effort of the bank.
3. Will be called upon from time to time to participate with community organizations and in community projects.

JOB DESCRIPTION: Computer Operator
DEPARTMENT/DIVISION: Data Processing
REPORTS TO: Assistant Data Processing Officer
SUPERVISES: Has no supervisory responsibility.

JOB SUMMARY

Operates all computer equipment and processes all data for bank and Service Bureau.

DUTIES

1. Mount disk packs.
2. Mount magnetic tapes.
3. Clean tape drives.
4. Submit jobs.
5. Post totals.
6. Balancing (occasional).
7. Run transits (checks, deposits, etc.).
8. Print special forms.
9. Mount forms.
10. Film data.
11. Trim and burst data.
12. Deculate data.
13. Send out microfiche (occasional).
14. Sort data.

ORGANIZATION

Has an inherent duty and responsibility to make recommendations to supervisor concerning possible methods to improve department.

FINANCES

Has the responsibility to make recommendations to supervisor concerning the budgetary needs of the department.

RELATIONSHIPS

1. Responsible to the Assistant Data Processing Officer for the fulfillment of functions, responsibilities, and authority and for their proper interpretation.
2. Will have extensive contact with customers and the public, and is to conduct relationships in a manner that will enhance the overall marketing effort of the bank.
3. Will be called upon from time to time to participate with community organizations and in community projects.

JOB DESCRIPTION: Data Entry Operator
DEPARTMENT/DIVISION: Data Processing
REPORTS TO: Assistant Data Processing Officer
SUPERVISES: Has no supervisory responsibility.

JOB SUMMARY
Punches and verifies all work processed by the Data Processing Department.

DUTIES
1. Key and/or verify: payrolls, trust, bonds, general ledger, accounts receivable, deposit advice, repurchase agreements, Christmas Club, rejects from reconciliation runs, amortization schedules, safe deposits, career interest, programs for programmers, changes to the central information file, labels, DDA, savings, and automatic savings transfers.
2. Balance: City Hospital, and Christmas Club.
3. Balance: payrolls, accounts receivable. After they're processed, separate and check, then deliver to customers. Deliver: quarterly reports, tapes to UPS, pick up payrolls at bus station, carry back up tapes to off-site location at University branch.
4. Call customers toward the end of each quarter for quarterly reports, pull date cards and changes dates for O/E; after reports are processed, check; then separate and deliver to customers.
5. At year end, call customers for an OK to run W-2's, pull date cards, change dates; after processed, check; then separate and deliver to customers.
6. Set up all date cards, deduction cards, 941 and W-2 cards for new customers.
7. Make all necessary changes or updates on payroll, 941 and W-2 cards.
8. Train new employees.
9. Fill out supply requisition for data entry and operations; go to supply room for supplies.
10. Help customers with accounts receivable or payroll related problems.
11. Design and write new applications on Keymaster for Data Entry. Make changes to existing applications.
12. Fill in for Data Processing Secretary, call customers to give net payroll totals, balance secretary's work and take to proof for processing. Code charge tickets for customer billing, take amortization schedules, sign payroll checks.

ORGANIZATION
Has an inherent duty and responsibility to make recommendations to supervisor concerning possible methods to improve department.

FINANCES
Has the responsibility to make recommendations to supervisor concerning the budgetary needs of the department.

RELATIONSHIPS
1. Responsible to the Assistant Data Processing Officer for the fulfillment of functions, responsibilities, and authority and for their proper interpretation.
2. Will have extensive contact with customers and the public, and is to conduct relationships in a manner that will enhance the overall marketing effort of the bank.
3. Will be called upon from time to time to participate with community organizations and in community projects.

JOB DESCRIPTION: Computer Operator I
DEPARTMENT/DIVISION: Data Processing
REPORTS TO: Assistant Data Processing Officer
SUPERVISES: Has no supervisory responsibility.

JOB SUMMARY

Responsible for production runs; balancing and control of the daily and periodical work load; maintains stock room and records vault. Familiar with operation of all existing data processing equipment. Exercises a minimum of judgment under maximum supervision.

DUTIES

1. Operate the following equipment:
    A. 1419 check reader.
    B. 3505 card reader.
    C. 3525 card punch.
    D. 3330 disc drives.
    E. 3410 tape drives.
    F. 1403 printer.
    G. Forms burster.
    H. Filmer.
    I. Decolator.
    J. Key punch.
2. Keep records and files in stock room.

ORGANIZATION

Has an inherent duty and responsibility to make recommendations to supervisor concerning possible methods to improve department.

FINANCES

Has the responsibility to make recommendations to supervisor concerning the budgetary needs of the department.

RELATIONSHIPS

1. Responsible to the Assistant Data Processing Officer for the fulfillment of functions, responsibilities, and authority and for their proper interpretation.
2. Will have extensive contact with customers and the public, and is to conduct relationships in a manner that will enhance the overall marketing effort of the bank.
3. Will be called upon from time to time to participate with community organizations and in community projects.

JOB DESCRIPTION: Documentation Librarian
DEPARTMENT/DIVISION: Data Processing
REPORTS TO: Special Services Manager.
SUPERVISES: Has no direct supervisory responsibilities.

JOB SUMMARY

Responsible for the control, retention, storage and distribution of master documentation files.

DUTIES

1. Review documentation of new systems to ensure adherence to standards.
2. Control and maintain storage of acceptable documents.
3. Receive documentation revisions and update files.
4. Release documentation as per proper authorization (i.e. program status and control form, PSAC)
5. Maintain files of documentation release authorization.
6. Serve as backup for Security Scheduler.
7. Review console logs daily for operation exceptions.
8. Maintain CICS, ICCF, CIF, and Doscheck Security files.
9. Control ICCF source module libraries to ensure modules are not lost/destroyed.

ORGANIZATION

Has an inherent duty and responsibility to make recommendations to supervisor concerning possible methods to improve department.

FINANCES

Has the responsibility to make recommendations to supervisor concerning the budgetary needs of the department.

RELATIONSHIPS

Some personal contact with bank personnel.

Auditing Division

JOB DESCRIPTION: Auditor
DEPARTMENT/DIVISION: Auditing
REPORTS TO: Examining Committee, Board of Directors
SUPERVISES: Secretary
                    Assistant Auditor

JOB SUMMARY

Review Internal Controls operating in all areas of the bank.

DUTIES

1. Schedule audits.
2. Assign personnel.
3. Review work performed.
4. Coordinate audit work with external auditors.
5. Coordinate audits with regulatory authorities.
6. Conduct special audits (robberies, embezzlements).
7. Represent bank in legal matters, including special audits above.
8. Coordinate activities of the examining committee in an attempt to aid them in the discharge of their duties and responsibilities as directors.
9. Participate in the feasibility studies including purchase and design of new systems.

Auditor (continued)

ORGANIZATION

1. Initiate changes in the basic organization structure and complement of the planning function in order to accomplish objectives as developed in concert with the Examining Committee, Board of Directors.
2. Activate new work procedures and systems to accomplish planning and bank development objectives more efficiently.

FINANCES

Prepare the annual budget for Auditing, administering allotted funds in accordance with the budget and approved fiscal procedures; and, recommend capital expenditures for planning and bank development.

RELATIONSHIPS

1. Responsible to the Examining Committee and Board of Directors for the fulfillment of his or her functions, responsibilities, and authority and for their proper interpretation.
2. Will advise and assist department managers, officers, and staff in their respective functions associated with the areas for which he or she has direct responsibility.
3. Will have extensive contact with customers, the public and the community, and is to conduct relationships in a manner that will enhance the overall marketing effort of the bank.
4. Will be called upon from time to time to participate with community organizations and in community projects.

JOB DESCRIPTION: Secretary
DEPARTMENT/DIVISION: Auditing
REPORTS TO: Auditor
SUPERVISES: Has no supervisory responsibility.

JOB SUMMARY

Performs general secretarial/clerical responsibilities as needed for the Auditing Department.

DUTIES

1. Balance daily trust work.
2. Record teller's cash differences daily.
3. Monthly cash limit exception report.
4. Monthly teller's overage and shortage report.
5. Monthly teller's year to date overage and shortage report.
6. Balance Travelers Check Statement.
7. File Bait Money Listing and Reports.
8. File cash difference $10.00 or more reports.
9. Balance and reconcile teller's cash count sheets to the general ledger.
10. Type monthly reports.
11. Checking account confirmations.
12. Saving account confirmations.
13. Dormant saving account confirmations.

14. Charge off report and confirmations.
15. Accountant confirmations.
16. List employee overdrafts.
17. Prepare list of employee opened and closed accounts.
18. Stock supply cabinet.
19. Record and mail returned coupon books.
20. Reconcile time deposit open accounts.
21. Type Examining Committee and Board of Directors reports.
22. File miscellaneous files.

ORGANIZATION

Has an inherent duty and responsibility to make recommendations to supervisor concerning possible methods to improve department.

FINANCES

Has the responsibility to make recommendations to supervisor concerning the budgetary needs of the department.

RELATIONSHIPS

1. Responsible to the Auditor for the fulfillment of functions, responsibilities, and authority and for their proper interpretation.
2. Will have extensive contact with customers and the public, and is to conduct relationships in a manner that will enhance the overall marketing effort of the bank.
3. Will be called upon from time to time to participate with community organizations and in community projects.

JOB DESCRIPTION: Assistant Auditor
DEPARTMENT/DIVISION: Auditing
REPORTS TO: Auditor
SUPERVISES: Audit Clerk

JOB SUMMARY

Ensures that assets are properly safeguarded and liabilities are properly recorded through review of internal controls within the department and the bank.

DUTIES

1. Write and revise audit programs.
2. Perform audit procedures.
3. Review work of assistants.
4. Write audit report.
5. Assist external auditors.
6. Work with bank examiners.
7. Assist in budgeting and planning.
8. Perform special reviews at management's request.
9. Supervise audit clerk.

Assistant Auditor (continued)

ORGANIZATION

1. Initiate changes in the basic organization structure and complement of the planning function in order to accomplish objectives as developed in concert with the Auditor.
2. Activate new work procedures and systems to accomplish planning and bank development objectives more efficiently.

FINANCES

Prepare the annual budget for Auditing, administering allotted funds in accordance with the budget and approved fiscal procedures; and, recommend capital expenditures for planning and bank development.

RELATIONSHIPS

1. Responsible to the Auditor for the fulfillment of his or her functions, responsibilities, and authority and for their proper interpretation.
2. Will advise and assist department managers, officers, and staff in their respective functions associated with the areas for which he or she has direct responsibility.
3. Will have extensive contact with customers, the public and the community, and is to conduct relationships in a manner that would enhance the overall marketing effort of the bank.
4. Will be called upon from time to time to participate with community organizations and in community projects.

JOB DESCRIPTION: Audit Clerk
DEPARTMENT/DIVISION: Auditing
REPORTS TO: Assistant Auditor
SUPERVISES: Has no supervisory responsibility.

JOB SUMMARY

Advanced clerical work requiring prior work experience or training. Deals with moderately complex operations. Requires some specialized knowledge of auditing procedures. Prepares various reports and reviews some departmental records. Handles complete audits of small operational areas under direct supervision. Assists Auditor and Assistant Auditor in audits of all areas of the bank. Work is performed under minimum supervision in most instances. Certain aspects of the job require some degree of independent judgment.

DUTIES

1. Prepare Accountant's Confirmation Inquiries.
2. Schedule customer account verifications.
3. Review teller differences and prepare monthly reports.
4. Review loans charged off, trace amounts to loan department records and prepare monthly reports.
5. Reconcile weekly reports from Federal Reserve Bank of securities being held for our bank.
6. Review all Trust Department security transactions and control all pending entries.

ORGANIZATION

Has an inherent duty and responsibility to make recommendations to supervisor concerning possible methods to improve department.

FINANCES

Has the responsibility to make recommendations to supervisor concerning the budgetary needs of the department.

RELATIONSHIPS

1. Responsible to the Assistant Auditor for the fulfillment of functions, responsibilities, and authority and for their proper interpretation.
2. Will have extensive contact with customers and the public, and is to conduct relationships in a manner that will enhance the overall marketing effort of the bank.
3. Will be called upon from time to time to participate with community organizations and in community projects.

JOB DESCRIPTION: EDP Auditor
DEPARTMENT/DIVISION: Audit
REPORTS TO: EDP Auditor.
SUPERVISES: Has no direct supervisory responsibility.

JOB SUMMARY

Analyzes computer systems to discover problems and then implement solutions.

DUTIES

1. Study new EDP equipment and programs.
2. Verify external back up for computer processing data.
3. Review internal EDP bank programs.
4. Recommend possible alternatives for new programs.
5. Verify legitimacy and propriety of all internal bank program changes.
6. Evaluate possible future EDP problems.
7. Determine procedures employed by each EDP system.
8. Coordinate and assemble new system designs in both soft/hardware.
9. Furnish audit personnel with information on same.
10. Analyze individual programs comprising the systems' procedures.
11. Facilitate work between user and computer systems.
12. Design generalized audit software.
13. Perform acceptance testing of new EDP system, i.e., before installation of system, (review of controls).
14. Perform post-installation audits of controls in an installed application.
15. Review audit workpapers of other EDP audit programmers.
16. Participate with EDP Audit Officer in evaluating and recommending changes for audit procedures related to EDP.

EDP Auditor (continued)

ORGANIZATION

Has an inherent duty and responsibility to make recommendations to supervisor concerning possible methods to improve department.

FINANCES

Has the responsibility to make recommendations to supervisor concerning the budgetary needs of the department.

RELATIONSHIPS

Considerable personal and telephone contact with audit personnel, trainees, and other bank employees.

JOB DESCRIPTION: Account Receivable Auditor
DEPARTMENT/DIVISION: Audit
REPORTS TO: Senior Accounts Receivable Auditor.
SUPERVISES: Has no direct supervisory responsibility.

JOB SUMMARY

Examines books of Account Receivable client companies.

DUTIES

1. Visit client's premises.
2. Examine, verify, and analyze collateral, books, records, management and physical facilities, balance sheet accounts, i.e. account receivables, inventory, and cash transactions.
3. Interpret financial statements.
4. Write examination report including significant trends, adherence to contract requirements, and unusual transactions or situations.
5. Assist in determining companies' collateral value and account administration.
6. Complete special audit examinations as requested.
7. Assist officers in liquidation of account receivables.
8. Review adequacy of verification and posting procedures involved with accounts receivable companies.
9. Assist Senior Account Receivable Auditor with new business surveys.

ORGANIZATION

Has an inherent duty and responsibility to make recommendations to supervisor concerning possible methods to improve department.

FINANCES

Has the responsibility to make recommendations to supervisor concerning the budgetary needs of the department.

RELATIONSHIPS

Considerable personal contact with customers and bank personnel.

JOB DESCRIPTION: Account Receivable Clerk
DEPARTMENT/DIVISION: Audit
REPORTS TO: Account Receivable Supervisor.
SUPERVISES: Has no direct supervisory responsibility.

JOB SUMMARY
Maintains ledgers, files, and records on Account Receivable loans.

DUTIES
1. Receive and record payments on assigned invoices, and contracts in ledgers.
2. Settle same daily.
3. Verify aging of collateral assigned.
4. Verify calculations on documents for assignment and notification of assignment.
5. Maintain (daily) record of availability of funds.
6. Post assignment and collection data to same.
7. Reconcile (daily and monthly) customer's balance to control.
8. Run tapes on sales invoices supporting individual assignment.
9. Maintain general ledger accounts on same.
10. Maintain files on credit information, interest accrual ledgers, yearly loan interest, service charges, audits, contract fees, loan balances, financing statements and credit insurance policies.
11. Calculate daily interest on loans.
12. Decrease or increase loan rate changes as instructed. Assist other department personnel as necessary.
13. Maintain (daily) restricted bookkeeping accounts for payments on loans.
14. Buy and sell loans as instructed.
15. Maintain detail receivable ledgers, aging reports received, and note portfolio.
16. Enter in journal (daily) loan transactions and rates for other bank departments.

ORGANIZATION
Has an inherent duty and responsibility to make recommendations to supervisor concerning possible methods to improve department.

FINANCES
Has the responsibility to make recommendations to supervisor concerning the budgetary needs of the department.

RELATIONSHIPS
Some telephone contact with bank personnel.

Purchasing Department

JOB DESCRIPTION: Check Imprinter
DEPARTMENT/DIVISION: Purchasing
REPORTS TO: Check Imprint Supervisor.
SUPERVISES: Has no direct supervisory responsibility.

Check Imprinter (continued)

JOB SUMMARY

Operates MICR Check Imprinter to print customers' name and account numbers on checkbooks and deposit tickets.

DUTIES

1. Receive mail and telephone orders for checks and deposits tickets.
2. Sort orders.
3. Pull plates to match orders.
4. Verify addresses and account numbers.
5. Print checks.
6. Staple backs to same.
7. Mail checks to customers.
8. Maintain record of checks printed.
9. Test quality of magnetic coding via MICR Tester.
10. Remove and destroy plates for closed accounts.

ORGANIZATION

Has an inherent duty and responsibility to make recommendations to supervisor concerning possible methods to improve department.

FINANCES

Has the responsibility to make recommendations to supervisor concerning the budgetary needs of the department.

RELATIONSHIPS

Occasional telephone contact with customers and bank personnel.

JOB DESCRIPTION: Stock Room Clerk
DEPARTMENT/DIVISION: Purchasing
REPORTS TO: Stock Room Supervisor.
SUPERVISES: Has no direct supervisory responsibility.

JOB SUMMARY

Stores and distributes bank forms to various bank departments and branches.

DUTIES

1. Receive bank forms and supplies from print shop and outside suppliers.
2. Store same within stock room.
3. Distribute stock items within building per requisition for same.
4. Wrap and send stock items to other offices as requested.
5. Assist in maintaining inventory record of supplies.
6. Inform supervisor of stock reaching predetermined minimum quantity for re-order. Substitute for Supervisor as necessary.

ORGANIZATION

Has an inherent duty and responsibility to make recommendations to supervisor concerning possible methods to improve department.

FINANCES

Has the responsibility to make recommendations to supervisor concerning the budgetary needs of the department.

JOB DESCRIPTION: Coin Machine Operator
DEPARTMENT/DIVISION: Purchasing
REPORTS TO: Coin Supervisor.
SUPERVISES: Has no direct supervisory responsibility.

JOB SUMMARY

Operates Coin Machines to sort, count and wrap loose coin.

DUTIES

1. Sort, count, and wrap loose coin from tellers, correspondent banks, customers and Federal Reserve shipments.
2. Review coins for slugs, foreign coins, mutilated coins and shortages in bags of coin received.
3. Load and unload coin transported by armored service.
4. Unload delivery shipments of coin tubes, wrapping paper and other supplies from delivery truck.
5. Inventory and store supplies received.
6. Package coin for shipment to branches and other banks.
7. Assemble bulk coin shipments to branches and customers.
8. Stack sufficient rolled coin for future orders.
9. Receive, sort, and forward cloth money bags to branches and other banks.
10. Repair minor equipment malfunctions as possible.
11. Open and close coin vault compartments in conjunction with Coin Room Supervisor.
12. Assist Supervisor in daily vault settlement.
13. Assist Lottery Clerk in sorting and receiving lottery return tickets.
14. Assemble and package same for shipment to lottery headquarters.

ORGANIZATION

Has an inherent duty and responsibility to make recommendations to supervisor concerning possible methods to improve department.

FINANCES

Has the responsibility to make recommendations to supervisor concerning the budgetary needs of the department.

JOB DESCRIPTION: Currency Proof Clerk
DEPARTMENT/DIVISION: Purchasing
REPORTS TO: Coin Room Manager and Senior Currency Proof Clerk
SUPERVISES: Has no direct supervisory responsibility.

JOB SUMMARY

Counts, sorts and proves bulk currency deposits received.

DUTIES

1. Sort mutilated currency in deposits received.
2. Maintain and operate Fast Cash Machine to bundle currency for payrolls.
3. Sort, verify, and bundle finished bands of currency.
4. Package same with Heat Sealer.
5. Prove payroll currency.
6. Open, verify, count, and settle deposits from Abbotts Dairies.
7. Locate and correct errors in same per specific instructions.
8. Count and verify food coupon deposits.
9. Settle same (daily) per deposit.
10. Assist Senior Currency Proof Clerk in Currency settlement.
11. Perform duties of Safe Deposit Clerk and Senior Currency Proof Clerk as necessary.

ORGANIZATION

Has an inherent duty and responsibility to make recommendations to supervisor concerning possible methods to improve department.

FINANCES

Has the responsibility to make recommendations to supervisor concerning the budgetary needs of the department.

JOB DESCRIPTION: Receiving Teller
DEPARTMENT/DIVISION: Purchasing
REPORTS TO: Coin Room Manager.
SUPERVISES: Has no direct supervisory responsibility.

JOB SUMMARY

Receives and proves deposits from armored delivery and customers.

DUTIES

1. Prove bulk deposits received.
2. Locate and correct errors in same.
3. Notify customer (by phone) of deposit differences on same.
4. Receive (by phone) instructions from customers on same.
5. Refer same to Coin & Currency Supervisor.
6. Sort checks in deposits.
7. Forward same to Clearing.
8. Charge coin and currency to appropriate departments.

9. Count small deposits and "odd lots" of coin and currency.
10. Verify and prove same.
11. Mail receipts to customers for deposits.
12. Remove previous nights deposits from night depository (dual control function).
13. Maintain records of same.
14. Prove food coupons received from deposits.
15. Credit same with currency deposit.
16. Sort bond coupons in deposits.
17. Forward same to Collection.
18. Credit appropriate account with same.
19. Maintain and complete settlement of receiving function.
20. Assist with department settlement.
21. Assist (daily) in removal of tellers boxes from vault.

ORGANIZATION

Has an inherent duty and responsibility to make recommendations to supervisor concerning possible methods to improve department.

FINANCES

Has the responsibility to make recommendations to supervisor concerning the budgetary needs of the department.

RELATIONSHIPS

1. Some personal contact with armored delivery carriers.
2. Some telephone contact with customers.

13

INTERNATIONAL DEPARTMENT JOB DESCRIPTIONS

International trade, money flows for investment and payments, and loans to governments and official institutions as well as to the private sector are all critical aspects of the international department of a bank.

The job descriptions which follow detail the particulars of two key positions in the international department.

JOB DESCRIPTION: Standby & Export Letter of Credit Issuer
DEPARTMENT/DIVISION: International
REPORTS TO: Assistant Vice President
SUPERVISES: Has no direct supervisory responsibilities.

JOB SUMMARY
Issues standby letters of credit and export letters of credit and their amendments. Deposits and withdraws standby letter of credit collateral to and from safekeeping facilities and maintains collateral history records.

DUTIES
1. Issue standby letters of credit after reviewing letter of credit application form and any additional legal wording submitted and possibly revising text. Prepare covering letters to beneficiary and accountee and line of credit officer approval form. Compute commission and prepares all

liability and commission ticket entries. Maintain ticklers for expiration dates of standby credits and advises account officers and customers of same.

2. Receive all export letters of credit and amendments by mail or telex and prepare necessary forms and letters to advise beneficiary and acknowledge receipt to issuing bank. Telexed credits may necessitate transcribing the wording from a correspondent bank code book to our export letter of credit advising form.
3. Maintain negotiable and non-negotiable collateral records for collateralized standby letters of credit, deposits and withdraws same from vault and department safe. Maintain ticklers for maturities of savings instruments and for clipping bond coupons etc.
4. Compose and send telex messages for above matters and for other members of the International Division.
5. Answer customer requests for guidance on rules and regulations regarding letters of credit.
6. Perform the International Division's daily settlement of general ledger entries on a rotating basis with other personnel.
7. When time allows perform the import letter of credit issuance and amendment duties.

ORGANIZATION

Has an inherent duty and responsibility to make recommendations to supervisor concerning possible methods to improve department.

FINANCES

Has the responsibility to make recommendations to supervisor concerning the budgetary needs of the department.

RELATIONSHIPS

Frequent telephone contact and mail communication with customers and other bank personnel.

JOB DESCRIPTION: Documentary & Foreign Currency Supervisor
DEPARTMENT/DIVISION: Commercial-International
REPORTS TO: Vice President and Assistant Vice President.
SUPERVISES: 3 International Clerks, 1 International Clerk-Teller, and 1 Clerk-Typist.

JOB SUMMARY

Supervises function of document checking and foreign currency control.

DUTIES

1. Record (monthly) documentary and foreign currency activity.
2. Maintain controls on same.
3. Buy and sell foreign currency.
4. Issue foreign drafts.
5. Transfer funds by cable and air mail.
6. Examine and verify documents including transmittal letters, commercial and customer invoices, drafts, bills of lading, etc. against letters of credit.
7. Authorize cashiers checks on letters of credit and payment orders from abroad.
8. Compute bank commissions.

Documentary & Foreign Currency Supervisor (continued)

9. Advise (by phone and mail) customer of same.
10. Attend (monthly) International conferences.
11. Solicit new business at same.
12. Answer (phone, mail, and in person) inquiries from customers and bank personnel on exchange rates, regulations governing foreign exchange, and import-export regulations regarding foreign currency.
13. Assist supervised personnel with difficult customer inquiries and settlement problems.
14. Complete entries on foreign currency to General Accounting and Checking.
15. Recommend salary adjustments for supervised personnel.
16. Substitute for Letters of Credit & Foreign Collections Supervisor as necessary.

ORGANIZATION
Has an inherent duty and responsibility to make recommendations to supervisor concerning possible methods to improve department.

FINANCES
Has the responsibility to make recommendations to supervisor concerning the budgetary needs of the department.

RELATIONSHIPS
Frequent personal, telephone, and mail contact with customers, other banks, bank institutions, and bank personnel.

PART THREE

Appendixes

Appendixes I-IV feature many items which might help you in putting together useful job descriptions. The appendixes are all arranged alphabetically for easy reference.

The action verbs list in appendix I lists many action verbs which are relevant to bank job descriptions. Since the effective job description uses action verbs to clarify duties and responsibilities, this list can be a good starting point for you.

The words to watch in appendix II, while not all-inclusive, includes many words that are either tricky or often used incorrectly. If you have a question about how a word or phrase should be used, consult appendix II.

The grammar hotline directory in appendix III consists of names of various universities and colleges across the country which offer help with grammar problems to people who call. You might find it useful to turn to one of these hotlines if you are stumped by grammar or usage problems when writing your job descriptions.

The bibliography lists articles and books which might help you when you begin your job description program. Much has been written about job description format and usage. The publications listed in appendix IV highlight a few of the better references available on the subject.

APPENDIX I

ACTION VERBS LIST

A

Accept
Acquire
Act
Activate
Add
Adjust
Administer
Advise
Allocate
Alphabetize
Analyze
Answer
Arrange
Assign
Assist
Attend
Audit
Authorize

B

Balance
Bill
Buy

C

Calculate
Call
Cancel
Carry
Cash
Change
Charge
Check
Clean
Clip
Close
Collate
Collect
Communicate
Compile
Complete
Consult
Contact
Control
Convey
Cook
Coordinate
Correct
Correspond
Counsel
Count

D

Deal
Delegate
Delete
Deposit
Design
Determine
Develop
Dictate
Direct
Disburse
Distribute
Divide

E

Emboss
Encode
Enter
Establish
Evaluate
Execute

F

Figure
File
Film
Fold
Follow-up

G

Generate
Greet
Guarantee

H

Handle
Haul
Help
Hold

I

Improve
Initiate
Input
Install
Instruct
Insure
Interview
Investigate
Issue

K

Keep
Keypunch

L

Learn
Lift
List
Listen
Load
Log
Look

M

Mail
Maintain
Manage
Mark
Match
Meet
Microfilm
Monitor
Mount
Multiply

N

Notarize

O

Observe
Obtain
Open
Operate
Order
Oversee

P

Participate
Pay
Perform
Photograph
Place
Plan
Post
Prepare
Present
Price
Process
Provide
Pull

Q

Quote
Query

R

Read
Receive
Recommend
Reconcile
Record
Redeem
Refer
Refund
Reimburse
Reissue
Reject
Relate
Relieve
Renew
Report
Repossess
Represent
Request
Requisition
Research
Retain
Review
Revise
Route
Run

S

Schedule
Scratch
Secure
Select
Sell
Send
Separate
Serve
Service
Settle
Ship
Sign
Solicit
Solve
Sort

Staff
Stock
Structure
Study
Submit
Subscribe
Supervise
Supply
Survey
Synthesize

T

Take
Tape

Teach
Tear
Telephone
Throw
Trace
Train
Transcribe
Transfer
Transmit
Turn
Type

U

Undertake
Update

V

Value
Verify

W

Watch
Wire
Write

APPENDIX II

WORDS TO
WATCH

acknowledge with thanks or **acknowledge receipt of**   Using the words "thank you" is a more direct way of expressing gratitude after receiving something.

affect vs. **effect**   When used as verbs, affect means "to influence"; *effect* means "to accomplish." Both words can also be used as nouns. Affect, as a noun, is usually only used in a psychological context. When the construction calls for a noun, and you are not using the word in a psychological sense, you will almost always use effect.

aforesaid   Write "named" or "mentioned earlier."

after the conclusion of   Write "after."

along these lines   Another trite expression to avoid.

all right   Always written as two words.

allude vs. **elude**   You allude to a piece of literature. You elude someone chasing you.

a lot   Always written as two words.

alternative   Means the choice between two possibilities. In constructions such as "no other alternative," the word "other" is unnecessary.

amounting to or **in the amount of**   Write "for" or "of" or "totalling."

and/or   Avoid the use of and/or unless it is absolutely necessary as a legal term. It destroys the flow of a sentence and causes confusion or ambiguity.

anybody   An indefinite pronoun meaning "any person." Should be written as one word, as should "somebody," "nobody," and "everybody." If you are writing about a body that was looked for but not found, you could write, "The investigators did not find any body." Such usage would be rare in banking.

anyone   Best written as one word unless meaning, "any one of them," as in the sentence: "He didn't like any one of them."

arrived enclosing   Write "enclosed with."

as of even date herewith   Unclear. Merely give the date.

as per copy   Instead of writing, "We wrote you last Friday as per copy enclosed," it is clearer to write, "We have enclosed a copy," or "Enclosed you will find a copy . . .".

as requested   It is a little more personal to write "you requested," "you described," or "you mentioned."

as soon as possible   Give a specific date when possible.

as to   Write "about."

as to whether   Write "whether."

as yet   Write "yet."

at   Do not use after the word, "where."

attached hereto   Forget the hereto, write "attached."

at the present time or **at this time** or **at this writing**   Write "now" whenever possible, instead of these words.

attorney vs. **lawyer**   A lawyer who has a client is an attorney.

bad or **badly**   The adjective "bad" is used after verbs of the sense — smell, sound, feel, look, taste. For example, "he looks bad" or "it tastes bad." Badly indicates manner. For example, "he was hurt badly in the accident."

beside vs. **besides**   Beside means at the side of. Besides means in addition to or other than. Sometimes the use of besides can result in an ambiguous sentence, such as: "Something besides the defaulted loan caused us to sever business ties." It would be best to clarify by writing, "in addition to the defaulted loan," or "other than the defaulted loan."

between vs. **among**   Where the number exceeds two, use among for both persons and things. Between is a preposition which takes the objective pronoun.

bimonthly   Every two months.

biweekly   Every two weeks. (Sometimes bimonthly is used to mean "twice a month" and biweekly to mean, "twice a week." The preferred usages, however, are the ones I have given here.)

both alike   Both is superfluous. Write "alike."

by means of   Write "by."

calling for   Often used needlessly. In a sentence such as: "A proposal calling for seventy shares," the word "calling" can be omitted.

communication   Avoid using to mean a letter, telegram, or conversation. Use the specific reference.

contact   Use more specific words, like "talked to," "wrote," or "called."

data vs. **datum**   The plural form data is generally used, and it takes a plural verb. The singular reference is datum.

different from vs. **different than**   Things differ *from* one another. Write "different from."

direct vs. **directly**   Direct is both an adjective and an adverb. "The man was sent direct (or directly) to Chicago." The sentence, "The officer made a direct trip to Chicago," takes the adjective "direct." Directly is always an adverb, as in the sentence, "We remit directly to a beneficiary if there is no intermediary."

disinterested   Means impartial. Do not confuse with the word, "uninterested."

drop in or **drop a line**   Avoid using these colloquialisms in your letters.

due to the fact that   Write "because."

early convenience   Encourages delay. Be more specific.

enclosed herewith   Forget the herewith, write "enclosed."

enclosed please find   Write "enclosed is."

etc.   Don't use unless the omitted context is understood. Because the meaning of *et cetera* is "and so forth," you would never write "and etc." or "etc. etc."

equally as well   Write "equally well."

factor   Overused. Instead of writing "Good salesmanship is an important factor in loan administration," write "Good salesmanship is important to loan administration."

farther vs. **further**   Farther refers to distance. Further refers to discourse or to something additional. The distinction between these two words is blurred by many writers who also use further to refer to distance. Eventually, this usage may become acceptable.

for your information   Usually superfluous.

going over   Write "examine," "look over," "read."

hopefully   An adverb meaning "with hope" or "in a hopeful manner." It is used incorrectly by many writers to mean "I hope."

however   Best used in the middle of a sentence. When however is used at the beginning of a sentence, it usually means "to whatever extent."

i.e. vs. **e.g.**   I.e. is an abbreviation for *id est*, which means "that is" and is set off by commas in a sentence. E.g. is an abbreviation for *exempli grata* which means "for example" and is set off by commas in a sentence.

in position   Implies "at attention," or "standing around." Write "prepared," "ready," "willing," or "available."

in receipt of   Write "we (I) have received," or "we (I) have."

in reference to or **in regard to** or **in reply to**   Write "concerning," "proposing," "inquiring about," or "suggesting."

in the last analysis   Trite expression. Don't use.

in which you enclosed   Write "with which you enclosed." Information is given *in* a letter. You receive an enclosure *with* a letter.

irregardless   Not a word. The proper word is "regardless."

its vs. **it's**   Its shows possession. It's is a contraction for "it is."

like vs. **as**   Like is a preposition which introduces a prepositional phrase and is used to compare things: "He looks like his mother." As is usually used as a conjunction and introduces a subordinate clause (Clauses have a subject and a verb.): "He acts as his mother did."

matter   Too general a term. Use the specific word: "problem," "request," "subject," "question," or whatever you may be writing about.

most   Don't substitute for almost. Write "almost everyone," instead of "most everyone."

myself, ourselves, himself, herself, yourself (pronouns ending in -self)   Avoid using as the subject in a sentence. Write "Max and I are approving the loan," instead of "Max and myself . . .". Pronouns ending in -self are used for reference and emphasis in a sentence. In the sentence, "I approved the loan myself," myself emphasizes I.

neither, nor and **either, or**   These correlatives should be kept together.

party vs. **person**   Use party as a legal reference. Person should be used in ordinary reference.

people vs. **persons**   Use people when referring to large groups; persons for small groups.

per   Use of per is acceptable in an economic context, such as "twenty shares per dollar." Although it has been said to avoid mixing Latin and English, and "per" is Latin, if the construction is made less awkward by using per, use it. Avoid writing "per your letter" or "per my last letter," however, because this fills your writing with technical jargon.

please be advised that   Avoid this wordy construction.

previous experience   Write, "Our experience with this person," instead of "Our previous experience."

principal vs. **principle**   Principle refers to basic truths. Principal, as an adjective, means "leading" or "chief." As a noun, principal means either a person in charge or, in finance, capital.

shall vs. **will**   The rule that "shall" is the future indicative of to be in the first person and "will" in the second and third person, and that to express determination the forms are reversed, is no longer followed by most people in the United States. "Shall" sounds too lofty to many people's ears and is avoided. Most educated people use will instead of shall in their writing.

taking this opportunity   Instead of writing, "We are taking this opportunity to thank you," write, "We thank you."

than vs. **then**   Than is used for comparison. Then is used to indicate time.

that vs. **which**   A simple rule is to use the pronoun "which" if the clause it modifies can be separated from the rest of the sentence with commas. Otherwise use "that."

thereafter   Too lofty. Use "after that" when possible.

this will acknowledge receipt of your letter   An answer to a person's letter will let him or her know it was received.

transpire   Means "to become known." Used incorrectly to mean "occur" or "happen."

try and vs. **try to**   Write "try to."

under date of   Write "on," "dated," or "of."

under separate cover   Write, "we are sending separately," or "you will receive."

unique   There are no degrees of uniqueness. "Very unique," "most unique," or "extremely unique" are incorrect.

utilize   Inflated language for "use."

via   Means "by way of" (geographically), and is properly used as a railroad, airline, or steamship term. Write "by express," or "by parcel post."

we ask you to kindly   Write "please."

we wish to thank you   Write "thank you."

writer   Write "I" or "me."

APPENDIX III

GRAMMAR HOTLINE DIRECTORY

Because these services are staffed by colleges and universities, most close during college breaks. Unless otherwise noted, none accepts collect calls.

ALABAMA
Auburn 36830
(205) 826-5749, Writing Center Hotline
Monday through Thursday, 9:00 a.m. to noon and 1:00 p.m. to 4:00 p.m.; Friday, 9:00 a.m. to noon
Auburn University
Thomas Nash

ARKANSAS
Little Rock 72204
(501) 569-3162, The Writer's Hotline
Monday through Friday, 9:00 a.m. to noon (Central Time)
University of Arkansas
John Stratton

ILLINOIS
Charleston 61920
(217) 581-5929, Grammar Hotline
Monday through Friday, 9:30 a.m. to 3:00 p.m.
Eastern Illinois University
Jeanne Simpson

Normal 61761
(309) 438-2345, Grammar Hotline
Monday through Friday, 8:00 a.m. to 4:30 p.m.
Illinois State University
Janice Neuleib

INDIANA
West Lafayette 47907
(317) 494-3723
Monday through Friday, 8:00 a.m. to 5:00 p.m.
Purdue University
Muriel Harris

KANSAS
Emporia 66801
(316) 343-1200 (Kansas callers toll free 1-800-362-2578) Writer's Hotline
Monday through Thursday, 11:30 a.m. to 4:30 p.m. during spring and fall semesters
Emporia State University
Faye Vowell

MASSACHUSETTS
Boston 02115
(617) 437-2512, Grammar Hotline
Monday through Friday, 8:30 a.m. to 4:00 p.m.
Northeastern University
English Department

NEW YORK
Jamaica 11451
(212) 739-7483, Rewrite
Monday through Friday 1:00 p.m. to 4:00 p.m.
York College of the City University of New York
Michael G. Southwell

OHIO
Delaware 43015
(614) 369-4431, ext. 301
Monday through Friday, 9:00 a.m. to 5:00 p.m.
Ohio Wesleyan University
Dr. Ulle Lewes

SOUTH CAROLINA
Columbia 29208
(803) 777-7020, Writer's Hotline
Monday through Friday, 9:00 a.m. to 5:00 p.m.
University of South Carolina
Tom Waldrep

TENNESSEE
Memphis 38152
(901) 454-2665, Grammar Cool Line
Monday through Friday, 9:00 a.m. to 5:00 p.m.
Memphis State University
Fred Collins, Joan Weatherly

TEXAS
San Antonio 78284
(512) 730-2503, Learning Line
Monday through Thursday, 8:00 a.m. to 10:00 p.m.; Friday 8:00 a.m. to 5:00 p.m.
San Antonio College
Vivian Rudisill

VIRGINIA
Virginia Beach 23452
(804) 427-3070, Grammar Hotline
Monday through Friday, 10:00 a.m. to 2:00 p.m. (reduced hours during summer)
Tidewater Community College
Donna Friedman

APPENDIX IV

BIBLIOGRAPHY

ARTICLES

Gehm, John W. "Job Descriptions — A New Handle on an Old Tool." *Personnel Journal*. Vol. 49, No. 12, December 1970, pp. 983-985, 993.

Hemphill, John K. "Job Descriptions for Executives." *Harvard Business Review*. Vol. 37, No. 5, September/October 1959, pp. 55-67.

Henderson, Richard I. "Job Descriptions — Critical Documents, Versatile Tools." Parts 1-5. *Supervisory Management*. Vol. 20, Nos. 11-12, Vol. 21, Nos. 1-3, November 1975 — March 1976.

Industry Week. "Job Descriptions: Key To Hiring the Right Man." Vol. 173, No. 2, pp. 60–61.

Iron Age. "First Step to Getting a Good Man — Sound Job Description." Vol. 209, No. 25, p. 25.

Klingner, Donald E. "When the Traditional Job Description is Not Enough." *Personnel Journal*, Vol. 58, No. 4, April 1979, pp. 243-248.

Vance, Paul M. "How to Write an Accurate Job Description." *Supervisory Management*. Vol. 15, No. 9, September 1970, pp. 9-11.

Walsh, William J. "Writing Job Descriptions: How and Why." *Supervisory Management*. Vol. 17, No. 2, February 1972, pp. 2-8.

BOOKS

Appley, Lawrence A., and Keith L. Irons. *Manager Manpower Planning*. New York: AMACOM, 1981.

Beatty, Richard W., and Craig Eric Schneier. *Personnel Administration*. 2nd Edition. Reading, MA: Addison-Wesley Publishing Company, 1981.

Corns, Marshall C. *Organizing Jobs in Banking*. Boston: Bankers Publishing Company, 1967. (Out of print.)

———. *The Practical Operations and Management of a Bank*. Boston: Bankers Publishing Company, 1968.

Garcia, F.L., and Glenn Munn. *Encyclopedia of Banking and Finance*, 8th Edition. Boston: Bankers Publishing Company, 1983.

Handbooks for Analyzing Jobs. U.S. Department of Labor, 1972.

Looper, C. Eugene. *Banker's Guide to Personnel Administration*. Boston: Bankers Publishing Company, 1983.

Olson, Richard F. *Performance Appraisal*. New York: John Wiley & Sons, Inc., 1981.

Patten, Thomas H., Jr. *A Manager's Guide to Performance Appraisal*. New York: The Free Press, 1982.

Pigors, Paul, and Charles A. Myers. *Personnel Administration*. 9th Edition. New York: McGraw-Hill Book Company, 1981.

Seglin, Jeffrey L. *Bank Letter Writing Handbook*. Boston: Bankers Publishing Company, 1983.

Task Analysis Inventories: A Method for Collecting Job Information. U.S. Department of Labor, 1973.

Wortman, Max S., and JoAnn Sperling. *Defining the Manager's Job*. 2nd Edition. New York: AMACOM, 1975.